Cover Photograph

PEOPLE WALK PAST DESTROYED BUILDINGS in the Sadriyah outdoor market, located in a predominantly Shi'ite area of Baghdad on Sunday, February 4, 2007. The day before, a suicide bomber driving a truck loaded with a ton of explosives obliterated the market, instantly killing at least 135 people while they shopped. The total injured was nearly 350. It was one of the most deadly suicide attacks since the beginning of the U.S. invasion of Iraq in 2003. The author was walking inside the barricade wall of the International Zone (IZ) more than a mile from the explosion when it occurred. I thought a rocket had landed 50 feet away. All day a plume of black smoke from the burning buildings rose thousands of feet in the air. (AP Photo/Khalid Mohammed)

America's Failure
In Iraq

Michael M. O'Brien

authorHOUSE®

AuthorHouse™
1663 Liberty Drive
Bloomington, IN 47403
www.authorhouse.com
Phone: 1-800-839-8640

This book is a work of non-fiction. Unless otherwise noted, the author and the publisher make no explicit guarantees as to the accuracy of the information contained in this book.

© 2009 Michael M. O'Brien. All rights reserved.

No part of this book may be reproduced, stored in a retrieval system, or transmitted by any means without the written permission of the author.

First published by AuthorHouse 10/6/2009

ISBN: 978-1-4389-8795-8 (sc)
ISBN: 978-1-4389-8796-5 (hc)

Library of Congress Control Number: 2009905735

Printed in the United States of America
Bloomington, Indiana

This book is printed on acid-free paper.

To my Dad, the finest man I ever knew.

THIS BOOK IS BASED ON actual events. I use my real name. I have omitted the names of certain people and organizations I write about in a negative light for the sole purpose of avoiding a law suit. That by no means diminishes the things they did, or the consequences of their actions. I would like to include their names so the reader would know who they are, but that would create another battle I'm not ready to deal with. At least not today.

The only names I retain are those of public figures or organizations, the reader being able to deduce who I am referring to anyway.

INTRODUCTION

THIS IS A PERSONAL STORY. It is also a story of two places, of two countries half a world apart from each other. It is a story of how one very powerful country destroyed one very weak one, while all along it was professing to save it.

I went to Iraq in the summer of 2006 to work for a defense contractor based in Alexandria, Virginia. I spent 14 months there and came back a different person than when I left. My experiences there opened my eyes to many things I will discuss in this book. My eyes also opened to an even bigger problem right here in America that most people don't have any idea exists. That problem is the subtle, and sometimes not so subtle, abuse of power. This abuse is shared by both the civilian leadership, who then implements that abuse through the military it commands. But this abuse has to be fed. It is fed by the military industrial complex that President Eisenhower warned us about when he left office in 1961.

I love America. At least I loved the America of my youth. Before I left for Iraq I could honestly say that I was proud to be an American. In many ways I still am, but nowhere near to the degree that I was before. I'm *happy* to be an American. I'm *glad* to be an American. But I can't really say that I'm *proud* to be an American, at least not now. What happened to me? A word comes to my mind that describes this transformation: *disappointment*. The word *proud* connotes accomplishment, achieving something good. What have we achieved in Iraq? What have we accomplished there? Obviously, nothing other than the expenditure of money. So what do I have to be *proud* of. Sadly, not much. Maybe one day I'll be able to say I'm *proud* to be an American again, the way I used to be, but I'm not very optimistic.

When it comes to waging war and using its political and military might in a just manner, and for causes that make sense, the United States has failed. This began with the Korean conflict, but took on its own identity during Vietnam. We had a few minor excursions after that, but things picked up again with the Gulf War of 1991, and again with Operation Iraqi Freedom, the current conflict. We used to fight honorably and use our power to great effect, to win swift and clear objectives, but those days are long gone. They're for the history books. They ended on the final day of the Second World War in 1945. This book looks at the United States' involvement in Iraq beginning with the Gulf War of 1991, under President George H.W. Bush, and then onto the current conflict created by his son, President George W. Bush.

I am not a professional writer. I am not a politician. Nor am I a political wonk. I graduated from West Point and served in the Army as an Infantry officer, then left to enter private industry. I have spent the past 22 years in commercial real estate in the Washington, DC area. My professional experience was capped off by serving 14 months in Iraq as the Real Estate Advisor to the Iraqi Ministry of Defense in Baghdad. I was a contractor.

This book is partly my story, but it is also the story of how the United States of America has destroyed a country, the very country it professes to save. It has done this with mismanagement and botched planning on a scale never seen before, by people who are supposed to be smart and know what they are doing. However, to write a book about the problems in Iraq today, one must go back at least to the Gulf War of the early 1990's to see the beginnings of the domino effect the United States created there. To only look at the last 5 years would be to ignore the mistakes made earlier. The son picked up where the father left off.

I am not *proud* to be an American right now. The reason I am *disappointed* in America now is because of what I saw and experienced in Iraq. It is the reason I decided to write this book.

Two books provided background information on the conduct of the war, officially called Operation Iraqi Freedom. "Cobra II" by Michael R. Gordon and General Bernard E. Trainor, and "Fiasco" by Thomas E. Ricks. Both give an excellent and detailed description of the planning and conduct of the warfight, and the initial stages afterwards. "The Secret History of the CIA," by Joseph J. Trento, provided me with the foundation of our nation's covert, and mostly futile, involvement in the political, military and domestic affairs of other countries since World War II. In just about every case the results have been disastrous. And no account of our failure in Iraq could be written without reference to "Dereliction of Duty: Johnson, McNamara, the Joint Chiefs of Staff, and the Lies That Led to Vietnam," by H.R. McMaster. Written by an active duty US Army full colonel at the time, it is one of the best accounts of the total lapse in leadership, judgment, ethical responsibility and ethical accountability related to the Vietnam debacle. I also refer to the film "Obsession," produced by the Clarion Fund, as an excellent graphic source of reference about the true danger of radical Islamic terrorism in the world today. I highly recommend to every living soul who believes in freedom and western civilization to watch this one hour DVD. It gets right to the heart of the issue. ("Obsession" can be watched on-line at *www.obsessionthemovie.com/.*)

I also reference the book, "Crush the Cell," by my West Point classmate, and one-time roommate, Michael A. Sheehan. Mike was the last Ambassador at Large for Counterterrorism under Bill Clinton. His book provides an insider's story of the inner workings of our national leadership surrounding the issue of global terrorism, specifically during the Clinton administration.

Last, I would like to express my sincere thanks to Dr. Anita Gadhia-Smith, Psy.D, who gave me much needed advice on how to get my book published.

This story is based much on hindsight. But as the wise saying goes, "Those who do not study history are doomed to repeat it." I want the reader of this book to understand it is a *study* of America's Failure In Iraq, therefore it is a history text as much as anything else. The most important thing I hope to achieve by writing this book is to help my country avoid repeating mistakes made in the past, which we failed to do this time.

This entire book is my own writing. It is based on my own experience, and my opinion of the reality of events.

Mike O'Brien
Arlington, Virginia
August 2009

1

A Free Pass

ON THE EVENING OF APRIL 6, 1991, I dropped by to visit my mother at our family home in Bethesda, Maryland. The TV was on and suddenly the show was interrupted by the network announcing a Special Report about to be broadcast. Within a few seconds President George H.W. Bush came on the air and announced he was ordering the cessation of all hostile action in Iraq, and that he had ordered all American troops to stop any further advances and action against Iraqi forces. He went on to say he had ordered the immediate return of American soldiers home from the battlefield.

I was dumbstruck. I turned to my mother and said this was the worst news I had ever heard. Why on earth were we not going all the way to Baghdad? Why on earth were we letting Saddam Hussein go? Why on earth were we letting him off the hook for his invasion of Kuwait? I couldn't understand why we were stopping our troops half way to Baghdad, when we had Saddam by the short hairs, his troops sprinting back to Baghdad as fast as their "camels" could take them, and the world watching us as we kicked him from one side of the dessert to the other on CNN. What had gotten into the President? What had happened? Indeed, what was he smoking?

It seemed as if the nation had gone into a drug-induced euphoria over hearing the news. But I was not happy. To me this was the worst thing the President could have done. I remember saying it was probably the worst political-military decision of the century. I have never regretted my words.

Shortly afterward General Norman Schwarzkopf, the CENTCOM (Central Command) Commander and commander of all allied forces in theater, was making statements to the effect that the President's decision to end hostilities was a mistake. About two days later he was "taken behind the wood shed" by Bush and we never heard another thing from Norm about it being a mistake. But in the January 20, 1992 issue of Newsweek the story became very clear. The night before the President's announcement General Colin Powell, then the Chairman of the Joint Chiefs of Staff, and General Schwarzkopf, were directly asked by the President for their recommendations. According to the Newsweek story, Powell strongly recommended ending hostilities, while Schwarzkopf was ambivalent. He had the chance to say we should continue to press forward, which is what he thought we should do, but he wimped out and went along with Powell. That was why he was making his statements to the press. But it was too late by then. The cat was out of the bag. The horse was out of the barn.

Why did Bush do it? There are many reasons thrown about, but the one that has been heard the most is the "power vacuum" theory. I for one have never bought into it. The theory goes something like this: If we had captured Saddam Hussein and removed him from power that would have created a "power vacuum" in Iraq with the head of the country gone. The theory goes on that this would have led to the countries surrounding Iraq to swarm in, while at the same time civil unrest would have broken out inside Iraq itself. I don't buy that theory, and never did, for one very simple reason—we had about half a million allied soldiers right there, in Iraq and Saudi Arabia, at the end of the war. What were the odds that Iran and Syria would have invaded Iraq with half a million United States forces standing there with everything they had brought over with them? What are the odds that Sunni and Shi'ite radicals would have started fighting each other with that many US forces there to stop them? None of the power vacuum theories hold up against the fact there were 500,000 United States troops on the ground with the new M1A1/2 Abrams tank to stop anything that would have started in Iraq at that time.

There is another theory, equally as weak, that was being thrown around at the end of the Gulf War. That was the issue of the United Nations resolutions. True, the resolutions may have specifically prevented the US from continuing to pursue Saddam and his forces. But hadn't we already gone beyond the limits of the resolutions? And even if the UN resolutions specifically prevented pushing any further toward Baghdad, what would have been wrong with continuing to press Saddam and demand his surrender? What would have prevented the United States from getting another resolution from the Security Council to pursue Saddam until his capture, in order to prevent him from getting away with what he had done and doing something else later?

The fact is the UN resolutions were weak, they are always weak, they mean nothing in practical terms, and they are merely political props so heads of state can fall back on them to say they have world backing. States can always do what they want to do, and what they need to do, without UN approval. Why does the United States need the approval of the UN to do what it feels is necessary in the first place? Are we afraid of the UN and what it will say against us? You bet! That is exactly why we defer to the UN any time we want to do something to defend ourselves or our allies. When we have a weak leader in the White House he always has to go to the UN for permission to do anything. This is another reason for the decision of President Bush that fateful night. He wanted the world and the UN to like him, to think he was a nice guy, to let them know he really cared what they thought about his actions. He certainly didn't want to do anything that might upset the mighty UN.

In the final analysis President Bush stopped hostilities because he was a weak person and deferred to Colin Powell for decisions he should have had the capacity to make himself as Commander-In-Chief. In the end Powell simply told him what to do. Colin Powell is a liberal and a peace lover. Being a peace lover is not necessarily a bad thing, but it is disastrous if it is the main thing affecting his decisions as a four-star general and the Chairman of the Joint Chiefs of Staff of the United States. Not to say that generals don't love peace, but peace should not be a general's primary objective. A general's primary objective should be the total defeat of the enemy. With defeat he can assist his political leader achieve *his* primary objective, which is the peace that comes only after the enemy's total defeat. But Colin Powell never really knew what he was. He wore a uniform but acted like a diplomat. He tried to be both when he should he have focused on what he was being paid to do, wage war. Instead, he wanted to achieve peace before achieving military victory. He put the cart before the horse. His priorities were backward. And for that we are paying the price today, and will continue to for years to come. (Today Powell claims he's a Republican but acts like a liberal Democrat. He still doesn't know what he is.)

Colin Powell deserves credit for one major thing, however, the use of *overwhelming force* to defeat the Iraqi army during the Gulf War. When Iraq invaded Kuwait on the morning of August 2, 1991, the world stood in shock primarily due to its disbelief in Saddam's stupidity. He had been rattling his saber for months, but no one thought he would actually invade Kuwait. But when he did invade the response of the United States was to get UN approval to defend Kuwait and kick Iraq back across the border. It was Colin Powell who espoused the use of *overwhelming force* to do this. For this he will go down in history as a brilliant military leader, but the concept of *overwhelming force* is nothing new. It's been around forever. US Army doctrine and training has always called for a force ratio of at least 3/1 if attacking an enemy who is in a defensive position. This meant if we were going in to attack Iraqi forces in Kuwait and kick them back across the Iraqi border, we would have to go in with at least three times as many troops as they had on the ground. With complete air superiority and 37 days of non-stop bombing, the Iraqi army was devastated and no match for our forces. Powell knew this and still said we needed half a million soldiers there when the bombing ended and the ground attack began. He was completely correct.

Powell got his way, as he always did, and the troops were sent over. But then why didn't we use them to their full effect after all the trouble we went through to get them there? Why didn't we use them to capture and topple the Saddam regime when we knew he was a scumbag and was killing his own people? Did President Bush send half a million troops over there to kick Saddam out of Kuwait because he had invaded a neutral country, or was it so Kuwait could continue to ship oil to the US? If so, then our entire reason for going over there was truly disingenuous after all. It wasn't to rid the world of Saddam Hussein, it was to get him out of Kuwait so we could continue to get their oil. We really didn't care at all about Saddam Hussein. We just wanted Kuwait oil, and he was getting in the way. All the talk of atrocities committed by Saddam meant nothing to President Bush and Colin Powell because we could have taken him out then and there. We sent 500,000 troops there. Why did we bother? Instead, we left him alone after he went back to Baghdad with his tail between his legs.

The response to the "power vacuum" theory is this: we had enough troops on the ground to stand up to anything that Iraqi insurgents, Iran, or any other threat could have thrown against us. The reasons Bush gave us for pulling out and leaving Saddam in power don't hold up. We had the forces in place.

What is the use of massing overwhelming force if you don't use it? The United States had nearly half a million troops on the ground in Kuwait, Saudi Arabia, and later in Iraq, and stopped. Why? We have never gotten a straight answer from anyone. The President said he couldn't go any further, but if the sanctions prevented him, as he said then, why did he ask Powell and Schwarzkopf what they thought? If the sanctions were that specific he didn't need their opinion. He asked them because he knew he had the option to continue if he wanted to, but he also asked them because he wanted to hear the answer they gave him, and they all knew it. The President, wanting to be loved by the media, stopped aggressive hostilities without giving any thought to what the consequences would be for anyone else. Colin Powell started off on the right foot by massing overwhelming force in Saudi Arabia, but then lost his nerve and backed off once we got ourselves into the fight and started killing Iraqi forces by the thousands. Isn't that what war is all about? Isn't that why Powell was a career Army officer? But Powell's media popularity had long since gone to his head by this time. He was their pawn now.

If we had used the troops we had sent there, captured Saddam Hussein, and waited for the dust to settle, we would not be in the mess we are today in Iraq, and in that entire part of the world. We would have had the forces in place to protect the Iraqi people while they decided for themselves what government they wanted, and then we would have been there to help them achieve that goal, with the number of US forces on the ground to protect them while they worked to get there. This could have been done, and only a fool would have thought otherwise. With half a million soldiers on the ground, who would have tried to stop us from protecting the Iraqi people while they decided their own destiny? The answer is—no one. Everyone knows it but is afraid to say so.

Then there's Norman Schwarzkopf. He had the opportunity to tell the President to continue on toward Baghdad, but he failed to do his duty. Then he had the nerve to blame the President for his decision after he was given the chance to speak his mind but didn't have the courage to. Too little, too late. General Schwarzkopf is looked upon as a hero. Perdue Chicken should use him as their spokesman. I hope he enjoys watching current events in Iraq on TV. He had a hand in creating these events along with Powell and Bush. There is no United States general officer who could have failed to achieve the success Schwarzkopf did with all the tools he had at his disposal. He was given 37 days of non-stop bombing by the US Air Force to soften up military targets in Iraq, and at the same time given half a million soldiers with their full complement of equipment to fight with, all while the Iraqi armed forces were being blown away by the US Air Force without any air cover of their own. Bozo The Clown could have gotten the same results that ol' Norm did. But when it came to really being tough, to stand up for what he believed in when the President asked for his opinion, he chickened out. Schwarzkopf is as much a weenie as Powell is, and they both got paid millions after the war to tell everyone how great they were.

The fact is, our modern day political and military leaders are not men of courage or fortitude. They "talk the talk," but can't "walk the walk." They are collectively afraid of the media and what people will think of them if they make the tough, but necessary, decisions needed of men in their positions. They can't cut the grade. Military officers become increasingly afraid and weak as they advance in rank, for the simple reason they don't want to upset their careers from further advancement. One has to wonder where their loyalty to their soldiers lies. Making full colonel is a very hard thing to do, and making Brigadier General is just about impossible. To rise to the rank of 1-star general is a feat few achieve. But making it to 4-star general is harder to do than getting struck by lightning. There is only one way to get there and that is to never, ever, say anything that will raise eyebrows, anything that is against the "party line." To say what is really going on is professional suicide if one wants to become a general officer. It has been this way since the Second World War.

General officers were not as timid and shy during the Civil War or later. They were often very courageous and spoke their minds. Grant was a perfect example. President Lincoln gave him command of all the Union Armies, even though he was known to have a drinking problem, because he got results. Lincoln was heard telling his senior military staff that he would buy a case of liquor for any officers who would fight as well as Grant did. Military results, military success—that was what Grant got and delivered to his political commander, because Lincoln stayed out of his way. Lincoln took those results and transformed them into political goals and objectives. One did his job, while the other did his. They worked well together, and stayed in their respective "swim lanes" where they each belonged.

But things started to change during World War II and Korea. The strong generals started to get slapped down by the weak ones, or by politicians who had their priorities backward. Look what happened to General George Patton, who was furious when Eisenhower wouldn't let the US Army go into Berlin. "Ike" wouldn't let him because he was a political general. Roosevelt had cut a deal with Stalin allowing the Russian army into Berlin first, and also giving Eastern Europe to "Uncle Joe" as a bonus. Look where things ended up. Was Patton wrong? General Douglas MacArthur wanted to go after the Red Chinese army during the Korean War. Granted, he was talking about going nuke, which wasn't the greatest idea, but he had a point about addressing the communist Chinese and North Korea while we were there to do something about them. He got sacked by Truman, the same guy who had gone nuke a few years before, but that was OK. And then we went into Vietnam to stop the very thing MacArthur was trying to prevent more than a decade earlier—communist Chinese expansion. So who had it wrong, MacArthur or Truman?

Today it's totally different. Today's generals, like weak politicians, want to be liked by a media that will always hate them and be anti-military. Colin Powell is the best example of this. Today's generals testify before

Congress and give flowing speeches that have been prepared in advance by their staff officers and tested for response and reaction by their PR people. Decisive military results are not as important as looking and sounding good on TV, especially in front of Congress, and getting good newspaper coverage the following day. These are the important factors to generals now. Powell and Schwarzkopf were not real military leaders. They were four star generals who were in reality high level executives of a large corporation whose staffs did all the work while they spoke in front of cameras. Remember Schwarzkopf on TV day after day during Desert Storm. He was in love with himself. When they had the chance to be real generals, which meant waging war toward the total defeat of the enemy, they failed miserably. If Powell and Schwarzkopf were really doing their jobs they would have told the President to press on. There would have been no question in their minds what the answer was. If they were real generals, they would have asked the President why he was asking them the question in the first place.

Their jobs were to advise the President on how to destroy Saddam Hussein and his military forces, not to advise him of the political ramifications of continuing the attack. But it was the President himself who failed the American people by feeling the need to ask Powell and Schwarzkopf for their opinions. It was his decision to make, not theirs to advise him on what political decision to make. If Powell and Schwarzkopf were doing their jobs it is very conceivable they would have replied, when asked for their opinions, that they could not imagine why he would want to stop aggressive actions against Saddam's forces. It was up to the President to say to them he had decided to stop, but instead he asked them for their opinions on something he shouldn't have asked them in the first place. It would be like a doctor asking a patient what their opinion was for their surgery and medical care. My aunt was asked this by her doctor after breast cancer surgery. He asked her what follow-on treatment she would prefer to have, the more intense and painful, or the lesser. She opted for the lesser and died a year later. For similar reasons Powell and Schwarzkopf share the blame, along with President Bush, for the disastrous way the Gulf War ended in 1991.

But the Gulf War did not simply end that night when the President got on TV and announced the cessation of hostilities. That was the end of Phase I. The next phase would prove far worse for the Iraqi people. It would have been better for them if we had never gone back.

It is an accepted fact by rational people that the United Nations is an ineffective organization. It's only purpose is to employ educated and connected fat cats from third world counties who live the "life of Reilly" in Manhattan while the their countrymen back home starve. It is an organization made up of people who accomplish little, but who say a lot, and are given far more importance than they deserve. (It also employs half the country of Fiji, whose population has become a UN peace keeping army that is sent by the UN to conduct police actions around the world. The UN must be the major employer of the Fiji Islands. UN security forces from Fiji, with their nifty blue berets, were all over Iraq.)

When the Gulf War ended President Bush could report back to his titular superiors at the UN that he had ended the war according to their resolutions. He then spearheaded the follow-on sanctions that embargoed the Iraqi economy, effectively destroying it and the lives of average Iraqi citizens. When I went to Iraq in the summer of 2006, I saw the effects of the sanctions with my own eyes. Iraq became a black market economy, with people who would never have taken a bribe or a kick-back before now openly accepting whatever it took to feed their families. Before the Gulf War the Iraqi dinar, the unit of currency, was about three to the dollar. At present it is approximately 1350 dinar to the dollar. Iraqis get paid in cash that is handed to them in piles too large to carry in their pockets. They have to put their monthly pay in bags to carry home.

The sanctions didn't hurt Saddam in the slightest. Most of Saddam's 21 or more palaces were built by foreign construction companies with money he hauled in under the eyes of the United Nations during the sanctions after the Gulf War. Saddam personally became richer than he was before the Gulf War. The money coming in from the food-for-oil program was scratch. It wouldn't feed a dog. But if he fed his people with the money he was raking in with illegal oil sales, the world would have wondered where it came from. He was happy to keep it all himself. And why not, especially if the UN and the US knew all about it anyway? It was all a big act by Saddam to make it look as though the sanctions were really hurting Iraq. They were hurting the Iraqi people, but not him. He was living a great life and building one palace after the next with the money he was being paid by illegally selling oil to Kofi Annan's son and others.

But the sanctions did far more than just destroy the Iraqi economy and destroy the Iraqi way of life. They also created unrest and desolation, perfect recruiting grounds for future terrorist organizations and insurgents bent on destroying the Iraqi government and anything else they could. When men have jobs and can support their families they aren't going to jump at the chance of becoming terrorists and killing their neighbor. But when young men have no job, nothing to do, see no reason to start families, and the western world has left them instead of saving them from their dictator, they'll take the best offer they can get. This is exactly what happened after the Gulf War.

The "No-Fly Zones" were created to stop Saddam from sending his aircraft into Kurdish areas in the north and Shi'ite areas in the south. But when he wanted to fly his helicopters into them to "deal" with things, Norman Schwarzkopf let him do it. What did Schwarzkopf think Saddam was going to do once his aircraft flew in, drop off toys? Saddam sent his aircraft into the No-Fly Zones to bomb and gas his own countrymen while Schwarzkopf, Bush and Powell watched. It was easy for the world to gasp in horror at the atrocities they saw, but how could Bush, Powell and Schwarzkopf sleep at night knowing what they had done by letting Saddam off the hook, and the opportunity they had lost? The generals didn't do their jobs as generals, and the President didn't do his as Commander-In-Chief and the leader of the free world.

As the years passed by after the Gulf War, Saddam Hussein rose to power again, but this time to even greater power than before the war began. He was now a "player" on the world scene, where he had only been a small actor before. He declared himself to be the victor in the Gulf War for one simple reason—he was still alive. In his world and culture, that was all that mattered. By letting Saddam live, but far worse stay in power, he could declare himself the victor. His countrymen, and the countries surrounding Iraq, had to admit that he was right. This gave him greater power than ever because he had "beaten" the United States. All over Baghdad we saw murals and paintings showing Saddam and his forces kicking our butts during the Gulf War. That's what the Iraqi people believe happened. He was also allowed to gas his own people with our permission, which stoked his ego even more. On top of that, he could keep all of his country's oil money for himself because of the sanctions we and the UN had imposed, and his people were now weaker than ever for the same reasons. The true winner of the Gulf War was the very man we were supposed to defeat, and should have destroyed—Saddam Hussein. Is there any wonder he got worse, and not better? He truly got away with murder. By 1992 Saddam was on top of the world.

For the way he allowed the Gulf War to end, which set the stage for things to come, George H.W. Bush has been getting a "free pass" from the media, the American people, and from world opinion. Whenever I fly into Houston International Airport and see the snappy statue of him in the terminal, I have to turn away. The current situation is as much his fault as anyone alive, but his son came in to "finish the job," and proved to be a bigger disaster than his father.

2

September 11, 2001

I was lying on my hotel bed at around 8:30 in the evening trying to get to sleep. I had gotten food poisoning the night before and hadn't been able to go to work that day, so the rest of the team went on without me. The phone rang and I picked it up. It was Michael Jackson on the other end. Not the Michael Jackson we all know and admire for his clean living, but Michael Jackson the Administrative Officer from the US Embassy in Dacca, Bangladesh, where I was at the time. I'll never forget what he said to me: "Mike, are you watching TV?" I remember thinking that was a strange thing for him to say, but figured he may have been asking just to see if I was OK and that I had something to do. I said I wasn't, to which he replied, "Well, you need to turn the TV in your room on right now. A plane just slammed into one of the towers at the World Trade Center, and another one just hit the second tower. We're under attack." That's how it started for me.

Mike told me to stay at the hotel until the Embassy notified me, and to keep the team I had brought with me to Bangladesh at the hotel too. No one was allowed to go anywhere without the Embassy's permission.

I was a political appointee in the administration of George W. Bush, having worked on his campaign at its national headquarters in Austin, Texas. I had taken part in the vote recount in Florida, being flown in the middle of the night with a dozen other people to Miami to begin working the next morning with several hundred other Republican operatives observing the recount at the Miami-Dade County office building in downtown Miami.

The entire recount process and the grounds surrounding it are a topic for another book and another time. Suffice it to say, from one who was there, the Gore campaign wanted human error and the popping chads to overturn the election of Bush. The more the vote cards were handled, the more the likelihood that the chads, which were pre-punched little squares perforated into the cards, would pop out and call the vote into question. That's exactly what the Gore campaign wanted to happen. They wanted the election to be overturned by man-handling the cards, which was tantamount to tampering with previously fine vote cards. It was all a scam. I personally caught the county employees who were doing the recount making several mistakes, all in favor of Gore. The reason was because Gore was doing the recount *only* in predominantly Democrat counties in the state, which would mean that any mistakes and un-counted ballots would likely go in favor of Gore. Human error played a big role in it all. Every time the cards were held up and the county employee called the results out, they were calling mostly for Gore. They got into the habit of doing this and ended up mistakenly calling Gore's name out, when the vote was not for him. I stopped this when it happened, and the county employees were shocked they had made the mistake. They didn't even know they had done it. Such were the tactics of Gore's camp. To this day, every time I see the liberal bumper sticker, "Hail to the Thief," it makes my skin crawl. Gore tried to steal the election, not the other way around. He just went about it the wrong way, and didn't pull it off. When Gore failed to call for a recount in the entire state of Florida, but only in the four (later three) most heavily Democrat counties, he showed his real intentions and the recount for the scam it was.

We never even got to see all the ballot cards in Miami-Dade County. The democrat-controlled County Election Commission had already gone through and done their own recount (there were at least three recounts, for a total of at least four times that the vote cards were handled. It's no wonder chads were popping out all over the place). If the Commission looked at a vote card and could not determine who the vote was for, then it went ahead and made its own decision who the voter "intended" to vote for. In other words, the democrat-controlled Miami-Dade County Election Commission had been given the gift of clairvoyance and was casting the vote on behalf of the voter whose intention the Commission couldn't determine in the first place! Of course, if a vote card had half a dozen chads popped out, then the Gore camp could say it was impossible to determine who the person intended to vote for. It was all nonsense. Because the vote cards had been handled so many times *after the original vote had been cast*, now there was no way to determine who the vote was meant for *the night of the election*. But the Gore camp twisted and turned this scenario on its head with the help of the liberal media. The real story, which is being told here, never came out. Now we're just left with "Hail to the Thief" bumper stickers by liberals who haven't got a clue what really happened, and wouldn't care if they did. They just wanted Gore to win and Bush to lose, whatever the cost to the dignity of the election process that they don't care about either.

The Commission decided who got these mystery votes, weeks after the voter had made their own decision in the privacy of the voting booth, and then placed all these special vote cards in sealed envelopes by precinct. No one was allowed to open these envelopes, and if we did we would be thrown out of the room where the recount was taking place. No one ever saw these cards, but what we did see was the tally of these votes written on the outside of the envelope. Someone from the Election Commission had written in a magic marker what the vote tally was of the cards sealed inside the envelopes, and that was that. The predominant majority of these votes were for Gore, but we'll never really know who the votes were for. It was not open to the public to see what these cards even looked like. We never got to make our own determination of what we thought the vote was. It was a completely closed process.

Al Gore should be ashamed of what he put this country through for 35 days. He didn't care about the American people. He only cared about himself and getting into the White House. And he certainly didn't care one bit, and neither did his "lawyers," about tampering with the voting process and with the vote cards. His lawyers just cared about the incredible money they were hauling in. The entire Gore-inspired recount was a mockery of the sanctity of the American voting system and the honor of the individual's right to vote for who they want. The

Gore campaign, with the able assistance of the Florida Supreme Court, openly and willingly tampered with valid vote cards and ballots for the purpose of overturning the original vote in only three counties in the state. If Gore really thought the state of Florida was messed up, why then didn't he contest the count in the entire state? He said the state's process was wrong, but then he only asked for recounts in four counties (later dropping one of them), the most heavily democrat counties in the state. He showed his real intentions when he did this. He didn't think the votes were messed up in the state of Florida, he just wanted a recount in four counties to surpass the 1,000 vote margin Bush had over him. That's all the recount was to Gore. It was never about the integrity of the voting system in Florida, or possible abuses of it. It was just about how much abuse *he* could get away with, with the permission of the Florida Supreme Court, in order to steal the election from Bush who always had the majority of votes from the night of the election. With Gore in 2000, and Al Franken today in Minnesota, it's the same. If you are a Democrat and within 1,000 votes—steal it. Or at least give it one hell of a try.

After the election was finally decided I was given a job on the Presidential Inaugural Committee back in Washington, DC. Because of what Gore had put everyone through, the Bush Inaugural Committee had less than half the time to prepare for the numerous inaugural balls held throughout Washington. There were nine balls that night, with the ball for everyone from Texas held at the old DC Convention Center, which has since been demolished. (This was not the "Texas Ball" people hear so much about. That's the one where the "Who's Who" go to look cool in their tuxedos and their brand new boots they just bought the day before. All the hot single women in DC want to get a ticket to it to grab some stud with money from the Lone Star State who flies in for the event on daddy's jet.)

When George W. Bush was sworn in everyone was scrambling for a job in the new administration. I was no exception. I landed a job at the Department of Agriculture where for three months I did absolutely nothing for eight hours a day, and then split as fast as I could before my head exploded. But one day I got a call from Presidential Personnel, the office that places political hacks in jobs in the new administration. (By the way, all new administrations do the same thing, Republican and Democrat.) The person at the other end of the line asked me if I would be interested in going over to the State Department, to the office called Foreign Buildings Operations, or FBO. This is the branch of State responsible for the design and construction of US embassies and consulates around the world. It's a huge operation, almost like a global real estate development firm. Having been in commercial real estate for over 15 years at the time, I jumped at the opportunity. But what really amazed me was that someone at Presidential Personnel had actually read my resume.

I interviewed with a retired US Army 2-star general named Charles Williams, who was a Colin Powell worshipper. When Powell was tapped to be the Secretary of State, he called Chuck Williams in to do an assessment of FBO, ostensibly to determine the condition of its installations around the world, but really to pull him into the job of running it. To his credit, Powell saw the need for an overhaul of FBO, which would entail an overhaul of the infrastructure of all United States diplomatic facilities around the world. Because real estate, and commercial facilities in general, isn't given much thought by diplomats, this was commendable on Powell's part. I tend to think, however, that he had been given a heads up as to the terrible condition of our facilities around the world prior to taking on the job at State. Not being a real estate person, how would Powell know these things about our diplomatic facilities? Maybe he actually listened to diplomatic staff on his many travels around the world, and actually took notes and promised to fix things. More likely, General Williams sold Powell on the need for this, in the process creating a job for himself in the glory of Colin Powell. Either way, I give Powell a lot of credit for seeing this need, and General Williams credit for responding as he did.

General Williams had been busy in the time between retiring from the US Army and taking over the job at State for his good friend Colin. After leaving the Army General Williams went to New York City to take over as head of the City's School Construction Authority. "He left the New York job after an audit found he had given misleading information on the progress of projects he was overseeing." (Glenn Kessler, Washington Post, August 17, 2007) After that he came to Washington, DC, to head up the renovation of all the facilities owned by the DC School System. He had been hired by Julius Becton, also a retired US Army general and head of the DC Public Schools, which is another story of complete disaster. "He left the D.C. job after an audit said he authorized shoddy contracting procedures and left the school system vulnerable to waste and fraud." (Kessler, WP, 8/17/07) What is interesting is that General Williams does not mention the DC School job on his bio, most likely because the effort was a failure. He doesn't allow his name to be associated with failure, even if it happened. He just leaves it off his resume. After the DC Schools fiasco he took over the construction of the Dulles Toll Road, called the "Greenway," in suburban Loudoun County, Virginia. This is the recently completed road that extends past Dulles International Airport west of Washington, DC, and goes to Leesburg, Virginia, where it ends. The road is beautiful and is expensive as hell. It is a great way to avoid taking the more narrow, traffic-filled back roads of modern day Loudoun County, which are awful. General Williams completed the project and has its success well documented in his resume, likely with the accompanying photographs of the ribbon-cutting on his basement wall, which I will describe shortly. (General Williams' bio states he "has had an exemplary engineering and construction management career, first in service to his country in the military and now as a civilian. His outstanding leadership, innovative abilities and vision have contributed dramatically to the engineering and construction management profession." It also states he is a graduate of the Senior Manager in Government Program at Harvard University. According to the bio he received a "BS Degree" from Tuskegee Institute. There is no indication what his major was. I was informed while at OBO that General Williams doesn't have an engineering degree. He had been a 2-star general in the US Army Corps of Engineers.)

It was after the Dulles Toll Road completion when Powell asked Chuck Williams to do an assessment of the State Department's overseas facilities, and then asked him to take the job permanently. (General Williams described the offer from Powell as one he simply couldn't refuse.) Then General Williams, after what he called "careful deliberation" with his wife, decided to accept the job as Director of FBO for his good friend Colin. In fact, if Powell had asked him to jump off a roof he would have run for the edge. I tend to think General Williams was the one who planted the bug in Powell's ear about the need for an overhaul of FBO and our country's diplomatic infrastructure around the world, and then begged Powell for the position. What a great job this would be for General Williams as he went into retirement. As I got to know him and the tremendous ego he has, I tend to think this is more likely what happened. When he took over FBO, he did so with vigor. But then again he was used to being in charge. He was the type of "leader" who would make changes for change's sake in order to leave his "mark" on the organization. FBO would be no exception.

General Williams began to run FBO like a military unit. Anyone who's been in the military, especially officers, knows there are many different ways to manage and lead people. There is leadership by example, and there's leadership by shear presence of the person's personality. But then there's leadership by authority, whereby the person in charge dictates and the rest must, and will, follow. That's the style of General Williams. He didn't ask, he ordered. He didn't request, he demanded. That's OK in an army unit, but in a civilian organization it stinks.

The senior staff was invited by General Williams to his house for a Christmas party. We were greeted at the door by he and his wife, and then he asked us to go directly downstairs to the basement where there was an open bar. But upon reaching the bottom of the stairs we were hit in the face by a pictorial history of General Williams' career, of his entire professional life. Nearly every picture on the wall, and there were a lot of them, was of him. Every promotion throughout his long career was photographed, with the picture mounted on the wall along with a brief description of the rank he was achieving, the date and other key information about the photograph. Only someone planning a wall like this would have made sure these pictures were taken in the first place, and then saved all of them over a period of 30 or more years. There was an artist's sketch of the general with his staff at one of his last commands. It was a humorous caricature of him on an Alaskan dog sled, holding a whip, and his staff were the sled dogs! Of course, General Williams has a big grin on his face. He loved that sketch. Such was his "leadership" style. It wasn't until the end of the "tour" of his basement wall that we saw photographs of his wife and his children. One picture of each, if I recall. How touching.

Wanting to leave his mark on the organization, what better way to do this than change its name. Instead of FBO, for Foreign Buildings Operations, General Williams changed it to OBO, for Overseas Buildings Operations. Now everyone calls it "OBO."

Morale at FBO went down the tubes because bureaucrats do not like change in any way, shape or form. People wanted to quit, but the ship didn't sink because in the end government employees will go through hell rather than give up their job security and their retirement. They'll bitch and moan and count the days until they retire, in some cases counting days into the thousands. This was the situation when I started to work for General Williams. He was able to talk the Sectary of State into promoting his position, which forever had been a Deputy Assistant Secretary. The general's position was elevated to Assistant Secretary, befitting of his ego. He was allowed by Powell to attend the Secretary's morning briefings, which no Director of FBO had ever been able to do. I'm sure he has a picture of his promotion to Assistant Secretary somewhere on his basement wall too.

I was asked by General Williams be the Director of a new division he had created under his new reorganization. FBO never had a branch strictly devoted to planning. In the past FBO reacted to needs that came up, waiting for a roof to fall in before a new one was put on the building. But General Williams created a new organization just for planning, devoted strictly to determining where facilities were in their "life cycle," and making a list of all facilities throughout the world based on this research. What was developed was a new 5-year plan for FBO, with posts (the State Department refers to all its locations as "posts") listed in descending order based on need of renovation, repair or complete replacement. To his credit, this was a very good thing for General Williams to have initiated at FBO. Based on this list my staff would go to the post, perform an assessment of the condition of the Embassy or consulate facilities there, to include ancillary buildings such as residential housing and warehouses, and produce a report for the architects and engineers back at FBO to decide what to do. This was why I was in Dacca on September 11, 2001.

I left Dacca about three days after the attacks, after meeting with the US Ambassador, Mary Ann Peters, to say goodbye. She and I had a very interesting conversation about the events of the past few days, the main point being her contention that the world would never be the same again. I left with one of the members of the team who went there with me. We flew to Bangkok, and then arrived at London's Heathrow Airport, which was a mob scene. I've never seen an airport in the condition I saw Heathrow the day we arrived there, which was September 14th. We got in at 8:00 in the morning, and had a connecting flight to Dulles at around 11:00, three hours later. Of course, all flights had been cancelled for the preceding three days, but we were told they might start flying again later that day. My coworker and I were waiting in one particular line, when one of the American Airlines employees told us to wait in another line across the way. She walked us over to it, and we proceeded to wait again, but this line wasn't too long, so there was hope. When we got to the counter the young lady asked us for our tickets and passports, and when she saw "DIPLOMATIC" across the top she took them, asked us to wait, and then disappeared. We waited there for about 20 minutes. When she came back to the ticket counter she handed us our boarding passes and wished us good luck. I asked her how we had gotten on the flight. She pointed to the word across the top of our passports, and said two people had been bumped to get us on the next flight out, which was scheduled for about 5:00 that evening.

The staff at Heathrow Airport were wonderful. I've never met such nice people in my life. This was the first of many instances where I would see goodness in people, total strangers. Everyone felt sorry for Americans then, and for what we had suffered. It brought out the good in just about everyone, with one exception, which I will mention shortly. The hotel staff in Dacca were wonderful too. They kept offering their sympathy to us and saying how sorry they were for what our country was going through. It was a beautiful thing.

Sure enough, we got to the gate and the word got out that flights were going to start again. One flight left for Chicago before ours, but then ours left for Dulles—the first to land there from Heathrow since the events of the days before. I sat next to a middle eastern man who never said one word the entire flight. He must have been scared to death. He never left his seat to go to the bathroom. I can't blame him. When the wheels touched the ground the entire plane started clapping and cheering. It felt great to be home, but greater still to be an American. The guy next to me disappeared.

I would return to the States to hear stories of what people had experienced that fateful day. FBO (now OBO) was located in Rosslyn, Virginia, the part of Arlington County just across the Potomac River from Georgetown, the trendy area of Washington, DC. When the plane hit the Pentagon people in my building who worked on the upper floors saw it hit. One of my friends was on the phone talking to a friend in New York City, who was describing the planes slamming into the World Trade Center towers, when she looked out the window and saw the plane hit the Pentagon. She went into shock and walked out of the building, taking 12 flights of stairs to the ground floor, and pulling a fire alarm on the way out to clear the building. She walked all the way home, and didn't come back to work for a week. She was still in a mild state of shock when she told me her story two weeks later.

After the April 18, 1983 US Embassy bombing in Beirut, Lebanon, followed by the Marine barracks bombing on October 23, 1983 in that same city, the State Department asked retired Navy Admiral Bobby Inman to chair a commission on improving security at U.S. foreign installations around the world. According to Wikipedia, "The commission's report has been influential in setting security design standards for U.S. Embassies." Well, sort of. Because our country has the habit of freaking out every time a disaster happens, then in no time flat everyone forgets all about it, the "Inman Report," as it became known, was being used as a paperweight at the State Department. However, by 1:00 in the afternoon on September 11, 2001, every copy of it was being pulled off the shelves at FBO and dusted off. All of the sudden, the Inman Report *was* influential in setting security standards for U.S. Embassies around the world. But because the events of 9/11/01 were so incredible, the report was only a beginning.

After the attacks of September 11, 2001, the State Department had a new mandate—the physical security of its facilities around the world. Now the State Department had a whole new set of problems as far as its buildings were concerned, and they weren't just leaky roofs and bad plumbing. For example, what would happen to buildings located in cities like Paris, where they sat right along the sidewalk and anyone could reach out and touch the walls with their hands, where any terrorist could pull a car loaded with explosives up against the wall of the building and set it off, killing everyone inside and outside of the facility within hundreds of feet? What would the US do with these buildings, located around the world and worth billions of dollars not only for their historical value, but also for their incredible locations in the most important cities in the world? We couldn't just look at buildings for their repair or replacement any more, but for their entire relocation outside city centers where they had been located for decades. The costs would be enormous. OBO had an annual budget of $1 billion dollars. The cost of relocating embassies would be astronomical, take years to accomplish, and would call for a whole new way of doing business for the State Department. This was the situation during the time I spent there.

Although he had a rough start when he took over OBE, there couldn't have been a better person in charge of it than General Williams after the terrible events of 9/11 happened. The Department of State needed a military leader to run that operation. We were at war. We didn't have time for debate or discussion. We had to get things done. Who better to lead us than a retired 2-star general from the US Army Corps of Engineers? Before 9/11 his style didn't work at OBO. After 9/11 it was exactly what was needed.

When 9/11 happened I saw for the first time the cost we would pay for the many failures of the new administration of George W. Bush. When Bush was elected he kept George Tenant in his job as Director of Central Intelligence. Why he did this was beyond my comprehension. I remember wondering at the time, well before 9/11, why Bush would keep Tenant, a Clinton hack, in this immensely important job. The conventional wisdom around Washington was that his father, Bush the First, recommended Tenant stay in his job at CIA because Bush liked him. If that is indeed true, it is another example of the flakiness of Bush the First, and his desire to be liked by liberals. George Tenant was a flaming liberal from way back, with no practical experience to run the CIA. He had been the head of the Congressional committee staff responsible for the oversight of the CIA—that was all. He had never been a "spook," had never been directly involved in the collection of intelligence. All he had ever done was run the committee staff that reported to the members of

Congress who provided oversight of the CIA, the committee that gave the CIA the money it needed to run. He was a glorified administrator and office manager.

But the real stinker was the affect this decision of George W. Bush's had on the people who had worked so hard to get him elected—people like me who had fought in the trenches in Florida on the recount. Why does someone vote for a presidential candidate? Well, one of the reasons is because of the people they hope he will place in his administration. A good example is a pick for a Supreme Court Justice. This single selection is one of the main reasons we vote for a presidential candidate, because it will have lasting implications for years to come. The Director of Central Intelligence may not be a Supreme Court Justice, but the position is certainly one of the most critical in the Cabinet. Allowing George Tenant to remain the Director of the CIA was a slap in the face of everyone who had worked to get Bush elected in 2000, contributed to his campaign, voted for him, and fought in the states Gore was trying to steal away from him. We did not expect to get stuck with Tenant, a Clinton holdover. I for one didn't do all that I did, to include fight in the trenches in Florida during the recounts, to get stuck with a Clinton hack like Tenant.

Another point that must be made here, and that was first seen after 9/11, was Bush's complete and utter failure to hold people accountable and responsible for their mistakes. I worked on his campaign in 2000. I was at his national headquarters in Austin. One of his major points during the entire campaign was the issue of "personal responsibility." Bush stressed over and over the need for people to be responsible for their actions, as if he was placing personal responsibility back on the shoulders of the average American, and we liked what we heard. It was "Reaganesque." Personal responsibility is one of the touchstones of the conservative movement, and was so at the time of the founding of this country. Stand up for yourself, and take responsibility for yourself. These are the hallmarks of what made this country great. They embellish capitalism and a free market society. Work hard and reap the rewards of your labors. They are also the battle cry of those who are against big government and the liberal-socialist movement. But when 9/11 happened what did Bush do in this critical area? He did absolutely nothing. Did a single person lose their job? Did a single federal employee in a position of responsibility for the security of our country get fired? To the best of my knowledge not a single person lost their job, got fired, or was forced to resign. That wasn't "Reaganesque," it was the same thing that would have happened in Moscow if a high level member of the Communist Party screwed up. Nothing would happen to him either. Needless to say, those same people still either have their secure federal jobs, or have since retired with no loss of their precious pensions. This is despicable. We suffered because senior FBI agents and managers in Phoenix failed to heed the warnings of their own agents, because there was no coordination between domestic and non-domestic intelligence agencies, and because peoples' jobs and careers were more important than raising the red flag and digging into things that were beginning to pop up and raise eyebrows.

For the last two years of Bill Clinton's administration his Ambassador at Large for Counterterrorism was my West Point classmate, and onetime roommate, Michael Sheehan. Shortly after the *USS Cole* was attacked in the port of Aden, Yemen, a meeting was held with Madeleine Albright, the Secretary of State. Also at the meeting were Richard Clarke, Clinton's Counterterrorism Advisor, Secretary of Defense William Cohen, Director of Central Intelligence George Tenet, Attorney General Janet Reno, Mike Sheehan, and others. Clarke wanted to go after al Qaeda, and had a plan in place to do so that he had been working on for months. A vote was taken of the participants at the meeting and he was the only one in favor of retaliation against Osama bin Laden. According to a September 11, 2003 report by Kathryn Jean Lopez of National Review Online:

"Reno thought retaliation might violate international law and was therefore against it. Tenet wanted more definitive proof that bin Laden was behind the attack, although he personally thought he was. Albright was concerned about the reaction of world opinion to a retaliation against Muslims, and the impact it would have in the final days of the Clinton Middle East peace process. Cohen, according to Clarke, did not consider the *Cole* attack "sufficient provocation" for a military retaliation. Michael Sheehan was particularly surprised that the Pentagon did not want to act. He told Clarke: "What's it going to take to get them to hit al Qaeda in Afghanistan? Does al Qaeda have to attack the Pentagon?"

"Instead of destroying bin Laden's terrorist infrastructure and capabilities, President Clinton twice phoned the president of Yemen demanding better cooperation between the FBI and the Yemeni security services. If Clarke's plan had been implemented, al Qaeda's infrastructure would have been demolished and bin Laden might well have been killed. Sept. 11, 2001 might have been just another sunny day."

Based on what happened at this meeting, no one thought the attack on the *USS Cole* was worth doing anything about, other than Richard Clarke and Mike Sheehan. All of these people were responsible for the defense of our country and the protection of our people, and going after anyone who killed our citizens, especially our armed forces overseas. Yet, Muslim opinion was more important to most of them than the lives of United States sailors, and the sovereignty of one of our ships. To take it a step further, it's OK if Muslim extremist scumbags murder 17 of our sailors, but God forbid we go after the bastards who did it and offend other Muslims. The only conclusion that can be reached is that Madeleine Albright, William Cohen, George Tenant and Janet Reno felt the sensitivities of Muslims was more important than the lives of our dead sailors, and our nation's honor. What other conclusion can anyone come to? From his comment to Clarke after the meeting, it would appear Mike Sheehan would have voted in favor of retaliation as well, but maybe he didn't vote at all.

Then when 9/11 happened Madeline Albright had the audacity to accuse Bush of not doing anything to prevent it. Bush had been in office for 8 months when it happened, yet Clinton had been in office for a full eight years before it happened. During Clinton's time in the White House we had the attack on the USS Cole, the Embassy bombings in Africa, the explosion at the World Trade Center, and other attacks. Yet he did nothing. So when 9/11 happened, Bush could have done something to show the American people he wasn't going to allow those in positions of responsibility to get away with their failures, like Clinton had done, yet he did nothing as well. This was the beginning of an era where no matter what happened, or how bad things were planned and executed, George W. Bush would not do a thing to punish the people responsible, and worse, would back them to the hilt in the face of overwhelming evidence that they were completely incompetent. His loyalty to his staff, a great asset when times are good, would prove his undoing when times were bad.

As mentioned above, one of the problems with the events of 9/11, indeed one of its causes, was the lack of coordination between the intelligence agencies of our government. The Federal Bureau of Investigation, for example, is responsible for domestic intelligence, for tracking and apprehending individuals who are spying on the United States within our borders. During the Second World War the FBI was famous for apprehending German and Japanese spies found in the United States. On the other hand, the Central Intelligence Agency is the primary asset responsible for ensuring our nation's security beyond our borders, our own "James Bonds." Because he was so out to lunch and out of touch with the realities of the murky world of "human intelligence" collection, Bill Clinton enacted official policy that essentially barred our intelligence-gathering agencies from dealing with people of "unpleasant character." Look at what the results of this have been, and add 9/11 to the list.

The Clinton administration went a step further to diminish our intelligence collection capabilities, in other words to help 9/11 happen. A memo was written by Jamie Gorelick of the Clinton Justice Department, who served under Janet Reno of Branch Davidian massacre fame. The Gorelick memo in effect stated there had to be a complete separation of intelligence collection and intelligence sharing between the domestic and international intelligence agencies of the United States government. The memo was the single main reason for our intelligence agencies' failure to coordinate their efforts leading up to 9/11. Yet this same Jamie Gorelick was a member of the select panel appointed by the President to investigate the circumstances surrounding the events of 9/11! During the course of the hearings it was discovered that the person who was one of the single most important players in the events that led up to the tragedies of that day was in fact a member of the same panel investigating what led up to the events of that day—Jamie Gorelick. Being an attorney, why didn't she recuse herself from membership on the panel? They say the criminal likes to return to the scene of the crime. Maybe Jamie wanted to be on the panel so she would know firsthand how close it was to finding out about her role leading up to the events the panel was investigating. What better place for her to be.

When this came out she cried in outrage that her integrity should not be subject to question, when in fact all anyone wanted to ask her was why the memo needed to be written, and why it was written by her. Instead, the Chairman of the panel, Governor Thomas Kean, got in front of the microphones and blasted everyone and anyone who would dare to even so much as ask about the memo and why Jamie Gorelick wrote it. She was placed off limits by the Chairman of the very panel assigned to investigate the events of 9/11, thereby preventing forever the dissemination to the American people of any information about the memo, why it was written, and what effect it may have had on the events leading up to September 11, 2001. With Ms. Gorelick on the panel she was declared immune by its Chairman from being questioned about her own memo, which was one of the single most important pieces of evidence the panel needed to look at. So it never did. The memo and its effects leading up to 9/11 were put off limits by the Presidentially-appointed panel called to investigate the events leading up to 9/11. If they couldn't discuss the Gorelick memo, why bother to have the panel at all? It was nothing more than a whitewash and a sham.

Throughout all the 9/11 investigations the President did nothing, or if he did anything he spoke in platitudes about how great a person was, how great their service to the nation had been, etc., etc., etc., blah, blah, blah. In the case of Jamie Gorelick, all we got was BS about what a great person she was, and that her integrity was beyond reproach. So much for the American people getting the full story, or even close to the full story, about how 9/11 was able to happen, how we might have been able to prevent it, and certainly what was being done about it now. One thing is for sure, no one lost their job or their precious pension as a result of the biggest intelligence and security disaster ever to happen to this country. And they all worked for the man who campaigned on the platform of personal responsibility. Not only did George Tenant keep his job after the election of George W. Bush, he kept it after 9/11 too. We would see over and over again how Bush would fail to enforce that same promise, and fail to hold people in his administration responsible for one screw up after another. We've all seen it when select people get to a certain level, no matter how bad they screw up nothing happens to them. We were now beginning to see this happening every day.

But in order to make the leap from the events of September 11, 2001, to our attacks in Afghanistan and later Iraq, another critical failure of George W. Bush must be brought to light. After the attacks on the World Trade Center and the Pentagon, and the plane crash in Pennsylvania, George Bush could have done anything he wanted. He could have gotten anything he asked for, and the American people would have given it to him. Even Rosie O'Donnell backed him! If she would, that speaks volumes for the support he had, if he had only used it. But instead of grabbing the bull by the horns and doing what he should have done, what he could have done, George Bush squandered the best opportunity any president since Franklin Delano Roosevelt had after Pearl Harbor to bring the country together in the face of catastrophe. Because Bush is a weak president, like his father, he failed to act. He failed to do the one thing he should have done—he failed to reinstitute the draft.

Some will say this is crazy. But their reaction is the same knee jerk we always get when the word "draft" is mentioned. The President went on about the "global war on terror" after 9/11. If indeed we were now involved in a global war on terror, how were we going to fight it with the Army half the size it was only ten years before? During the Clinton years the armed services were decimated. When I left the Army in 1982 there were 16 fully operational combat divisions. At that time a division consisted of about 20,000 soldiers, and was either an Infantry or armor division. (In a division there are three combat brigades, as well as support units. If at least two of the three brigades are Infantry, then it is an "Infantry-heavy" division. If at least two of the three are armor, it is an "armor-heavy" division. If all three brigades are Infantry or armor, then it is an "Infantry" or "armor" division.)

If the President declared to the country that we were in a global war on terror, and of course our own country had been attacked, how could he possibly think this war could be fought with the post-Clinton manning strength that now had the Army at around 10 operational divisions. It was Bush's perfect opportunity to reinstitute the Selective Service System, whereby men and women would have to register during the month of their 18th birthday, as I did when I turned 18 in 1972. I never served in Vietnam, but I registered for the draft in case the country needed me. But today our country is locked into the "all volunteer Army," which is nothing more than a social welfare system that throws money at kids who want to buy a new car. We pay our soldiers out the nose to enlist, and then pay them out the nose to stay, and then pay them out the nose to go to college, and then offer huge bonuses to re-enlist. True, most are there because they want to serve, but how many would be there without the financial incentives? The true patriot is one who serves but really doesn't want to. The true patriot is the guy who was drafted during Vietnam and had a million things he would rather have been doing, but went because he had to. The true patriot is the one who went to Vietnam totally against the war and paid the ultimate sacrifice. Is today's "volunteer" soldier a true patriot like the Vietnam draftee, when he gets paid out the nose for everything and was probably unemployed in the first place? It's easy for today's volunteer to say he joined to serve his country. But would he have joined without the money and the bonuses? We're just paying for their services. We have a mercenary force, not a volunteer force. If it was a true volunteer force, our soldiers would serve for their basic pay and nothing more. Every time I see commercials on TV for college and the like, it turns my stomach. A volunteer force—where?

One huge reason why the draft is so unacceptable is because the country doesn't want to see women registering for it, as they would have to do, and then actually getting called up. This is the last thing the feminists want, even though they want women to do everything men do, so we can't take the steps needed to protect our country from further disaster in the post-9/11 world we live in today. Something has to be done about this, but people in power refuse to look at it. They are afraid and won't act, and the country is weaker and less defended for it.

Today's soldiers, all good and decent people, are bought and paid for. The majority of those in the service today—other than our true combat forces who really want to serve their country—are there because it's the closest alternative to being unemployed. Yet during Vietnam, because we had a draft, the services were made up of men from all walks of life, all levels of the economy, and all levels of education. The flaw with the

Vietnam draft, like it was during the Civil War, was that there were too many ways to avoid it as Bush, Cheney and Clinton did. Yet, even though there were ways for cowards to get out of Vietnam many, like Tom Ridge, Al Gore and John Kerry did serve. Ridge enlisted as a common Infantry soldier after having graduated from Harvard, and Gore served even though he was the son of a United States Senator and could have gotten out of it with a phone call from his dad. And John Kerry, even though he faked his decorations, did serve in combat and was in the thick of things (albeit for only three months) in the Mekong Delta. Gore and Kerry both served their country in Vietnam, while Bush and Clinton avoided it. And Cheney got married to get a marriage deferment.

It never ceases to amaze me how men who avoided military service have no problem sending young men, and now women, into combat and possibly to their death. How can they look themselves in the mirror every day? But then, they don't really care, so it doesn't bother them. What they really care about is themselves, their egos, and their position in life. They say they care about others, especially our soldiers, but their actions speak otherwise. President Bush goes on about "the troops" he cares for so much. But then he admitted he gave up golf so it wouldn't look like he was enjoying himself too much as the body count continued to climb during this current conflict. How nice. Soldiers' lives are the moral equivalent of a golf game? Can't he come up with a better sounding "sacrifice" than that?

The draft is the last resort when the country is faced with catastrophe. Who would not agree we were in just such a situation after 9/11, and are so today? With a draft the Army and Marines could have grown in strength, and we would have had the forces needed to go into both Afghanistan and Iraq. To think we could pull off both operations without resorting to the draft is insane, yet that is exactly what Bush has done. He never declared war, because that is politically incorrect today as well. So, we went into both Afghanistan and Iraq without a declaration of war, i.e., without a clearly defined enemy, purpose, objective and mission, and without the troops to accomplish any of it. The result has led to the disaster we have now.

3

THE OFFICE OF HOMELAND SECURITY

AFTER THE 9/11 ATTACKS THE President asked Tom Ridge, the Governor of Pennsylvania, to come to Washington to head up a new office in the White House, the Office of Homeland Security. Governor Ridge had been a close advisor to George Bush during the campaign the previous year, with talk of him possibly being Bush's Vice Presidential running mate. But Ridge is pro-abortion, so that idea never went far.

Tom Ridge was sworn in as the nation's first "Advisor to the President for Homeland Security," his official title. Unknown to many, he was actually Condoleezza Rice's counterpart: she was the President's Advisor for National Security, and he the Advisor for Homeland Security. Another little known fact outside Washington was the setup of the Office of Homeland Security, which by its nature was designed to be completely impotent.

The Office of Homeland Security was made a part of the Executive Office of the President, the staff assigned directly to the White House itself. This was done because the President has the power to do most anything he wants with his own immediate staff. If he had tried to create the Office of Homeland Security outside the Executive Office of the President, Congress would have been able to get involved and it would have taken forever to create the office, if at all. Due to limitations of space, most people assigned to the Executive Office of the President don't work in the West Wing itself, but across the drive in the Old Executive Office Building. Some are a block away in the New Executive Office Building on 17th Street. The Old Executive Office Building (the "OEOB") is one of the most beautiful buildings in Washington, having been at various times the Navy Department, the War Department, and the State Department. Today it is an extension of the West Wing, housing staff of the Executive Office of the President. So, when someone says they are on White House staff and work "in the White House," they are on the staff of the Executive Office of the President and very likely don't work in the West Wing, but in the Old Executive Office Building next door.

But there was more to the structure of the Office of Homeland Security (OHS) than just where it was on an organization chart. Being a part of the Executive Office of the President, and not a stand-alone agency, OHS had extremely limited powers. In effect, it had no real power at all. For example, when OHS was established it could not direct any other component of the United States Government to do anything. It was merely a staff element of the White House. And rather than being in the OEOB next door to the White House, its offices were physically located several miles away from the White House at a US Navy facility called the Nebraska Avenue Complex (the "NAC"), located at Ward Circle across from American University. The NAC had been the headquarters of Naval Intelligence during the Second World War, and was the home of the Navy's international arms sales division at the time of the 9/11 attacks. There is a residence right next to Ward Circle located on the NAC grounds, which is home of the commander of the Navy's nuclear program. It used to be the home of Admiral Hyman Rickover, the eccentric "father" of the modern nuclear Navy. Homeland Security kicked out the occupants of one of the buildings on the NAC grounds and completely renovated the interior. It was quite an impressive task, and done in minimal time.

Being a political appointee at the State Department's Overseas Buildings Operations, I was a square peg in a round hole. I had civil servants working for me. One of them went out of her way to make my life and that of everyone around her as miserable as possible. She had a reputation in the State Department for being a total malingerer (i.e., a pain in the ass). She didn't work, but instead complained to the

Federal Employees Union whenever someone tried to make her do her job, which I had the nerve to do. With the Federal Government being what it is she wasn't going anywhere, but I could. I got no support from General Williams with this malcontent, after he had hired me and put me into the job, or from my direct superior, a career Senior Foreign Service Officer who made it very clear he didn't like Republicans, and who I shouldn't have been reporting to in the first place. Never having been in a high level political job before, General Williams didn't realize he was feeding me to the wolves when he placed me in direct charge of bureaucrats. Being a political appointee I should have been in a policy position, where I would report directly to him. It could have worked out if it hadn't been for this woman, but the general didn't care about how much she was destroying the cohesion of the office and the staff, so I was on my own. I saw the writing on the wall and asked for a transfer.

The one person who showed her true colors the days after 9/11 was this woman, who was on my team in Dacca, Bangladesh. The morning of September 12, 2001, she was making a joke of the attacks of the day before. We were eating breakfast in the hotel restaurant and she started joking about how "afraid" she was to be an American, and how she better hide her passport, ha, ha, ha. She thought it was all very funny. The rest of us just looked at her.

I decided to visit the State Department's White House Liaison office. The White House Liaison in a Federal agency is the person responsible for all political appointees placed in that department. I asked one of the staff if I could get another job, either within the State Department or elsewhere. The next thing I knew I was being asked if I would like to work for Tom Ridge in the new Office of Homeland Security (OHS) in the White House. Of course I said yes. Who wouldn't want to do that? I interviewed and was selected to be the Senior Director for Administration in OHS, in charge of Personnel, Security, Information Technology and Facilities for Tom Ridge. I was on loan from the State Department to OHS for one year. In the Government this is called a "detail." Because OHS didn't have budget authority to have its own permanent staff, save for about a dozen people, all of its staff were people from other agencies on detail like me. The entire homeland security of the United States was being coordinated by a dozen full-time staffers and about 50 other people, political and full-time employees, all on loan from their other government jobs.

One of my responsibilities was for the building that OHS occupied at the NAC. Inside the building was a large room set up with plasma screens and a wide array of communications equipment. It was set up just like an Operations Center, but because OHS had no direct authority over anyone, or any other government agencies, we couldn't even call it what it was, so instead we called it the "Coordination Center." To call it an Operations Center would have meant we had the operational authority to tell agencies what to do. All we could do was "suggest" what they should do and monitor them. If an agency didn't want to do what we "suggested," they didn't have to. OHS was a lion without any teeth. All of this was because of where the Office of Homeland Security was placed, which was within the organizational framework the Executive Office of the President. If it had been placed outside that, and had been made a department of the Executive Branch of the Federal Government, things would have been completely different. The results of not doing this were felt everywhere. We had no budget, we had no authority, we had no permanent staff beyond about 12 people, we didn't even have the ability to call our operations center what it really was.

The Office of Homeland Security had essentially two missions. The first was to set up a national homeland security staff and organization to coordinate the efforts of the rest of the government. This involved bringing other agencies together to begin working toward a common goal. This also included bringing together the federal, state and local "first responders" into the effort. And it also involved bringing together federal, state and local governments, and private industry, to coordinate the latest in technology to fight the "enemy." Private industry would soon prove to play a major role in the effort to protect the homeland due to the wonderful way our country works. In a classic win-win effort, private industry stood to gain financially by bringing to the government the latest in technology, thereby making huge amounts of money, while at the same time the government would get what it needed to fight terrorism with the latest technology available. At least it is supposed to work that way in theory.

The second mission of the Office of Homeland Security was to draft the formulation of the new cabinet "Department of Homeland Security" that was only being talked about then, but was well on its way to becoming reality. The staff of OHS spent most of its time doing both of the tasks mentioned here. Some, however, spent all of their time entirely devoted to drafting the legislation creating the new department, although officially they weren't supposed to be doing anything but the first of these two missions. One of my colleagues at OHS was a 30-something PhD and university professor named Richard Falkenrath. Dr. Falkenrath was the primary drafter of the legislation that created the new Department. Included in the law was merging all of those 22 agencies into one Cabinet Department, to include FEMA and the US Secret Service. Why these were brought into the new Department is anyone's guess. It makes no sense to me, but then it wasn't my job to write the legislation, nor to approve what Dr. Falkenrath wrote. Other than these two glaring examples of fluff mixed into the new Department, Dr. Falkenrath did an incredible job at OHS, especially for such a young person. His knowledge of government and the workings of its institutions is remarkable. He is currently the Deputy Mayor of New York City for Counterterrorism, the post most recently held by my West Point classmate, and former Clinton Ambassador at Large for Counterterrorism, Michael Sheehan.

As the months went by the new department became the most talked about topic in Washington. How many agencies would be folded into it? How many employees would it have? How much authority would it have? Where would it be located? How many regional offices would it have? The list went on. I was involved in many meetings on the future location of the new department headquarters. Would it be in Washington or located outside the city, even in another part of the country? Would it be a federally owned building, or leased by the Government for 10 or 20 years? Who would get the deal, who would win this huge procurement, standing to make hundreds of millions in land and development fees? The Congressional delegations from Maryland, DC, and Virginia all got involved, wanting the new agency headquarters to be located in their jurisdiction for employment and business revenue. Federally-owned buildings don't pay real estate taxes. But if the building was leased, the owner would have to pay real estate taxes to the local government, raising millions in revenue for its coffers.

The District of Columbia was at the forefront of these discussions, mainly due to its standing as the jurisdiction most in need. This is primarily because its inept administration, corrupt institutions and socialist government are always in need of Federal cash to operate and make political payoffs. As a result, the bleeding hearts in Congress usually give the District what it wants, only to see US tax dollars poured down the drain because of the bribes, payoffs and bloated bureaucracy of the District Government. The leader of this effort was Representative Eleanor Holmes Norton, the current member of the US House of Representatives in Congress from DC. She has the distinction of having been elected to her first term years ago after it was brought out by her opponent a week before the election that she and her husband had not paid their taxes for years. Their combined income was well over $500,000, yet they couldn't pay their taxes. And they are both lawyers, "officers of the court." She blamed her husband for not filing their taxes, and took no responsibility for the fiasco at all. If Marion Barry could get elected term after term, when everyone knew he was a crack head, what did it matter that Eleanor Holmes Norton didn't pay her taxes?

Having spent nearly 10 years at the US General Services Administration (GSA) involved in leasing and construction for the Federal Government, the planning for the new department headquarters building was right up my alley. This was especially true in light of the fact that the 22 agencies merging into the new Department of Homeland Security all had existing space and real estate. What would happen to these assets when they got combined into one department? You can move the personnel files from one department to another and tell the employees where to report to work on Monday morning, but you can't put a building into a Bankers Box and move it from one location to another. Most of the space the Federal Government occupies is leased. These leases aren't just going to expire because the Government wants them to. I had been a Contracting Officer at GSA, with warrants to execute real estate leases and construction contracts. I would have been a valuable asset to the newly forming Department of Homeland Security, especially working with GSA, my old agency.

Once the law creating the department was signed by the President all the heavies started rolling in, to include a Republican hack named Janet Hale, who was the designee to be the new Under-Secretary for Management. She would be responsible for all of the department's real estate and facilities. This would be a huge undertaking, and I knew it. I asked her if I could assist in any way, but she never gave me the time of day. I wasn't one of "her people." So much for my big plans of getting a high level job in the new department.

I have since seen the effects of Janet Hale's "leadership" as the DHS Under-Secretary for Management first-hand at the Federal agency where I recently worked as a consultant after returning from Iraq. The agency is a component of the Department of Homeland Security. I was employed there by a large firm under contract at the agency. When I arrived at the agency I was told one of the policies she had implemented at DHS was the concept of "shared services," whereby one agency does work for one or more others in addition to itself. It's supposed to trim costs and increase efficiencies. It all sounds good, but makes absolutely no sense in the real world. The problem is the agency doing the work is going to concentrate on its own needs before doing anything for the other agencies it's supporting. It also creates problems because one agency isn't familiar with the space needs of another, causing miscommunication and poor development of space requirements. This added an unnecessary layer of bureaucracy to a process that is already time consuming and extremely complicated, which anything to do with real estate is. It drastically affected the acquisition and delivery of the facilities needed by the agency where I worked, numbering hundreds of individual projects per year. There is an agency that provides real estate services for all Federal departments—GSA—where I happened to work for nearly a decade. Janet Hale saw this on my resume in 2003, but I guess not being one of her people superseded the needs of a brand new cabinet department whose facilities requirements would be gigantic. The new Department of Homeland Security would need staff on hand its first day of operation who had the skills to deal with this dilemma, not the least of which would be working with GSA to acquire and manage the space needed for its 22 sub-agencies.

But Janet Hale was a budget person, not a real estate person, so how would she know this. I did, and was standing right in front of her offering to help in this critical area. One of the traits of a good manager is to use the resources available, especially when you don't have experience in the area yourself. A negative trait is to ignore a person with skills you don't have but that you desperately need, especially if the reason is frivolous.

Since 2003, whenever the agency where I worked needed any space it had to go to the other agency first, which then went to GSA, rather than my agency going directly to GSA itself. Within the last year the agency where I worked canned Janet Hale's "shared services" idea entirely, which was slowing down its space acquisitions by months, and causing needless confusion and duplication of effort. And it had to pay the other agency for its services! The policy didn't cut any costs or save any time. It just made everything worse, wasting time and money instead of saving it.

By 2008 the agency where I worked was just starting to form its own facilities branch from scratch, five years after DHS had been created. It is the second largest law enforcement agency in the federal government after the FBI, but because of Ms. Hale's "shared services" management style it was created without its own facilities staff. My company was brought in as the de facto facilities staff of the agency until it could get its own facilities program on its feet, costing hundreds of thousands of dollars in consulting fees, in addition to what was being paid to the other agency for its services. Some savings.

Ms. Hale is currently at one of the largest consulting firms in the country, no doubt getting highly compensated for her management expertise. Her firm recently acquired my old company, the same one that was under contract to the DHS agency where I worked. And, like General Williams, Janet Hale is also a "graduate" of Harvard. She has a Master in Public Administration from the John F. Kennedy School of Government there. The JFK school might want to take another look at its curriculum for would-be Federal executives.

Present at many of these meetings over the new headquarters building were senior staff from the General Services Administration, GSA, the agency responsible for real estate for the Federal Government. GSA's Chief of Staff, David Safavian, would walk in and start running the show at these meetings, while the rest of us watched in awe. Safavian was a Bush "wunderkind," having come up the ranks of the conservative lobbying world in Washington, and at one time working for Jack Abramoff, who would later be indicted and sent to prison for bribery. During the Abramoff scandal, it came out that none other than David Safavian had sold his position as the GSA Chief of Staff to help his old buddy Abramoff in his attempt to get some sweetheart deals on Government-owned land in DC. Safavian, the wonder boy, had e-mails of the deals on his Government computer, and was indicted too. He went to Federal prison for perjury and using his GSA position for financial gain, but his conviction was later overturned. In the end Tom Ridge decided not to do anything regarding the location of the new department, and it is still located at the NAC. It has kicked out the Navy and the entire complex belongs to what is now DHS, the Department of Homeland Security.

DHS is soon going to move its headquarters from the NAC to southeast Washington, DC, to the area known as Anacostia, by far the most dangerous area in the Nation's Capitol. It's a combat zone. It's where all the murders happen. DHS is taking over a large part of the federally-owned hospital for the severely mentally ill called St. Elizabeth's. This is where John Hinckley, the man who tried to assassinate President Ronald Reagan, has been confined all these years. Why is DHS going to St. Elizabeth's? To make use of all the federally-owned land there that no one else wants. It makes sense financially, but who in God's name would want to work in Anacostia? They will have a tough time getting Federal employees to take jobs there. Maybe they should offer combat and hazardous duty pay.

While the new department was being planned inside the walls of OHS, Congress was busy debating over it and using its creation for its own political gains. Having an ego of my own, I already had plans of where my corner office would be in the new department's classy new building. But Congress, being what it is, blew everything out of that corner window. One day it was discovered that the draft legislation creating the new department had a little clause in it concerning the status of its federal employees. The legislation stipulated they would not be afforded the same "protections" as the rest of the federal government, whereby they could be terminated based on the most ridiculous of reasons—their performance. When this was discovered the AFL-

CIO, and every other major labor union went nuts, but the one that really blew its stack was the Federal Employees Union. (Yes, there actually is such a thing. See the discussion about the woman on my staff at the State Department, above.) They went all out, going to every Democrat in the Senate, and stopped the creation of this new cabinet department, dedicated to protecting our country and its citizens, dead in its tracks. The debate in Congress over the protections to be afforded federal employees in the new department lasted nearly six months, delaying the creation of the new agency by the same amount of time. To the Democrats in Congress, not pissing off the unions was far more important than protecting our country from terrorist attack. (At the time of this writing these same Democrats are trying to shove Barack Hussein Obama's health care bill down our throats so fast none of them have even read the bill. But defending our country at its most vulnerable could wait six months. That was less important to them than taking care of their precious unions so they could get re-elected. It's obvious what they consider more important.)

Being on loan from the State Department to the Office of Homeland Security, my one year ran out so I had to go back to the State Department. General Williams, being the guy he is, gave my job away to someone else. His personal secretary informed me he was telling people that he had advised me not leave him to work for Tom Ridge. This is totally untrue. But more than it being false, why on earth would he tell me not to work at Homeland Security if offered the opportunity? General Williams is a man very short in stature, probably about 5'4". The things he said about me leaving his staff at OBO showed he can be very "small" in other ways as well. Because I was leaving his "team," he was spreading false rumors about me, and refused to allow me back to OBO. Being a political appointee, which meant I was employed at the "will of the President," in this case at the will of General Williams, I found myself on the street. Thus ended my career as a political appointee in the administration of George W. Bush.

4

"A Slam Dunk"

I LEFT THE ADMINISTRATION AFTER working for it for two years, both at the State Department and the Office of Homeland Security in the White House. By the time I left, the new Department of Homeland Security was just getting started, but it will be years before it is on its feet. To the Department's credit, and that of President Bush, our nation has not had another attack on its soil. This alone speaks volumes for the new Department, and for the administration. They have done a commendable job in this area.

Of course, liberal federal judges will not allow the Department of Homeland Security (DHS) to protect us as well as it could. A perfect example was the recent decision by US Judge Charles Brayer (the brother of the Supreme Court Justice) of the Northern California District, who ruled against DHS in its effort to send out letters to business owners notifying them of the *possibility* they may be employing illegal aliens. All the DHS letter was going to do was notify employers that they may be employing these people, and that they needed to make sure their employees were in the country legally. It was a way for employers to assist DHS in doing its job. What could possibly have been wrong with doing this, especially when it would have required at least ten suspected illegals at the place of employment for the letter to be sent? What are the odds an employer would have that many workers who were illegal aliens and not know about it? And the group that went to the judge to stop the letter from being sent was the group that represents the interests of illegal aliens in this country. Of course they don't want the letters sent. That would mean the US was on to the employers who aren't doing what they are supposed to do—not employ illegal aliens—and the illegals would be sent back home. What is our country coming to?

President Bush has lent plenty of assistance in this area too. Does Vicente Fox have something on Bush that has caused him to fail us so much regarding illegal immigration? One has to wonder. Did Fox help Bush get reelected to a second term as Governor of Texas? We'll never know. But we do know that Bush has sold the country out to Mexico. He'll probably build his Presidential Library in Mexico City.

By the time President Bush started talking his nonsense about granting asylum to illegal aliens, just months after 9/11, another pot was brewing—Afghanistan. After 9/11 President Bush declared to the nation and the world he would pursue Osama bin Laden wherever he was, and it turned out he was in Afghanistan, hiding in the mountains of Tora Bora near the border with Pakistan. The assault on Al Qaeda in Afghanistan has been debated at length, but the prevailing wisdom is that it was necessary, that bin Laden was there, and that he needed to be pursued and destroyed. But it is this last point that has proven elusive, and has created as many questions as it has answered.

General Tommy Franks was at the time the CENTCOM Commander. To those not familiar with military acronyms, CENTCOM stands for "Central Command." The United States armed forces are located all over the world. The entire world is broken up into regions for purposes of designating who is the military commander in charge in the event of hostilities. Therefore, anything that involves US forces in the Middle East falls under the CENTCOM Commander, whose offices are actually located at MacDill Air Force Base in Tampa, Florida. When Bush declared he was sending forces into Afghanistan, which lies within the geographic region of CENTCOM, that meant the operation fell under the command of Tommy Franks.

Franks is an affable fellow. Adopted by two loving parents of simple means, he grew up in Midland, Texas, driving pickups and chasing girls, like any normal good ol' boy. He went to the University of Texas at Austin, flunked out and enlisted in the Army. This was at the height of Vietnam. He was a good enough soldier to be asked to go to Officer Candidate School, meaning that he could add 2+2 and polish his belt buckle, and off he went to Vietnam as a Field Artillery Second Lieutenant and forward observer. In his book, "American Soldier," Franks describes the highlight of his service in Vietnam as his ability to handle multiple radios at one time while flying passenger in an observation helicopter to call in artillery fire on enemy positions. He took great pride in devising a method by which he rigged the headphones and the radios in the aircraft to be able to do this, almost as if he wanted to patent the improvisation. That was the highlight of his Vietnam experience. He served proudly, came home, got married, and began a rise to the highest levels of Army service. He never mentioned in his memoir if he ever graduated from college.

Tommy Franks was one of those fellows who must have had friends in the right places. There is no other possible way he could have gotten as high up as he did with the minimal qualifications he had. One has to wonder if his connection to Laura Bush had anything to do with this. She and Franks went to the same high school in Midland, Texas. There is no way to make general in the United States Army without "being connected." This is typical. But for Franks to have gotten where he did without a college degree and being a dropout from UT is truly amazing. If he got a degree he never discusses it in his book, only that he was kicked out of school, almost as if he is proud of the accomplishment. Franks surely must have been an adequate officer, but he must have also mastered a particular skill absolutely essential to advancement in the Army. He must have been a true "yes man." The fact is, military officers will not do or say anything as they advance up the ladder that they think might piss someone off, thereby jeopardizing their career. I know this. I've been there. I have seen full colonels lie through their teeth to avoid saying something they don't think their superiors want to hear. In many ways they are like Iraqis, who do the exact same thing.

Tommy Franks was groomed to be the successor to then-CENTCOM Commander Tony Zinni. Zinni was a Marine 4-star general who had spent years in the Middle East and really knew the people and their culture. Franks had been Zinni's deputy commander, groomed to be his successor by simply showing up for work with the right boot on the right foot. When Zinni retired, Franks took over and turned out to be at the right place at the right time. It's a funny twist of fate that in both the Gulf War of 1991 and this recent conflict, the previous CENTCOM Commanders had been Marines, but then left the job to their Army replacements, who then got all the glory for leading the subsequent attacks. The Marines must have gone apeshit over this. The CENTCOM Commander before Schwarzkopf was Marine General George Crist, who resigned because he got upset when he didn't get promoted to Commandant of the Marine Corps after the CENTCOM job. I guess retiring as a mere 4-star general just wasn't good enough for him. He had to retire as Commandant of the Marine Corps or his career was a flop.

The planning for operations in Afghanistan began in earnest soon after 9/11, with Tommy Franks at the forefront. He describes in detail in his book how he did this, but the main point was that everything he did was done at the request of, and to the specifications of, Donald Rumsfeld. The entire operation was Rumsfeld's, from soup to nuts. The idea of going into Iraq originally came from Deputy Secretary of Defense Paul Wolfowitz, but it was Rumsfeld who pulled all the strings and demanded that the war be conducted the way he wanted it done. Franks was more than a willing water boy, carrying whatever Rumsfeld wanted, and dumping it all on his poor staff officers in Tampa. My heart goes out to those poor souls on the CENTCOM staff right after 9/11. If they still have their sanity it's nothing short of a miracle.

The planning for operations in Afghanistan was thorough. The numbers and types of our forces seemed to match the terrain and the size needed to destroy the enemy's. And most important, the original successes we achieved were substantial. But two things went wrong. The first was not capturing Osama bin Laden, and the second has been our inability to maintain the successes we initially achieved, and at great loss of life.

During December of 2001, US intelligence identified Osama bin Laden's location in the mountain range called Tore Bora, in the east of Afghanistan along the Pakistan border. Not only did the mountainous terrain provide ideal protection for bin Laden, but the location was very close to Pakistan, offering a quick escape route from approaching forces from the west. Tommy Franks knew where bin Laden was, but instead of sending in US forces to capture or kill him, he went the "politically correct" route and sent in Afghani warlords to make it look like the locals were pulling their weight, when in reality they were worthless and just wanted American money for their own gain. Their only allegiance was to the US dollar bill. The attack was a flop, and bin Laden escaped. We have never been that close to capturing him since. When I heard what had happened I was as shocked as I was the night Bush the First announced the cessation of hostilities at the "end" of the Gulf War a dozen years before. How could Franks let bin Laden go? Could Franks be that inept? Maybe. Then again maybe not. I heard a first-hand account from a West Point classmate who was at the command center in Afghanistan when the radio traffic came in the night bin Laden's location was pinpointed. US Army officers in the field were requesting everything higher headquarters could give them to throw at bin Laden, yet their requests went unanswered. The radio had not gone dead. Higher headquarters, CENTCOM Command, refused to answer their requests for support. Why? Did the administration want bin Laden to get away? No one knows. But he did, and the war goes on, and the contactors and the military industrial complex keeps grinding away. I am not a conspiracy theorist, but one has to wonder how this could have happened.

While Afghanistan was in full swing, the plans for invading Iraq were being worked on as well. Again, Franks was actively involved in this, soon to become the commander of two major military operations at the same time. This is a commanding general's dream. During all of this Franks would fly back and forth from the States to the Middle Eastern theater of operations on his jet with his close personal staff—and his wife! A commanding general in wartime does not travel around with his wife on his official aircraft, but that's exactly what Franks did. Not only was his wife everywhere he went, but she sat in the middle of classified briefings given to her husband when she had no authorization to be present because she didn't have a security clearance. No one said a thing, certainly not to the general's face. She might have gotten upset if she was asked to leave. What a shame. Eventually, one of his staff officers had the courage to file a complaint with the Army Inspector General. When does a staff officer ever do something like this against his commander? Never. It must have been infuriating to his staff, and it took one with balls to actually do it. Of course, nothing was done. Franks was, after all, the commanding general, and that was that. Sort of like what John Deutch, the former Director of Central Intelligence, did when he was caught taking his classified lap top computer home and downloading porn sites on it—and not going to jail for it. Or when Sandy Berger went to the National Archives to steal copies of Bill Clinton's secret testimony during the Monica Lewinsky hearings out of the building in his socks, and nothing happened to him either. The higher one goes, the more they can ignore the law and get away with it.

As the planning for the invasion of Iraq progressed, it became clear to all involved that Donald Rumsfeld wanted it to be as lean and mean as humanly possible—I call it "Invasion Lite." He initially wanted around 35,000 soldiers to invade Iraq! That was soon discarded for a higher number, but not nearly enough. When I was at West Point I took a course during my last year called "History of the Military Art." It was mandatory for all cadets to take during their First Class (senior) year. It was a fascinating course, starting with the Trojan and Greek wars, went through the Roman conquests, Napoleon, the American Civil War, and the major world wars. We studied strategy (the big picture) and tactics (the little picture). One of the founding principles of warfare is this: when on the offensive (i.e., attacking) never attack with less than a 3-1 advantage in soldiers and overall force. As the invasion of Iraq was being planned it appears this principle was never even mentioned. It can only be assumed that Tommy Franks had West Point graduates on his staff, but these would be officers of full colonel rank and higher who would never open their mouths and tell Tommy that he was out of his mind. If they did they would have had their heads handed to them. But it wasn't up to the officers on Tommy Frank's staff to be aware of this military doctrine, it was up to Franks himself. Any officer who has risen to the rank of 4-star general and does not know of this military principle, going back to the beginning of modern warfare, was not deserving to wear the uniform of the United States Army. But that's exactly what Tommy Franks did. It must have been more important to him to be liked by Donald Rumsfeld than it was to come up with a plan for the invasion of Iraq that would work. Franks, like all the rest of the "best and the brightest," must have thought that all of the sudden warfare had changed and Infantry soldiers on the ground were obsolete and no longer required—that we could win based on our superior technology alone. Warfare hasn't changed at all. We just have more technology available to support the foot soldier who is the one who fights the fight on the ground, where it matters.

But why this 3-1 ratio when on the offensive, when attacking? When one force is attacking another, the force being attacked is stationary, and if lead by competent commanders it is dug-in and doesn't have to move long distances like the attacking force does. It has "central position," whereby the attacking force has to come from multiple directions, with different forces attacking in different places. By "dug-in," it is in fortified positions in the ground in the form of "fox holes," or well placed inside fortifications using earth, wood, steel and concrete to improve its positions. In the case of Iraq, the enemy would be "dug-in" by being hidden in buildings in every town, and with large man-made sand and dirt earthworks to hide and protect their tanks and other crew-served weapons. Multiply this on a scale covering the entire country of Iraq, and you have hundreds of thousands of troops, with their tanks and other crew-served weapons, hidden in every conceivable place, hidden from plain view, and protected by earth, steel and concrete. The Iraqi army under Saddam Hussein was estimated to be as large as a million men in strength, yet Rumsfeld was initially planning to attack this force with about 35,000 soldiers. At most 20,000 of this attacking force would have been actual combat Infantry and Marines. Granted, the Iraqi army had its ass handed to it by the US Army during the Gulf War, but that was because we went into that conflict after a 37-day aerial bombardment that was equal to some of the bombings during World War II, and then we attacked with 500,000 soldiers supported by the new Army M1A1/2 tank. The Iraqis didn't have a chance. This time things would be different.

Rumsfeld continued to plan for "Invasion Lite," and Franks continued to suck up and give him whatever he wanted. The facts spoke undeniably against going into Iraq with anything fewer than half a million men—again—but who cares about facts! Besides, it had been so easy the last time, why would it be any different now? Things don't change, do they? Who would expect the Iraqis to adapt to the beating they had received before and come up with new tactics? They're too stupid! When asked by the President for his opinion of the attack plan George Tenant, a real military wizard, said it would be "a slam dunk." Not only should Tenant have been fired by 12 noon on September 11, 2001, he was still around and able to give these nifty little assessments of how he thought the invasion of Iraq would go. He was saying what Rumsfeld and the President wanted to hear. Bush was out to lunch, and Rumsfeld's plans continued to be implemented by Tommy Franks, who would do whatever he could to please his boss, at the expense of soldiers' lives and the assurance of victory on the battlefield. Sounds like Powell and Schwarzkopf—"déjà vu all over again."

For his part the President allowed all of this to go on without the slightest show of stopping it or caring where it went—like Lyndon Johnson during Vietnam, who had no ability to control the hemorrhaging that McNamara had created. Harry Truman had a sign on his desk in the Oval Office that read "THE BUCK STOPS HERE." Well, that is indeed the case when it comes to the President of the United States. It is the President who is ultimately responsible for all that goes on in the government and what the government does. He has been elected to run it. He is the Commander-In-Chief. Rumsfeld would not have been allowed to do anything if Bush had not approved it, or had told him to come up with a better plan. Well, as they say, "You don't know what you don't know." The saying applies to Bush. He didn't know a good plan from a bad one, but Franks should have. The simple fact is this: Bush knew nothing about waging war, being a de facto draft dodger himself, nor did one of the chief architects of the war, Vice President Dick Cheney. Both had avoided the Vietnam War, Bush by joining the Texas Air National Guard, and Cheney by getting married. Yet both of these men had absolutely no problem waging a war that was fraught with failure: from the lack of troops, to the lack of intelligence about the enemy we were going to fight. With the intelligence capability that our country has, there is no reason why we did not know the facts about the enemy we were about to attack, yet we didn't. However, with Clinton's watering down of our intelligence capabilities, especially our human intelligence capability (our spies working with "bad people") it really isn't too surprising that we didn't know more about the enemy than we did. Tenant must have known this. So how could he then tell the President it was going to be a "slam dunk" when he knew our human intelligence was lousy? The only conclusion is that George Tenant didn't have a clue what the result of our invasion of Iraq would be.

Either Tenant thought he had enough intelligence, but didn't, or he was pulling that assessment out of thin air. I would tend to think it was the latter. He didn't have a clue what we were going up against or getting ourselves into, but wanted to say what he thought his boss wanted to hear. Just like Tommy Franks telling Rumsfeld what he thought Rummy wanted to hear. And these were the "best and the brightest" people we had at the absolute highest levels of our government and military. It's scary to think about. They all fell to the belief that the war would be a cakewalk like the Gulf War, which had a 37-day aerial bombardment before an attack by 500,000 US troops. Rummy thought the results would be the same with an aerial bombardment the opening night of the invasion and an attack by around 125,000 total strength (US and other countries), which the number eventually rose to. In reality no one had done any homework on the enemy, its capabilities, or even what the enemy looked like.

5

OPERATION IRAQI "FREEDOM"

To get public support and buy-in for the war, the President told the country that Saddam Hussein possessed weapons of mass destruction, the "WMD" that has become a part of our vernacular. The President had established the doctrine of "preemptive attack," thereby attacking the foe before the foe had the opportunity to attack us. This is what we were told. Yet, after the war began the President had the nerve to say that he never told us he was attacking Iraq because Saddam possessed weapons of mass destruction! Like the day his father stopped the Gulf War those years before, I couldn't believe what I was hearing. All I could think of was the propaganda machine of Dr. Joseph Goebbels, Hitler's Minister of Public Enlightenment and Propaganda in Nazi Germany—lie to the people long enough and they will start to believe it. I know what I heard before we invaded Iraq: it was the President of the United States telling me, and the world, that Saddam Hussein possessed weapons of mass destruction and that he was just about to start using them, with the implication he would start using them against us. We were even told he had small planes that were equipped with spray nozzles under their wings that might be used to emit poison gas and nerve agents over our cities. Was Saddam going to fly them across the ocean and then start spraying gas over our heads? How was he going to get them that far, ship them Federal Express so they would be here in time for his "attack!" I never felt the case for invading Iraq was solid or had been proven, yet

I supported my President because I had worked on his campaign, and because he was a nice guy. He wouldn't lie to me would he? Nice guys who go to church don't lie—do they?

President Bush told us we were going into Iraq to eliminate Saddam's weapons of mass destruction and to overthrow his regime. We were told the United Nations sanctions and the inspections of potential WMD sites after the Gulf War had been complete failures. The President told us that Saddam Hussein had left him no choice but to invade. Many of us believed him, and the President got the required number of votes from the Senate to attack. Many of those votes were cast by liberal Democrats wanting to be seen by the American people as being tough on national defense. In reality they don't want anything to do with national defense, only pork that gets them votes. To them votes are obviously more important than anything, especially their principles and national security, especially in an election year. John Edwards at least had the courage to say he made a mistake voting for the war, but of course by doing that he also implied that he was disingenuous and voted for the war when he really didn't want to. He had the choice and he took it, and for that he will be remembered and he will be judged. If he had any principles he would have voted his conscience (which is why people elected him in the first place), and voted against the war. But he wanted to be looked upon as a "hawk" simply to get votes for his next run at the White House. Since then he has been exposed for his affair and his love child, a big fall for a former US Senator. The little head was doing the thinking for the big head once again. Clinton could pull that off, but he already had the job. And why all the fuss, anyway? It's only sex. Who cares if Edwards' wife is fighting cancer while he's nailing a young blonde?

But the main event was when Colin Powell, who knows everything, was ordered by Bush to go to the United Nations to prove to that august body and to the world that Saddam had weapons of mass destruction and was about to "push the button." (Bush probably begged Powell to go.) For several days before he went to the UN, Powell poured over documents at the CIA and asked hundreds of pointed questions of the staff there. We are told by his adoring media that he did this to get all the facts. I tend to think it was for another reason—to make sure he was not going to put his foot in his mouth at the UN, or at least minimize the size of his shoe. The media plays this out like Powell was being the good student and going over everything to do the best job he could. I'm not so sure.

When Powell presented his "evidence" before the UN Security Council it was pretty clear he was grabbing any straw he could to make a case to invade Iraq. He probably suspected we didn't have a case to make in the first place. He knew Bush wanted to go to war and he was serving Bush's cause, even though he most likely didn't believe in the cause himself. Sounds like McNamara "supporting" Johnson during Vietnam. But if the case for WMD was as strong as the President was telling us it was, and if Colin Powell is the smartest man alive (after, of course, Barack Hussein Obama), why did he have so many doubts about our reasons for going to war up until the day before he flew to New York, which was evident by the amount of time he spent at the CIA? It is pretty clear now that the President and Powell were pulling the case for war with Iraq out of thin air. I recall Powell's testimony that day at the UN. He played a recording of a cell phone conversation between two Iraq army officers that had been intercepted by the National Security Agency (NSA). This is the agency located at Fort Meade, Maryland that has the electronic capability to tap anyone's phone and look at objects the size of a postage stamp from miles in space. We were told this information was so secret that Powell had to insist on the cell phone call being "declassified" so he could share it with the world. The call didn't prove squat. The conversation didn't say anything. It was a couple of Iraqi clowns jabbering over the phone about a "weapon." It didn't prove anything, yet the UN approved a resolution "allowing" the US to invade Iraq. The only reason the UN did so was not because of the bogus "proof" they had received, but because it came from the mouth of Colin Powell. If he said the sky was falling everyone in the Security Council would have run out of the room. No matter what he said everyone believed it to be the Gospel, the word of God himself. So much power was placed in the hands of this one man. Way too much power. No one ever questioned anything Powell ever said. If Powell said it, then it must be true. It had to be true! Like the Gulf War 12 years before, Colin Powell sold our country down the river—again.

With UN backing (i.e., permission) the plans for the invasion of Iraq continued. George Tenant said it would be a "slam dunk," and we all know now how accurate his assessments were. Colin Powell had succeeded in blowing smoke up the UN's ass, and Tommy Franks and Donald Rumsfeld continued with their plan for "Invasion Lite." Not allowing for anywhere near a ration of 3-1 in the invasion plans, the numbers of forces was slowly increased to around 125,000 US Army soldiers, Marines and other Coalition forces. The plan called for the land transit across Turkey of the 4th Infantry Division, commanded by a West Pointer with a shaved head (who doesn't even have parachute wings on his chest) named Raymond Odierno. Because Turkey screwed its ally, the US, and would not allow transit across its territory, the 4th Division sat in boats on the Mediterranean Sea for weeks twiddling its thumbs while the initial invasion of Iraq, and the real fight, went on without it. Odierno must have been climbing the walls in his "command ship." Later, when his division finally got involved the initial fighting was already over, so he would have to make up for it by creating some "fighting" of his own. There is speculation that many Iraqis were needlessly killed because Ray Odierno and his division had been left out of the initial stages of the fight. He probably felt he had to mix things up when he got there so he could say he hadn't missed all the "action." (*Fiasco*, pp. 232-233)

When the invasion and the initial ground fighting began it consisted primarily of two main attacks, one Army and one Marine, coming north from Kuwait. The ground commander of all US forces who reported to Franks was US Army Lieutenant General (3-star) David McKiernan. Because the Marines can't stand being under the command of an Army general, they sent Lieutenant General (3-star) James Conway over. He was there so the Marines would have a general in Iraq of equal rank to the Army general who was in charge, and also because they wouldn't have to take orders from an Army general. Whenever McKiernan wanted to say anything to the general in command of the Marines on the ground, Major General (2-star) James Mattis, he had to go through LTG Conway, thereby creating another layer of bureaucracy in the middle of a war. But the Marines didn't care. Their Marine ego is far more important than military efficiency by cooperating with the other services in a warfight. Conway is now the Commandant of the Marine Corps, having done such a great job as a messenger between McKiernan and Mattis. This arrangement flew in the face of another military doctrine of warfare, "unity of command." The Marines didn't want to report to an Army general, so they slid in a 3-star of their own. That meant that Mattis had two people to report to, Conway and McKiernan. Apparently, McKiernan was very upset about this, but Franks didn't have the balls to correct it and kick Conway out the door, which is exactly what he should have done. In the military politics is as important as it is in Washington. Besides, the Marines would have probably gone crying to Rumsfeld and gotten what they wanted anyway. Of note is the fact that LTG Conway was also responsible for the creation of the Fallujah Brigade in April 2004. This neat little operation, where the Marines would pull out of the area so the place would quite down on its own, turned out to be a complete disaster. Instead, the insurgents jumped on the opportunity Conway gave them and killed more of the Marines he was in command of. He wanted to be another Colin Powell and negotiate with, instead of kill, the enemy. All the insurgents did was take advantage of Conway's "kumbaya" nonsense to kill more of his Marines. That's what happens when generals lose their focus: their soldiers get killed and the enemy gets away. And more often than not the general gets a promotion because he's got a grasp of the "complexities of the situation," and is "thinking outside the box." Again, as we have seen from the opening days of this conflict, once a senior military officer has been selected for advancement it doesn't matter what he does or how bad he screws up, he is on his way.

On the very first day of the invasion the first casualty was an Army soldier killed in a drive-by shooting from a mini pickup truck. He wasn't killed in a conventional fight with regular Iraqi army soldiers. He wasn't killed by Iraqi artillery fire. He wasn't killed by an Iraqi soldier. No, he was killed by a guy dressed in civilian clothes driving by in a pickup truck. Some conventional war we were in. Some "slam dunk." This would be the case throughout the entire ground battle leading up the road to Baghdad—no conventional Iraqi forces or soldiers in uniforms like the Gulf War, no Iraqi tanks like the Gulf War, no conventional lines of defense by the Iraqi army like the Gulf War. Yet our commanders, and most of all Rumsfeld and Franks, never got the hint that this was their new enemy. They never figured out that we were up against guerrillas in a street-by-street, building-by-building fight, who wore civilian clothes and road in civilian cars. Instead, the entire campaign all the way to Baghdad was fought by the US with M1A1/2 tanks blowing up anything firing a bullet or an RPG (rocket propelled grenade), and continuing the move forward without killing the bulk of the enemy's ground forces.

The United States M1A1/2 tank is the most powerful tank ever built. Nothing can stop it except another tank, which the Iraqis don't have, or an anti-tank rocket fired from the shoulder of a man hidden behind an obstacle, which they do. If you have enough M1A1/2 tanks, you are likely to get where you want to go. There is only one problem with a concept of warfare that relies completely on tanks, as this concept did. With enough M1A1/2 tanks you will reach your objective, but you won't kill the enemy hiding in the buildings you pass along the way—if you don't have Infantry. The enemy will still be there after the tanks roll through. In Operation Iraqi Freedom, the assault of M1A1/2 tanks up the road from Kuwait was like a car driving through a puddle of water—the car will drive through the water, but after it does the water will just go right back into the puddle where it was before. You have to eliminate the puddle! Because we didn't kill the fedayeen, the new Iraqi enemy, as we advanced north to Baghdad, they were still there as we continued up the road toward the next town. All they did was pick up their weapons and ammunition and follow our tanks. The US was in such a hurry to move toward Baghdad that all "mopping up" (killing the enemy in house-to-house and door-to-door fighting by Infantry) was avoided because Rumsfeld and the President wanted to declare "Mission Accomplished!" as fast as possible. Franks just went along for the ride.

The cause of the problem is simply this—we invaded with too few Infantry soldiers. The problem existed when we first invaded Iraq in the spring of 2003, and it still exists today. The United States invaded Iraq in the spring of 2003 with a fraction of the number of ground combat soldiers needed to do the job right the first time, all because Donald Rumsfeld thought he was smarter than Tsun Tzu, Clausewitz, and all the military scholars who have studied warfare throughout history. He thought the US could defeat any enemy, of any number, anywhere, and at any time regardless of the number we brought to the fight. We can only do this with the right number of soldiers and equipment to do it with. Rumsfeld's plan for the invasion of Iraq was wrong, and we will be paying the price for his stupidity (and his ego) for years.

But Tommy Franks is equally to blame. He was the 4-star general in command, a veteran of Vietnam who had attended all the US Army's staff colleges where they do nothing but study the art of warfare, from the Greeks through Vietnam and Desert Storm. These courses look at planning attacks on a major scale, because the students are being groomed for the senior commands in the next war. What did Franks do when he attended the US Army War College in Carlisle, Pennsylvania—party like he did at the University of Texas? With the results we got out of him during this campaign, he probably did just that. What was Franks thinking, or was he thinking at all? Did he ever stand in front of Rumsfeld and say the plan was a risky? Did he ever say the plan had holes in it? Did he ever say to the Secretary of Defense that his plan to invade a country with an army as large as a million men, albeit a crappy one, with 125,000 US and Coalition forces was taking a chance? Did the attack include a 37-day bombardment like the Gulf War? And who was the enemy? Did the CIA have a real grasp of who we were going up against? It would seem the answers to all these questions would be "no." And if Franks didn't ask any of these questions, did he ever think of them in his head? How could he not have with his years of military experience, the training he had, with his rank and the high level of responsibility he had been entrusted with?

To invade a country without using all the forces at our disposal is a crime. We obviously didn't plan for the enemy we would be fighting against, or the fight itself. How could we with the results that we have gotten? This war is like driving a car and someone in the next lane pulls into your lane and hits you. After the accident the driver of the other car swears they looked before they made the move. But they couldn't have looked because if they did they would have seen you. You were right there. So they are making it all up. This is what "Slam Dunk" Tenant did. He was making it all up and hoping it would be a "slam dunk," because how on earth could we be beaten by the Iraqi army. It's like the driver of the other car. Change lanes and hope the other car isn't there! But we never went up against the Iraqi army. We were up against the fedayeen from the first day of the war. Yet our leaders and military commanders never adapted to the situation that they hadn't foreseen and planned for, and they never changed their strategy. If they didn't plan for it, then it was treated as though it wasn't happening, as though it couldn't happen. This is the biggest mistake of the entire war. The entire administration from the President on down, to include Rumsfeld, Powell, Tenant and Franks, all did the same thing. They all thought it would be a pushover, without having taken any time to really find out what they were getting us into or what was happening after we got there. **The United States failed far too long to adapt to the changing situation on the ground in Iraq.** Getting the United States into the war on flimsy grounds was one thing, coming up with a flimsy invasion plan was another, but not adapting to the changing environment and the realities of the war on the battlefield is inexcusable.

As the advance progressed towards Baghdad, the soldiers and Marines were taking a real beating. The only reason we made it to Baghdad at all was because we had the M1A1/2 tank and the Iraqis didn't. But what about the unconventional plain clothed forces we were up against, the fedayeen? Who were they and where did they come from? And where was the Iraqi army, the guys whose butts we handed them on a platter 12 years before? They were gone. It was just fedayeen now, yet our tactics never changed. Like the car driving through a puddle of water, what good was it to blow through a small Iraqi town with tanks, fighting every inch of the way, only to leave the fedayeen behind as we drove up the road toward Baghdad at 40 miles per hour? Did we kill the enemy? No, we didn't. We just pushed him out of the way and left him there to fight us another day in another Iraqi town closer up the road to Baghdad. And where were they getting their weapons and ammunition? Saddam had been hiding tons of it in small towns all over Iraq just for this occasion, yet when we found these caches we left them instead of destroying them in-place because we were afraid there *might* be WMD inside the stockpiles that would spread contamination if exploded. Without human intelligence from the CIA, there was no way for us to know the caches were there before we invaded. And if we didn't know the caches were there, we sure as hell didn't know there might be caches with WMD buried underneath them. It was all a big surprise to everyone, I bet George Tenant most of all. But if we were going after

WMD, as the President and Colin Powell told us, why didn't we have the chemical and biological experts with the advancing troops to detect WMD if and when we came across them, which could have happened anywhere or any place? There's only one explanation: the invasion was planned so fast and so poorly that the basics were never considered, such as what specialized soldiers to send over. So the stockpiles of weapons and ammunition were just left where we found them, for the fedayeen to go back and take with them as they followed behind us up the road to Baghdad.

If the reason for invading Iraq given to us by the President was Saddam's WMD, why didn't we have enough WMD experts, soldiers trained to deal with these threats, with the advancing troops in the initial phase of the war as they came upon these weapons stockpiles? The only conclusion can be President Bush gave us the WMD threat as the excuse to go to war. But once he got the votes he needed from the Senate, and the approval (again, "permission") from the UN, he didn't even bother to staff our invading units with WMD experts because he really didn't care. The WMD thing was just a ploy to get us into the war, just like the attack on Pearl Harbor was the excuse FDR needed to get the US involved in World War II.

This proves the fallacy of the WMD excuse to invade Iraq. We were told we were attacking Saddam because he possessed weapons of mass destruction, but we didn't even have WMD experts with the advancing units to make the WMD determination if and when we thought we may have come upon some. Tons of weapons, ammunition and explosives were simply left where they had been found, with thousands of fedayeen left alive because we didn't have Infantry with the tank columns moving north from Kuwait, whose job it would be to kill them. The result was more fedayeen following our tank columns as they advanced toward Baghdad, with more fedayeen waiting for them up the road, all armed with weapons and ammunition we left behind. As we got closer to Baghdad we were hit from the front, from the rear, and from the flanks, by fedayeen we left alive in towns our tanks had rolled though without Infantry to mop-up, shooting at us with the same ammunition our forces had left in those same towns because we didn't have WMD experts to make the decision to destroy it. This is remarkable. As the title of Colonel H.R. McMaster's book so aptly phrases it, this is gross "dereliction of duty." It placed the lives of our soldiers at tremendously greater risk than they ever should have been in. Our commanders, from the President on down, are to blame. This is not the way to fight a war, but this is the way Rumsfeld and Franks planned it, and how we fought it anyway.

As our tank columns approached Baghdad the fighting got incredibly intense. The fedayeen put up a fierce battle on the outskirts of the city. Finally, one tank brigade commander, Colonel David Perkins, decided he would just plow his way into the heart of the city, without approval from his higher command. On his own, Colonel Perkins sent his units forward on what would be known as the "Thunder Runs." The enemy casualties caused by these swift advances were immense. But so were ours. The US units achieved their objective, reaching the center of the city where Saddam's government buildings were located, and which would later be called the "Green Zone." These advances also reached Baghdad International Airport, where the headquarters of all Coalition forces in Iraq would later be located. It was when these advances reached Baghdad that the President declared "Mission Accomplished!" on the deck of the aircraft carrier USS Abraham Lincoln. But all that had really been achieved was the presence of US forces on the ground in the center of Baghdad. That was it. We no more had command of the situation on the ground in Iraq than we had a prayer of finding any WMD. We were there, and holding onto our grip of the few Baghdad city blocks that we "controlled" with our fingertips. This was victory?

From the first day of the assault, when the first US casualty was killed by a plain clothed "civilian" from the back of a pickup truck, until the day the President declared that our mission had been accomplished, we had not come across any regular Iraqi army units of any appreciable size or force. Yet our tactics never changed. We were partially using the same World War II armored tactics the Germans had used during the Blitzkrieg in the opening days of the war in western Europe. In this case Franks was using half of what he had learned from his dusty history books. But during the Blitzkrieg the Germans also had Infantry to kill any dismounted (not in tanks) enemy they came across, and to hold onto anything their advancing tanks had captured and destroyed. We were fighting with the same armored tactics, only without the Infantry to kill all the fedayeen the tanks had missed, and to control and maintain what we had captured. So tenuous was our "victory," it could have been achieved if we had simply conducted an airborne (parachute) assault at the very same location in the center of Baghdad that our tanks had "captured." The President could have declared "Mission Accomplished!" just the same. Our "hold" of the objective was as slim as it could be because we didn't have enough Infantry to maintain it. Tank soldiers are not Infantry soldiers. They like to ride and shoot big projectiles and blow things up, and they do this very well. Infantry are the foot soldiers on the ground, who go house-to-house and door-to-door and kill anything that shoots at them. That's the *only* way to fight a war and to win a war. Every other part of the military exists to support the Infantry to include tanks, planes and boats. Without an Infantry soldier holding and securing a piece of ground you haven't "won" anything. Tanks only have a crew of two or three men. They may arrive somewhere, and even blow the place up, but then what do you have? They're not going to get out of the tank, and if they do they'll be too few in number to do anything other than get themselves killed. Infantry units can hold ground the tanks have helped them capture because they have the manpower. But then again, if you are executing "Invasion Lite," you can't go in with tens of thousands of Infantry soldiers. The Infantry is heavy with people, and Rumsfeld didn't want that. He wanted the smallest number of soldiers going to Iraq so he could claim he was invading a county on the cheap, with tanks that could cause a lot of damage and make it to their objective. He thought the tanks would destroy everything, even soldiers dug into holes in the ground and hiding behind every wall. That's because he didn't know how to wage war. Tommy Franks, who is supposed to, just sat there and did nothing. He didn't want to piss off his boss. Holding on to his 4-star job and taking his wife for joy rides in his plane were more important to Tommy Franks than planning an attack that would work, and protecting his soldiers from unnecessary harm and high casualties.

    The biggest mistake Rumsfeld made was that he didn't really know what or who his enemy was going to be. This is inexcusable in modern warfare. Like the driver of the car in the lane next to mine who, if he looked and knew I was there, wouldn't have pulled into me. If Rumsfeld and Franks knew who and what their enemy was, they wouldn't have planned this war as they did. But they didn't know. They couldn't have known. Yet they went in anyway. As bad as that is, they then failed to adapt to the realities of the situation on the ground once they realized they were up against an enemy they hadn't planned for, who used tactics and stores of weapons and ammunition we left in place and didn't have the soldiers to fight against. But they refused to change the way they fought the war anyway. A tank can't kill a soldier in a hole. All it can do is fire a projectile over his head. A tank can't kill a man hiding behind a wall, unless it has infrared vision to "see" him. Rumsfeld just planned on there being no enemy left when the tanks exited the towns on their way to Baghdad. He thought they would drop their weapons and run away at the first sight of our tanks. And Tommy Franks went right along. Well, they were both wrong. But it's OK to be wrong as long as you change your original plan and adapt to the reality of the situation on the ground. But Rumsfeld's ego simply wouldn't allow him to do that. What makes a real warrior is the ability to do this. Rumsfeld wasn't one. Franks was supposed to be, but wasn't one either. Anyone who knows anything about warfare knows that tanks can only destroy so much. They can't destroy what they can't see. And thousands of fedayeen hiding in buildings in every small Iraqi town can't be seen as the tanks roll by. This is the way Franks fought the war Rumsfeld wanted him to fight. Franks should have known better. He probably did, but he allowed Rumsfeld to go on with his ridiculous plan, when he should have refused to buy into it, cost what it may to his career. But that would have taken courage, the kind of courage General Eric Shinseki, the Army Chief of Staff had. General Shinseki was the only general officer who told Rumsfeld the war could be fought, and won, with half a million men. For his opinion, Rumsfeld fired him. And as an added insult to this fine officer Rumsfeld refused to attend his "retirement" ceremony.

For his role in Operation Iraqi Freedom Tommy Franks will be remembered as one of the worst field captains in our nation's brief history. He rose to the position of CENTCOM Commander, he blew it, and he will pay the price in the history books. Franks was a "yes man" through and through. For the poor planning and execution of this battle, mostly due to the fact that we didn't have enough soldiers in the attack, primarily Infantry, we have paid dearly. But the ones who will pay the most, and have paid by the tens of thousands already, are the Iraqi people left in the crossfire.

The initial phase of Operation Iraq Freedom ended in this manner. We had reached the center of Baghdad, had been severely bloodied on the way, and in the months and years to come would continue to fight a new foe that is fierce, has plenty of firepower, is willing to die for his cause, and blends into the population. This is what we had waiting for us the day the President declared "Mission Accomplished!" on the deck of that aircraft carrier.

Is the fighting over now? Are there no more bullets being shot at our troops, or IED's (improvised explosive devices) blowing up our HUMVEE's? Is the enemy in capitulation to our numerous demands and wishes? Is there complete and unconditional surrender like we used to demand of our enemies after we had vanquished them? Are our soldiers greeted as conquering heroes everywhere they go, with Iraqi children waving little American flags that we were actually thinking of giving to them when we invaded? The answers to all of these questions is an obvious "no." We are not welcome by everyone in Iraq. Our soldiers are in firefights every day, being shot at from every direction. There is no end in sight, and the streets of Baghdad aren't much safer today than they were the day the President declared "Mission Accomplished!" How could President Bush say such a thing with a straight face? We were no closer to a real victory the day he said that than the day the invasion began when our first soldier was killed by a man in plain clothes firing from a pickup truck.

What is the definition of victory? Of a free Iraq? Is that what existed the day the President declared victory on the deck of the aircraft carrier, or was that just a "feeling" he had? Or a wish? How can victory be declared, in this or any war, when the fighting is still going on? How can victory be declared when that same day our soldiers are being killed and there is no sign at all of the fighting coming to an end? The victory was a temporary lull in the carnage, nothing more. We were sold down the river by George W. Bush. And I helped him get elected.

6

Paul Bremer

WITHIN WEEKS AFTER THE INITIAL ground combat ended the President sent retired US Army Lieutenant General Jay Garner to Iraq to oversee the reconstruction of the country. He was there only a few months when he was sacked by Rumsfeld and replaced by Paul Bremer, a career State Department Foreign Service Officer whose ego, arrogance and stupidity has led to the deaths of tens of thousands of Iraqi civilians.

Charged with the reconstruction and governance of all aspects of Iraqi society, Bremer proceeded to reinvent Iraq, in effect to create a new Iraq complete with a constitution, a rule of law, civil works, and something resembling a democracy. Many of the steps Bremer took were well intentioned, did a lot of good, and helped a lot of Iraqi people. But everything he did went down the drain when he made two decisions. In the effort to cleanse Iraqi society of any vestiges of Saddam's regime, he dissolved Saddam's personal political party, the Ba'ath Party. Anyone of consequence in Saddam's regime, and in Iraqi society, was a member of the Ba'ath Party, similar to being a member of the Communist Party in the former Soviet Union. A "Who's Who" of Iraqi society, one had to belong to the party to get ahead, regardless of what the party did. So, in an effort to rid the country of this cancer, Bremer "de-Ba'athified" it. But when he did so he purged anyone who had been a member of the party, down to its lowest ranks. The result was the firing of anyone who had any knowledge of the basic functions of government, e.g., the mid-level bureaucrats who ran the governmental institutions throughout the country, to include the provinces and towns.

But the other decision Bremer made was far more critical, making the one described above appear inconsequential by comparison. Without public notification, and in the face of overwhelming opposition from everyone on or off his staff who was aware of his plan, Paul Bremer dissolved the Iraqi Ministry of Defense and Ministry of Interior. With the stroke of a pen he eliminated the two institutions, the army and the national police, responsible for the security of the country and the Iraqi people. This decision would result in the deaths of tens of thousands of Iraqis. Without enough American forces to protect and secure the country because of Rumsfeld's inept plan to invade with a skeleton force, and now no Iraqi army or national police as well, the country was wide open for the violence and civil war that was to follow. What was left was a country not only without a head (Saddam) but without its arms and legs.

Bremer had to know the country was in a bad state of affairs. How could he not? How could he not know there were scant US forces to protect Iraq and that we had destroyed Iraq's critical infrastructure? Our forces could hardly protect themselves. How could he not know of the fedayeen and the violence they had been causing since the first day of the war? How could he not know of the civil unrest between Sunni and Shi'ite after 25 years of Saddam's rule? To make these two decisions was insane. It would have been enough if he had fired all the senior ranking generals and members of the Ba'ath Party, but to fire every member of the Iraqi armed forces and every member of the national police made absolutely no sense. In addition, he fired nearly every government official. Who, then, would patrol the streets, man the border crossing stations, and defend the country from outside attack from Iran and Syria—all at the same time? The Iraqi government? The US Army, which was only part of the total Coalition force of 125,000 soldiers, two-thirds of them support (non-combat) troops? In two actions, Paul Bremer eliminated the entire external and internal security infrastructure of the country, and fired all of the government employees who knew how to operate the dams, the electrical power systems, the water purification plants, the sewer systems, the streets and highways, the stop lights, and the schools. But he was Paul Bremer, a self proclaimed genius. By doing this he provided the insurgents, who were already raising hell with the US Army and Marines, the new recruits they needed. He gave the insurgents newly fired soldiers and policemen he had just sacked, all with their own weapons and ammunition, who now had a plausible reason to hate the United States and our presence in Iraq.

For a period of time after the initial fighting stopped Iraq was calm. Did Bremer think this was permanent? Who knows. But when he made the decision to disband the Iraqi army and national police, all calm went out the window. By 2004 things started picking up as a direct result of his decisions. Insurgents were going after Iraqi civilians and Coalition forces like ducks in a pond. US casualties were mounting up every day, and the word "Vietnam" was being heard on the streets of every city and town in America. But why were we still there? Saddam had been yanked out of a hole near his home town of Tikrit, and we couldn't find any weapons of mass destruction, although I'm sure the administration was hoping we would. How could it not? That was the reason we were given by the President for invading. If we didn't find WMD then the entire operation was put into question.

Around this time Cindy Sheehan's son was killed, and she became the symbol of parents who were angry that their children were being killed trying to find WMD when there was none. She also became an icon for the liberals who were against the war. I can't stand the sound of her voice. It makes my skin crawl every time she opens her mouth. But is she wrong for what she has done? If I lost a child under the same circumstances, especially after having lived through the debacle of Vietnam, I would have some questions too. If only we could have found some WMD then all would be well. But it was not to be. I remember talking with my mother about this. She is such a staunch Bush supporter that she would simply say that we would find the WMD, that Saddam had hidden them all. But as the months went by and we weren't finding anything, the best we could hope for was the occasional discovery of a few hundred artillery rounds with the chemical symbol stamped on them. They would flash the discovery of this "massive trove of WMD" on global TV, yet they would all be rusty and not possibly usable. Just old discarded mortar and artillery rounds from Iraq's war with Iran, or when Saddam used them against his own people after the Gulf War, all with our knowledge, of course.

So why were we still there after 2004? By this time the tension between the Muslim Sunni and Shi'ite factions in Iraq started to get worse. By 2005 we found ourselves right in the middle of an all-out civil war. We never should have stayed after we captured Saddam, and it was obvious by then we wouldn't find any weapons of mass destruction. But we stayed anyway. We were now starting to get sucked into a civil war that we had largely created ourselves with the dissolving of the Iraqi Ministries of Defense and Interior. We had to stay now because we had created the very "power vacuum" Bush the First was supposedly trying to avoid in 1991. Thanks to Paul Bremer there was no Iraqi army, so there could be no military security, and there was no national police, so there was no civil security on the streets. In his effort to wipe the slate clean and start from scratch, Paul Bremer had gone way beyond anything close to what might have been needed. He eliminated all the country's security institutions, and along with them the security and safety of the Iraqi people. Throw in the fact that we invaded with barely enough force to roll into central Baghdad, and you had a recipe for disaster that couldn't have been scripted better if it had been planned in the West Wing of the White House or the halls of the Pentagon. And it was all done with the acquiescence and the tacit approval of George W. Bush.

If we had invaded with the 3-1 ratio of an attacking force, which to his credit Colin Powell had done during the Gulf War, this never would have happened. I have classmates from West Point who were involved in the planning of Dessert Storm, the first Gulf War. The Iraqi army was so bad that we had parity against them even if we had a ratio of as little as 1-3 against us. That was when Iraq had a real, conventional army numbering as large as a million men, and even then we bombed the hell out of them for over a month before we crossed the border to invade. Given these numbers, even the worst planning for this invasion would have justified at least 350,000 soldiers. Rumsfeld first wanted to invade with less than 50,000 troops! Of these, only 20,000 or so would have been combat forces doing the actual fighting.

As previously stated, who would have dared try to start things in Iraq after the first Gulf War if there had been an *occupying* force of

400,000-500,000 American troops present on the ground? And who would have tried anything after our invasion in 2003 if we had the same number? Those who don't know a thing about military tactics don't know that there is a "break-even" point, where the more troops you have on the ground the fewer casualties you have, not more. Novices believe that the more soldiers you send into a fight the more casualties you will have. Nothing could be further from the truth. In Iraq we have had just enough troops on the ground to be easy targets, but not enough to mount an offensive campaign against the insurgents. But if we had 500,000 troops in Iraq the insurgency would never be able to get off the ground—there would simply be too many US forces present for it to get anything started. Whatever they tried would have been put down immediately. This is not just theory. Look at what has been happening in Iraq for the past four years. *The administration, with the war led by Donald Rumsfeld, went in with too few troops, but would not adapt to the changing situation in the field.* As soon as the situation in Iraq started to fall apart, which the world could see happening on cable news, the President should have made a decision to either pull out then, or send in more troops immediately in order to stop the hemorrhaging of the situation. Instead, he did nothing while we all sat there and watched, just like we did during Vietnam.

War is a confusing business, and the one thing that can be counted on is that it will not go the way you plan. This is a fundamental fact of warfare. Any soldier worth a grain of salt knows this. Tommy Franks certainly should have known it, and if he didn't he should never have gotten as far as he did in his career. We went into Iraq with barely enough forces to make it to Baghdad, and stayed there after Saddam had been captured but we had failed to find any weapons of mass destruction. By that time the insurgents (as the fedayeen were now being called) were picking off our soldiers by the dozens, so we decided to stay. In effect, we were now stuck there. Does the word "quagmire" come to anyone's mind? But then why stay without increasing the number of our soldiers? Why stay if we had achieved our objective of capturing Saddam Hussein and had found no weapons of mass destruction? Did we stay because the situation in Iraq was now different? Let's suppose that's why we did. If that was the case, why didn't we also decide to increase the number of soldiers we had there to adapt to the new situation? In effect the President, and Rumsfeld, decided to stay beyond the achievement of one of our objectives (Saddam), but then they didn't do anything to increase the number of troops we had there after the situation got terribly worse. Were we staying to "finish off" the insurgents? If so, we weren't doing such a great job. The more we pushed the insurgents, the harder they fought back and the more of our soldiers they killed. For the past five years the Iraq war has been a case of the US having just enough soldiers on the ground to be targets, but not enough to mass a *strategic offensive* to completely destroy the insurgency. This is all because of Bush and Rumsfeld, and their abysmal planning of the war before the invasion, followed by their lousy handling of the war since its opening day.

By 2004 the civil war between Sunni and Shi'ia, and the terror being inflicted upon Iraqi society by the forces of Al-Qaeda in Iraq (AQI) and infiltrators from Iran and Saudi Arabia, was in full swing. Now, instead of local Saddam zealots killing our soldiers, we had forces that were better trained and equipped coming from other parts of the Arab world, using the Sunni and Shi'ia factions within Iraq as surrogates. Now we were committed to a whole new war that we hadn't planned for, but for which we still hadn't changed our tactics in order to fight successfully. Not only had we been fighting fedayeen and not regular Iraqi army forces from the opening day of the war, which should have been a red flag that the plan of Tommy Franks and Donald Rumsfeld might have to be re-worked, but a year later we were up against insurgents that all indications showed were being equipped, supported and trained by the Shi'ite Iranians from the east, the Sunni of Syria and Saudi Arabia from the west, and Al-Qaeda forces from the Balkans and Central Asia from the north. Yet we still refused to bring in more troops to meet the demands of the situation. Instead, all we have heard since 2004 is that the "Iraqis are doing better," "they're doing a good job," and that "our strategy is working." This is all nonsense.

Paul Bremer added to this disaster by eliminating the Iraq security forces, thereby forcing the entire situation onto the United States to fix. Yet we keep saying it's the Iraqis' problem. It's not. **As soon as Bremer eliminated the Iraqi National Police and the Iraqi Army he made it our problem.** It is our problem because we created it, and it is our obligation to fix it. But we are doing neither. We are going to remain in Iraq at abysmally low troop levels, saying the Iraqis are "coming around," while the ones who suffer are the Iraqi people who are getting slaughtered by the thousands every month, all because George Bush wouldn't admit he planned things wrong, or change the way he was doing them once he got there. We should have either left Iraq after declaring that our objectives had been accomplished (we captured Saddam and found no WMD, although we sure wanted to), or if we were going to stay we should have poured in 200,000-300,000 more troops to adapt to the realities of the situation on the ground. Bush did neither. The irony is that his father, Bush the First, pulled out in 1991 when he should have stayed, and his son was staying when he should have pulled out!

The combination of the following factors created the current situation in Iraq:

1. Not invading Iraq with enough ground forces to kill the enemy, and trying to finish the mission too fast. We went in with plenty of armored units, but not enough Infantry to mop-up, i.e., kill every enemy soldier (fedayeen) in every village and town the tanks were going through. In addition, the President and Rumsfeld were in such a rush to declare victory, the advancing units were practically sprinting to Baghdad, passing insurgents every step of the way.
2. Not adapting to the realities of the situation on the ground. We should have added more forces as soon as it became clear that we were not up against conventional Iraqi army forces—as it had been *assumed* we would be—as soon as it became obvious things were not going to be the "slam dunk" George Tenant predicted. Instead, our forces were up against thousands of plain clothed guerilla fighters who were hiding behind every tree, rock, wall and doorway. This would have required 200,000-300,000 more troops then Rumsfeld had planned for. But if he didn't plan for them, they were simply not needed. The war would be won with what Rummy had planned, and that was that. But the generals knew better. They had to. If they didn't they should have been fired. If they did and didn't say anything they should

have been fired, or simply quit. But of course "Invasion Lite" was all Rumsfeld wanted, so they would have been fired if they said anything that didn't follow that line, like Shinseki. But Rumsfeld still wouldn't have changed his plan. At least these generals would have been able to look themselves in the mirror. But getting that next star and promotion is more important to most of them.
3. Paul Bremer's decision to eliminate the Iraqi Armed Forces and the Iraqi National Police. Doing this, combined with not having enough Coalition forces on the ground in the first place, was a recipe for disaster. This was the icing on the cake to creating a completely unsecure Iraq, an Iraq wide open for any terrorist organization to walk right through the front door and do what they do best—murder people.

This combination of factors has created the current situation, but this beast has continued to be fed to the present day. In later chapters this book will describe some of the ways this has been done. Suffice it to say, the situation in Iraq could not have been handled worse if it had been planned. Inept leadership from the President on down through Rumsfeld, Franks, Tenant and Bremer, and a host of military advisors, has led our country to this point half a world away. I say a host of military advisors. I purposely did not include "a host of civilian advisors" for a simple reason—I would not expect them to know any better. But senior military advisors should. It was shameful of any general officer, especially one who was old enough to have fought in Vietnam, to allow our civilian leadership to enter upon this disastrous course of action in Iraq without trying to stop it, or drastically alter the plan. Didn't they learn anything from that experience? How can a country invade another if it does not go all out with overwhelming force to achieve its objective and, yes, occupy it if that is what is needed to protect and secure the population. If I were a betting man I would say the lives of the Iraqi people just aren't that important to our national leadership.

The only senior ranking officer who said the correct thing was the Army Chief of Staff, General Eric Shinseki, who told Rumsfeld that it would take several hundred thousand soldiers to invade Iraq successfully.

Why would he have said this? Because he had studied military history at West Point, and he remembered what he had learned in Vietnam. He knew of the 3-1 ratio when attacking an entrenched enemy. He knew that you always attack with more than enough forces than you think are needed in case the unexpected comes up—which is to be expected in warfare. If you have more forces than what you need, then just send them home. He probably knew that our intelligence gathering capability stunk, and that whatever intelligence estimates we were getting could not be relied upon. After eight years of the dismemberment of our human intelligence capabilities by Bill Clinton, executed by George Tenant, and then with the continuation of that policy by Tenant as Bush's CIA Director, our intelligence on Iraq wasn't worth the paper it was written on. Look at what Powell went through trying to get straight answers from the CIA up until the night before he went to the UN. General Shinseki, being a Vietnam veteran and the senior officer in the United States Army, and also a student of military history at West Point, knew these things.

Tommy Franks' book, "American Soldier," was written at the same time he was leading us into the quagmire in Iraq, and he retired in order to publish it and cash in on the money. By the time Franks' book had been out six months the situation in Iraq was going down the toilet. Who's the one who didn't know what he was talking about, Franks or Shinseki? General Shinseki knew what would be needed, and he advised Donald Rumsfeld accordingly, which was his job (i.e., to advise the Secretary Defense and the President), and what did he get for his advice? Rumsfeld fired him and didn't even have the professional courtesy to attend the retirement ceremony of a man who had served his country in uniform for more than 40 years, from the day he entered the Military Academy at West Point as a new plebe. But the blame is not Rumsfeld's. It rests with the President. If George Bush had a grain of decency and respect, as we so often hear him say he has, he would have ordered Rumsfeld to knock off his childish behavior and attend Shinseki's retirement ceremony. But this is just another example of the hands-off leadership of Bush. Whatever Rumsfeld did the President turned the other way and didn't do a thing. It's been just like Johnson and McNamara the whole time. Rumsfeld even looks like McNamara.

The same could be said of Paul Bremer. By disbanding the Iraqi Armed Forces and the National Police he created the very "power vacuum" we kept hearing about after Desert Storm. It's as if the administration wanted to create it. But if a power vacuum had surfaced after Desert Storm, at least we would have been able to say we didn't plan for it to happen, and we would have had the forces in place to deal with it. But purposely disbanding the national police and the Iraqi army is a different matter. Bremer fired every single Iraqi soldier and national policemen (the Iraqi provinces have their own police forces). This "power vacuum" was entirely created by us—by Bush, Rumsfeld and Bremer. And where did many of these fired soldiers and policemen go, with their weapons and ammunition, and a new-found hatred of the Americans who just created their loss of a job and the inability to feed their families? We destroyed the Iraqi economy with the UN sanctions after the Gulf War, and then we did this? Many went right into the insurgency as new members of the same forces killing American soldiers. At least by maintaining the Iraqi army and national police we could have kept an eye on these men, trained them in ways we felt would be best for their country, and kept them busy instead of going off to join the insurgency. But Paul Bremer's stupidity stopped any chance of that ever happening.

Even though he was not a soldier, Paul Bremer would have to know that we didn't have enough forces when we invaded Iraq, and therefore not enough forces to protect the county after he disbanded the Iraqi army and national police. He was surrounded by military and former military advisors who should have known this. But rather than consult with his staff, Bremer never asked anyone for their opinion of his plans because he didn't want anyone to disagree with him. Being insecure, he was afraid of any feedback that did not conform to his decision. Instead of being open to other ideas, he made up his mind without consultation with others and then implemented his decisions with his staff unaware of what was coming and ill prepared to act upon it. The Coalition Provisional Authority, the CPA, became an organization famous for employing young people in search of adventure, old military retirees in search of something to do, and State Department civilians looking for advancement. All of them were looking for a lot of money. Paul Bremer became the classic example of an "egomaniac with inferiority complex."

Getting rid of Saddam Hussein we chopped off the head of the beast. Doing this we created a tenuous situation in a country known for backward thinking and backward ways of doing things—by comparison to us. But making the decision to disband the entire Iraqi Armed Forces and National Police, Bremer chopped off both its arms and legs. Now we were left with a beast with no head to lead it, and no arms and legs to get anything done. And by invading with a token force, we didn't have enough of our own soldiers on the ground to do anything about the situation we had created, other than fight to stay alive themselves. The fewer soldiers you have the more casualties you will have because they can't defend themselves. As you increase the number of soldiers, casualties may rise some simply because the enemy has more targets to shoot at. But once you hit the "break-even" point, you have so many soldiers on the ground the enemy goes into hiding or runs away, and the numbers of friendly casualties drops like a rock. We have never reached that point in Iraq. We have always maintained US troop levels that give the enemy just enough targets to shoot at and kill, but not enough to keep the enemy in hiding, or better yet, dead. We've never reached that point throughout the entire Operation Iraqi Freedom conflict because we have never increased our troop strength, other than the "surge."

The "surge" of 2007 is the one thing the administration has done right. The surge contributed an additional 25,000 troops to the fight. The reason the surge has been successful is the same reason why the initial phases of Operation Iraqi Freedom were a dismal failure—the surge consists of just INFANTRY SOLDIERS! US Army soldiers will destroy any foe in their path, if there are enough of them to do the job. There is no enemy force on earth that can stand up to the right number of American soldiers who are given a clear objective and a mission to accomplish. But the surge is too little, too late. It only has enough strength to contain a relatively small geographic area. When the surge went into Baghdad it was immediately successful because it was doing what the initial invasion forces should have been doing as the armored columns drove up the road to Baghdad. The surge is a mission that calls for its soldiers to go house-to-house and door-to-door to kill bad guys. We should have been doing this all along instead of going on meaningless "presence patrols" to show the people we were around, in cities and towns, but not concentrated enough or massive enough to constitute a meaningful fighting force, resulting in our soldiers getting constantly picked off. The surge clearly shows that we have learned from these lessons and has successfully cleaned up parts of Baghdad. But the enemy has simply moved northeast to Baquba and outlying areas, and continues to do the same thing there that it has been doing in Sadr City for four years. The surge is a good move, but all it is doing is moving the fight somewhere else, to a place that had been relatively peaceful. I'm sure the residents of Baquba don't appreciate the surge very much.

By being successful but too little, too late, the surge shows that there has to be much greater numbers than a mere 25,000 more soldiers. If it was we would be able to not only clean up Baghdad, we would be able to sustain the security of the rest of Iraq. But with only 25,000 troops, we can only clean up an area and then move on. Once we leave the area we just cleaned up the insurgents move right back in. Or, we could clean up an area and stay there. Then that area would be the safest place in all of Iraq, but it would just be a postage stamp-sized area in the middle of a country that is falling apart. The only way to really clean up Iraq is to "surge" the entire country, which would take at least 250,000 soldiers, 150,000 of which would be Infantry. Again, General Shinseki. The surge is a very good operation, but it can't sustain the successes it has achieved because it's too small to secure more than a neighborhood, or possibly a sector, of Baghdad or any other town in Iraq at one time. It's great for that sector or neighborhood, but what about everything else where it has no presence? What about when the surge force leaves? We're seeing this in Afghanistan now. It was a great operation in 2002-2003, but as soon as we drew down our forces the Taliban and Al-Qaeda came right back. Military success only works if maintained. That's why nothing happened in western Europe after the Second World War. We stayed there at high troop and unit levels for the purpose of keeping the peace in Germany, and preventing the Soviet Union from invading. Does anyone think for a moment it would not have invaded if the US Army didn't have a million men in Germany for 40 years? Is there that much of a difference between Germany after World War II and Iraq after we invaded in the spring of 2003? The size and scale are different, but not the strategy. Without a large force in Iraq we can't maintain what security we achieve, nor would we be able to fight off an attack from the outside, such as Iran, if it chose to do something by seizing the opportunity.

The low levels of our forces is also creating a terrible strain on the soldiers who are there. All of the fighting is being done by an incredibly small a number of soldiers and Marines because we don't have enough replacements to give them the needed rest. We keep sending our soldiers back but we don't bring in enough new recruits because we don't have a draft. Why will some young people volunteer for combat when they don't have to? It takes a very brave young man or woman to do such a thing, even with the money they get thrown at them. They may be brave, but we simply don't have enough of them to go around. The few we do have are doing all the work, with the help of the reserves and the National Guard, but all of them combined isn't enough. The fighting is done by the combat soldiers, which is a small fraction of the total strength of our armed forces. The reason the surge is successful is because it is a concentration of fighting soldiers. But we don't have enough fighting forces to do the same thing throughout Iraq what the surge is doing in parts of Baghdad.

At the end of the Second World War the United States, along with its other major allies, occupied Germany for decades. Why did we do this? To begin, after the war there were thousands of pro-Hitler sympathizers who wanted to continue the fight in his memory. For years after the war many Germans worshiped Hitler and wanted to continue what he had started. In addition, there was the very real fear after the war of the Soviet Union invading Western Europe and overthrowing the entire continent, as Hitler had attempted to do just a few years before. The United States had to remain in Germany for years to prevent all these events from occurring. Of course, as the years went by the pro-Hitler sympathizers dwindled, and about 40 years later the Berlin Wall came down. It took a while, but our occupation of West Germany was successful.

Fifty years later we are faced with an almost identical situation in Iraq, but we refuse to learn from our experience—and success—in post-war Germany. Just as in Germany, there exist thousands of pro-Saddam sympathizers in Iraq who thought he had the right idea about the Kurds and the Shi'ites. And just like Germany, Iraq stands to be overrun by its neighbor to the east, Iran. Yet, because our leadership is weak, we waffle. Instead of formally occupying Iraq and calling it just that, which we should do in order to maintain peace, we refuse to call our presence there an "occupation" because that isn't politically correct. And our troops suffer in the long run because we don't have a draft to replace them, much less occupy the country with the few forces we have there. Even though an occupation would require more of our soldiers to serve in Iraq, it would result in fewer casualties. Bush wouldn't do this because it was politically incorrect also. He wouldn't do this because he was afraid of the uproar from the liberal left. He received the votes he needed from the US Senate in order to invade Iraq, so what was he afraid of? But by 2004-2005 he knew it was too late politically to increase our forces in Iraq. He had the votes and had the chance to do it right, but Rumsfeld wanted "Invasion Lite," and the opportunity was lost. And, of course, the Iraqi people suffered the worst of all.

7

MNF-I

DURING THE INITIAL PHASE OF Operation Iraqi Freedom the coalition forces were called the Coalition Forces Land Component Command, or CFLCC. CFLCC was commanded by Lieutenant General David McKiernan, who reported directly to Tommy Franks in Tampa, Florida. Under McKiernan were all Coalition forces in Iraq, which comprised not only all the American forces but British, Australian, and all other allied forces who had joined the United States in what President Bush referred to as the "Coalition of the Willing." As time has gone by this Coalition of the Willing has dwindled down from around 25 countries to at most ten on a good day, and more like 5 on a bad one. Great Britain and Australia were being hard pressed by their people to pull out entirely, and only Tony Blair's strong support of Bush during most of this ordeal kept the Commonwealth nations involved as long as they were. The countries left include El Salvador, Mongolia, the Republic of Georgia, Korea and Japan. Not much of a fighting force. The United States, as always, makes up about 95% of all forces in Iraq today, although Australia and Great Britain had larger numbers of troops there until the latter's decision to pull out in early 2007. At the time of this writing, Australia has decided to pull out all of its forces, with Prime Minister Kevin Rudd stating former PM John Howard "misled" the Australian people into joining the conflict alongside the United States.

All Coalition forces in Iraq today fall under the command of the Multi-National Forces-Iraq, or MNF-I, commanded by General David Patraeus until the Fall of 2008, and now commanded by General Raymond Odierno. The previous MNF-I commander was General George Casey, who held the position for approximately two and a half years. The various subordinate commands that fall under MNF-I are:

1. The Multi-National Corps-Iraq, or MNC-I, formerly under the command of Lieutenant General Raymond Odierno prior to his assuming command of MNF-I.
2. The Multi-National Security Transition Command-Iraq, or MNSTC-I, under the command of Lieutenant General James Dubik, and which was formerly under the command of LTG Martin Dempsey.
3. Task Force 134, formerly under the command of Marine Corps Reserve Major General Douglas Stone.
4. The Joint Area Support Group, or JASG.
5. The Joint Special Operations Command-Iraq, or JSOC-I.

These commands and their missions will be described individually.

The Multi-National Forces-Iraq is the overall command of all forces in Iraq today, including US and other Coalition forces. As mentioned above, it was previously commanded by General George Casey. During the time that General Casey led MNF-I, the situation in Iraq deteriorated to the point where US casualties grew to weekly rates reminiscent of the Vietnam War, and Iraqi civilian deaths went into the tens of thousands. It was while General Casey was in command of MNF-I that the civil war within Iraq between the Shi'ia and the Sunni factions of Islam escalated, and the outside influence of Al-Qaeda in Iraq (AQI), Iran, Syria, Saudi Arabia and others increased. Also during Casey's command we witnessed the rise of the cleric Muktada Al Sadr, whose shenanigans went untouched, even while he taunted the United States and killed American soldiers by the hundreds. All of this occurred during General Casey's command, "on his watch" as they say, leading anyone to wonder how he held onto the job as long as he did, similar to George Tenant.

Yet what happened to General Casey when he left this position? Rather than be allowed to "retire" like General Shinseki, he was promoted to the highest job in the United States Army, its Chief of Staff. How could this happen? It is highly probable he was given this job in order to avoid the embarrassment (to him or the administration?) if he was ushered out of the Army, which is what should have happened. But instead of this he was promoted, most likely so the President could say he was given this new job as a reward for having done such a great job back in Iraq. General Casey's promotion to Army Chief of Staff was an implicit way for the President to say things in Iraq have to be going pretty good, otherwise why wouldn't the outgoing commander get promoted. It is another example of the "smoke and mirrors" the administration has subjected the American people to. Instead of calling it like it is, saying things aren't going well in Iraq and the commanding general there is going to "step aside," the President promoted that same general who did nothing during the period of turmoil described above. Rather, General Casey kept reporting to Congress that the situation in Iraq was improving, and the Iraqis were doing a great job. Nothing could have been farther from the truth during General Casey's tenure, but he got promoted as if that was reality. And, instead of refusing the job because his time in command was a disaster, General Casey gladly stepped in and is now watching soldiers get killed because he let two and a half years go by without asking for more troops to deal with the deteriorating situation on the ground.

His replacement was General David Patraeus, the former commander of the 101st Airborne Division. (The 101st used to be an "Airborne" unit, gaining fame at Bastogne during the Battle of the Bulge near the end of World War II. But since the Vietnam War it has been an "Airmobile" division, meaning it no longer parachutes into battle, but rides in helicopters. The "Airborne" on the shoulder patch is for nostalgic reasons only.) After leaving Iraq, General Patraeus came back to the States and was promoted to his third star and took command of Fort Leavenworth, the home of the famous federal prison, as well as home of the Army's Command and General Staff College. While there General Patraeus advanced the training in Middle Eastern studies, in order to better indoctrinate mid-level Army officers to the ways of fighting in this area of the world in the years to come.

When General Casey left for his nice new office in the Pentagon, General Patraeus, now a brand new 4-star general, stepped onto center stage in Iraq with a new vision and new ideas. Being an open-minded person, his new thoughts and ideas were a welcome change to the narrow vision of Casey, who was afraid to ask for more troops to do what was needed. (Or, being so out of touch with the realities on the ground in Iraq, General Casey didn't think anything was needed.) It was widely believed at the time that General Patraeus agreed to take the job only if the "surge" was implemented. (See below.) It is not known exactly how many soldiers were originally asked for, or if it was the 25,000 actually sent over. What is known, at least from the news accounts, is that the President said he would give Patraeus whatever he asked for. If this was true, it's too bad Patraeus didn't ask for more, but 25,000 was better than nothing. Anything would have been better than what Casey did.

It has now come to light that the "surge" was not even General Patraeus' idea, or that President Bush was really "giving the generals whatever they wanted." In his September 2008 Washington Post series on the turmoil inside the Bush White House in 2005-2006, Bob Woodward has described how it was Steve Hadley (one of the few civilians in the Bush administration who had a clue about warfare) and the National Security Council staff who realized the war was at a complete standstill, and told the President so. In a couple of satellite video teleconference calls, Hadley and others on the NSC staff asked General Casey, with Bush's permission, direct questions about the war and its current state at the time. Casey, Woodward reports, was livid he was being asked the questions at all, and furious at the insinuation he didn't have the situation in Iraq under control. The body count of US soldiers and Iraqi civilians must have meant nothing to him, but it certainly did to Hadley and the President. The arrogance and attitude of Casey, as portrayed in the Woodward series, say it all. Not only was Iraq going down the toilet on Casey's watch, but the mere fact he would be asked legitimate questions about it drove him over the edge. For the previous year he had been telling the President that Iraq would be able to stand on its own in 12 months, which was preposterous. In addition, he was telling the President we should be withdrawing troops, not adding more. It is clear from the Woodward series that General Casey was concerned only with his own skin and reputation, nothing more. It is also clear what the ego, arrogance and stupidity of incompetent senior officers and government officials can lead the country into. It is amazing General George Casey was promoted to US Army Chief of Staff. That single act by the President, and agreed to by the Senate, was a slap in the face of every dead American soldier and Iraqi during the time General Casey was in command of MNF-I. He was as clueless of the realities of the situation on the ground in Iraq as Donald Rumsfeld and Tommy Franks were in the planning of the invasion.

Lousy plan before the invasion.

Lousy execution of the battle theater afterwards.

When General Patraeus came into the job as Commander of MNF-I, the President went out of his way to tell the media that he was "listening to his generals," and "giving the generals in Iraq everything they ask for." Great, but why didn't he do that before we went over there when General Shinseki, the Army Chief of Staff, the senior US Army officer in the country, said we would need half a million troops? The President's statement that he was listening to his generals was too late—about three years too late. He should have listened to them before he ever went over there in the first place. He should have listened to his senior US Army military advisor, his expert on land warfare. Instead, all he listened to was Rumsfeld, who wanted the war fought his way, i.e., "Invasion Lite," and there was no other discussion about it. Tommy Franks was Rumsfeld's water boy who implemented Rumsfeld's plan when everyone, including the President, should have listened to Shinseki, who was the President's senior ground warfare advisor, not Franks. They were all listening to the wrong guy, who was not the senior ground warfare advisor to the President. Franks had only one thing going for him, and it was not the fact that he was the CENTCOM Commander. It was the fact that he was a "yes" man who did whatever his boss told him to do in the face of overwhelming historical evidence the plan he was executing was crap. If the two generals, Franks and Shinseki, had gone to Rumsfeld, working together as a team, and laid out a viable plan for the invasion and occupation of Iraq like they should have done, none of this would have happened. Instead, in his autobiography Franks calls the Chiefs of Staff of the armed forces of the Unites States "Title 10 mother fuckers" (referring to Title 10 of the United States Code, which addresses the role of the armed forces). In other words, to Franks the Chiefs weren't real field commanders like him, and didn't know what was going on in the "field of battle." He admits in his book he had no respect for the Chiefs of Staff, implying Shinseki, so working together for these two officers was out of the question. Franks sold Rumsfeld on his "leadership" because he was a yes man, and probably torpedoed Shinseki at the same time. Look where we ended up. Well, Franks had it the other way around. He thought he knew what was going on in the real world of warfare, when he was better at playing war games on computers than in real life. Tommy Franks should have stayed home in Midland, Texas pumping gas.

General Patraeus brought with him to Camp Victory (the name of the base where NMF-I is located on the western side of Baghdad, near the airport) a group of the "best and the brightest" army colonels, most with PhD's, who would transform the fight in Iraq into something better. One of these colonels was H.R. McMaster, who wrote the well-known account of Vietnam called "Dereliction of Duty." The book is a well documented account of the abominable planning and escalation of the Vietnam War, specifically the insanity of the McNamara policy of "limited warfare" and "limited engagement," which led to the deaths of 58,000 American soldiers. The amazing thing about Colonel McMaster's book is that it was written in 1998, five years before the invasion of Iraq. One wonders if Tommy Franks or Donald Rumsfeld ever read it. The similarities between Vietnam and Iraq are so numerous they are hard to count. Colonel McMaster is probably writing another book about this conflict, but he has to be careful, he is serving in it. I'm sure that's one of the reasons he took the assignment, and of course to get promoted to brigadier general. If he does write a book it should be a good one.

In "Dereliction of Duty" Colonel McMaster described how the Joint Chiefs of Staff acquiesced in almost every meeting with McNamara (that he invited them to) and the "best and the brightest" of the day. It was only General Green, the Marine Corps Commandant, who plainly told President Johnson and Secretary of Defense McNamara what it would really take to win in Southeast Asia. General Green gave them the number of soldiers and Marines that would be needed, and also the amount of time the war would last and the expected number of casualties.

But no one listened to him, just as no one listed to General Shinseki who fought in that war, and who said almost the same thing to his Secretary of Defense 40 years later.

The Chairman of the Joint Chiefs of Staff during Vietnam, General Wheeler, was a career Army officer who never fought in combat, but instead sat out the entire Second World War in the States as a training officer, sending soldiers into battle and their death. Wheeler was a complete desk jockey, going along with everything McNamara wanted and never saying a thing. There is a story that General Wheeler and the entire Joint Chiefs of Staff planned to resign "en masse" in protest of the way Johnson and McNamara were conducting the war. But they never did. They didn't have the courage to. Like Wheeler, General Franks went along with everything his Secretary of Defense wanted, in the face of overwhelming evidence that the plan would not work. McNamara's strategy of limited engagement in Vietnam is exactly like Rumsfeld's strategy of invading a country half a world away that possesses an army estimated to be as large as a million men with only 125,000 Coalition forces, the vast majority of whom are support troops and not combat soldiers. The United States didn't lose the Vietnam War. We were never "beaten." We just chose not to win it. The results of both wars will prove to end up the same, unless something is done with this one before it is too late.

Under MNF-I is the Multi-National Corps-Iraq, or MNC-I, formerly under the command of Lieutenant General Raymond Odierno, who is now the MNF-I commander. MNC-I is the command element that comprises all Coalition combat forces in Iraq. The Coalition forces involved in the fighting are broken down by regions of the country, such as MND-North, for Multi-National Division-North. As the name implies, this describes the forces in the northern part of Iraq that fall under the US Army division commander in that part of the country. As time goes by these divisions rotate out of combat, to be replaced by others coming from the States, but the designation remains the same. Therefore, if the 82d Airborne Division, as well as a smattering of other token Coalition forces, are located in the operational area to the north of Iraq, this combined force makes up the Multi-National Division-North. When another US Army division comes in to replace the 82nd, that unit will also be called "MND-North." The same goes for the forces to the south (MND-South), the east (MND-East), and central Iraq, or MND-Central. Because there is so much action near Baghdad in the center, this area is broken up into two sub-areas. All of these combat forces make up MNC-I.

What about the western part of Iraq, Anbar Province? Shortly after the initial phases of the conflict, the Marines replaced the Army in the area around Fallujah and Ramadi, two of the main towns in eastern Anbar Province along the Euphrates River, just a few miles west of Baghdad. The Army had been having a tough go of it for months, but the real problems were dealing with the local tribal leaders, most of them Sunni. When the Marines were directed to replace the Army in Anbar Province they publically announced that they would do what the Army had failed to do, e.g., turn things around and clean things up. This was a professional slap in the face by one service of the other, and was an open show of dislike of the Army by the Marines.

The Marines are jealous of the Army because they are not their own service (the Marines are part of the US Navy) and they don't get as much funding or equipment as the Army does. Not being its own service the Marine Corps has to go out of its way to be noticed and get attention. They have great looking dress uniforms and have neat commercials on TV. That's how they get attention, recruits, and the public thinking they are the only combat force this nation has. It's all good PR, just like a major corporation. You need it to sell your product. The Marine Corps is less than 200,000 strong. The US Army is over half a million, with 546,000 active duty soldiers. Yet, the average person (and most of the media) see an American in uniform and think he's a Marine, even if the soldier has "US Army" on his shirt. I've seen this in the papers countless times. The media, being so accurate, will have a caption under the photograph of a US Army soldier and refer to him as a Marine. The Marines must eat this up.

But does the product really work, or just look nice? The Marines are good, but they're not better than the Army, even though they may think they are. In the "joint forces" nature of warfare today the Marine Corps needs to check its attitude of superiority at the door and work with the Army to get the mission accomplished, rather than making every effort not to. This hasn't happened in Iraq since the opening days of the war, and the results speak for themselves. The Marine Corps is the smaller of the two land forces our country has, not the only one. We have two forces that do the same thing, and the redundancy constantly causes problems for everyone because the Marines refuse to work with the other branches of the service, primarily the Army because that's the other land component.

(At the time of this writing my classmate from St. John's College High School in Washington, DC, General Stanley McChrystal, is the commander of all US forces in Afghanistan. Under him is a Marine unit commanded by Brigadier General Lawrence D. Nicholson. General McChrystal recently flew to Helmand Province to discuss problems with the way Brigadier General Nicholson was handling things. What did BG Nicholson do the moment Stan McChrystal left on his helicopter? He called retired Marine Corps General Jim Jones, the current National Security Advisor, asking him to talk with General McChrystal. Essentially, he wanted General Jones to tell General McChrystal to get off his back. Stan McChrystal is a 4-star general and commander of all US forces in Afghanistan, but Marine Brigadier General (1-star) Nicholson just doesn't like being told what to do by an Army general, and his commanding officer. To a Marine like Nicholson an Army general isn't his commander. He only takes orders from another Marine. I was informed of this by a good friend of mine who is a former Marine himself, and who served in Vietnam. He told me this story with glee on his face. He loved what BG Nicholson did, and had no problem at all with his gross insubordination of General McChrystal. That meant nothing to my friend. He was proud of it. To him, it showed how the Marines don't take shit from anybody, even their superior officers if they are US Army generals. I guess to a Marine anyone other than one of them is the enemy. This type of nonsense gets us nowhere. We end up fighting two wars whenever the Marines and the Army are placed in the same theater of operations: one war against each other because the Marines refuse to work with the Army, and the other war against the enemy we're supposed to be fighting.)

If the Marine Corps' claimed area of expertise is amphibious warfare, where does it fit into our nation's war fighting capability if we don't do these any more? The Marine Corps has a lot in common with labor unions—they both served a useful purpose when they were created, but that was a long time ago. The US Army executed as many, if not more, amphibious landings during World War II as the Marine Corps did, but you wouldn't know that talking with a Marine. To a Marine, they're the only force that does these. Where was the Marine Corps on D-Day, the biggest amphibious operating in the history of warfare?

One of the Marines' main issues in taking over Anbar Province was their image and their professed ability to deal with any situation, be it fierce combat, or delicate inter-personal negotiations with whoever had the honor of being in their presence. They even went so far as to say that their combat uniforms would look different than the Army's, in order to show the Iraqis that they were different, and that now things would be so much better. This last point finally got under the Army's skin so much that the Marines had to back down and go in with their normal desert camouflage uniform.

The Marines entered Fallujah in eastern Anbar Province, and within a short time the situation went to hell. The primary flash point was the famous, and very tragic, Blackwater incident where four contractors were slaughtered by local militia. Their bodies were set on fire and dragged down the street, then hung from the steel beams of a bridge, all of it broadcast around the world later that same day. The word in Iraq was that the Blackwater contractors had pissed off the locals in Fallujah in the days preceding the incident by running people off the road and shooting at anyone who looked at them the wrong way. In addition, I also heard that the day before the incident the Blackwater team had asked for directions through the town, saying they needed it for a convoy the next day. This was a gross security violation on their part. It alerted the locals in the town of their intentions and their direction of travel, and also the time they would be doing it. They set themselves up by acting like jerks, alienating the local population, and then nailing their own coffins by committing security violations and broadcasting their intentions. The Blackwater contractors were acting cocky and arrogant, and it cost them their lives. After the incident the Marines, rightfully so, replied in kind and started kicking some insurgent ass, leading to months of some of the worst house-to-house and door-to-door fighting of the war. The glowing expectations of the Marines, and their cockiness, was a perfect example of the same flaws of the entire strategy of the Bush administration, highlighted in the famous words of George Tenant that the entire episode would be a "slam dunk."

To the present day the Marines still have responsibility for Anbar Province. But not to be just like everybody else (i.e., the US Army) their geographic area of responsibility is referred to as MEF-West, for Marine Expeditionary Force-West. The Marines do not want their sector to be named the same way as the Army's. But the Marine's disdain for the Army goes much farther than just a name. For example, when I first travelled to Al Asad, one of the main Coalition camps in Anbar Province, I flew there on a US Army Blackhawk helicopter, a UH-60. This is the primary helicopter of the Army, having replaced the famous "Huey," or UH-1 helicopter of the Vietnam War. The flight was uneventful, and we flew directly from the International Zone (formerly the "Green Zone") to Al Asad and back. It was about an hour each way, during daylight going out there from Baghdad, and in the middle of the night coming back. I did this a couple of times. Yet a few months later the Marine units rotated out, and the 1st Marine Expeditionary Force (MEF) was replaced by the 2nd MEF, whose commander must have really hated the Army. When this happened the 2nd MEF Marines stopped all US Army aircraft flights into Al Asad. They wouldn't let the US Army fly helicopters into a Marine base! I was amazed, but what really got me was they were allowed to get away with it. In order to get to Al Asad, a trip that lasted about one hour, we had to get on a Marine CH-46 twin rotor aircraft that made a round-robin trek from Marine base to Marine base. The entire one-way trip lasted 2-3 days because we had to spend the night at Taqadem, or "TQ," and then continue on our trek the following day to Al Asad. It was absurd, yet that was the way the Marines wanted it, and that's what the commander of MNC-I, LTG Odierno, let them get away with. When you consider we are at war, childish behavior like this is unacceptable. It shows the complete breakdown of command and control, simplicity, combat effectiveness, and rationality going on over there. It is no wonder our operations in Iraq are such a mess.

Task Force 134 is the element responsible for all the detainees captured by Coalition forces. A distinction has to be made, because detainees are captured by Iraqi forces too, yet they do not fall under the control of TF-134. There are so many detainees, especially since the start of the "surge" in February 2007, that housing and feeding them had become a monumental task by the spring of 2007. Facilities have to be constructed and contracts for things like food service need to be put into place to do this. TF-134 has this responsibility, and was working on these issues when I left Iraq in September of 2007.

The Joint Area Support Group, or JASG, is the command element responsible for the International Zone (IZ), formerly called the Green Zone. Essentially, the JASG is the "Mayor" of the IZ. After the United States and the Coalition "secured" central Baghdad, the Green Zone was established to protect all coalition personnel and facilities, not the least of which was the Republican Palace, the former headquarters of Saddam's government. Because the United States had no diplomatic relations with Iraq before the war, we needed a new Embassy building. Having spent time with the State Department in Overseas Buildings Operations, I found this solution to be interesting. One of Saddam's former palaces, the Republican Palace was taken over by the United States, its north wing being designated as the US Embassy. The rest of the building was used to house other State Department elements, such as the Iraq Reconstruction Management Office (IRMO), a Green Beans gourmet coffee shop, a short order deli, an internet café, and other facilities for the soldiers' (and contractors') morale. The Army calls these "MWR" facilities for "Morale, Welfare and Recreation."

The Joint Special Operations Command-Iraq, or JSOC-I, was the Coalition-trained (i.e., US-trained) Iraqi equivalent of our Special Forces, their most elite soldiers. It was basically a joke. JSOC-I wouldn't have been able to fight its way out of a wet paper bag. They just had fancier uniforms than the rest of the Iraqi army's.

Half way through my tour in Iraq the Embassy changed the rules for entry onto the compound. Now they would not allow any contractor who did not live in a trailer on the Embassy compound access through the checkpoint. Any soldier could walk right in, even if he/she didn't live there, but we couldn't. Now there was hardly anything to do with our free time. Things got worse from that point onward for those of us who lived on the other compounds in the IZ.

In addition, we were going to have our privilege to use the infirmary at the Embassy taken away from us as well. Contractors were not going to have any access to medical treatment at all, meaning we would have to fly back to the States or to Dubai if we really got sick. We were sent to Iraq on a DoD contract, but medical services were soon going to be pulled by DoD and the State Department. We simply weren't worthy of receiving adequate medical care as far as they were concerned. But DoD had no problem awarding contracts and sending us over there. Fortunately, I didn't get sick during the latter part of my tour.

I lived at FOB Blackhawk, across the street and down a block from the Embassy. This was where the former "Believers Palace" was located, having been completely destroy by our guided bombs the opening night of the war. It was beneath this palace that Saddam had his bunker. The bunker was amazing, having been designed by the granddaughter of the German engineer who built Hitler's bunker in Berlin, the one where he spent the last days of his life before killing himself. Saddam's bunker was so well designed and constructed that our bombs didn't make a scratch. We tried. The palace was completely destroyed above ground, but the bunker wasn't touched. It was the looting after Saddam left Baghdad that destroyed it. The entire bunker, about the size of a floor of a large office building, sat on shock absorbers with yards of reinforced concrete all around it. Saddam and his immediate staff could live there for over a month.

Also about mid-way through my tour in Iraq I began to hear about the "Negroponte Memo." John Negroponte, a career Foreign Service officer, was the US Ambassador to Iraq from June 2004 to April 2005. For whatever reason, he has been at the top of the heap as far as getting huge jobs since 9/11. Whatever a guy who made his career out of attending cocktail parties is doing in positions like National Intelligence Czar, I don't know. But then again, what does a Navy admiral know about securing facilities? It doesn't have to make sense. When I was in Iraq, from July 2006 to September 2007, the place was falling apart. Yet, I actually heard that the Coalition (the US) was going to give the IZ back to Iraq! In other words, we were all dead. I couldn't believe this, but then I heard when he was Ambassador, John Negroponte had written a memo stating at some point in time, specifically laid out in the memo, the Coalition (the US) was going to disband the IZ. That point in time was now approaching. There would no longer be any barricades, nothing. The portion of Baghdad where the IZ was would be just another part of the city. For a while after the initial fighting ended in the spring of 2003 Baghdad was relatively quiet. The shit hadn't hit the fan—yet—which meant the full effects of

Bremer's disbanding of the security infrastructure of the country hadn't taken hold. But by the time I was there the only thing keeping us alive was that the IZ was a fortress. If I had walked outside the gate I would not have made it 50 feet before I was killed. At the time the Negroponte memo was written the situation in Baghdad may have been better, but it wasn't any more. In such a rush to make everything seem like it was great, the Bush administration was trying to turn everything over to Iraq, purple thumbs and all, like it was just another day in good old Baghdad, with birds chirping and kids playing hop-scotch. It was decided by someone with a brain the IZ wasn't going anywhere. They took the Negroponte memo, that stellar piece of diplomatic nonsense, and stuffed it in a filing cabinet.

Most of Saddam's old palaces were constructed during the period of the UN sanctions imposed after the Gulf War. He built them primarily to show the world the sanctions weren't working, which they weren't, but also to thumb his nose at George H.W. Bush. It isn't difficult to understand why Saddam did this. After all, he was allowed to remain in power (i.e., alive) by Bush the First, and the sanctions had absolutely no impact on his lifestyle or his authority and grip over the Iraqi people. Bush let him get away with his invasion of Kuwait, and let him remain in power in Baghdad, so why shouldn't Saddam show the world he was alive and well, and more than able to build however many palaces he wanted. To do otherwise in his culture and in his mind would have made him look like he had been defeated in the Gulf War and was nothing more than a puppet of the US.

But we were too dumb to see what he was doing during the intervening years between the two wars, the wars fought by the father and the son. One war was fought with a terrible end, and the other fought with a terrible beginning, and without an ending in sight. The only ones who have suffered throughout all this are the Iraqi people. The sanctions were a joke, a waste of time, and hurt the people we said we were trying to help. What would have really helped the Iraqi people was not ruining their economy with the sanctions, but killing Saddam Hussein during the Gulf War in 1991 when we had half a million soldiers there to deal with any situation that may have come up later, such as the "power vacuum" we heard so much about. If we had done that none of the current situation would have occurred.

The other primary element of MNF-I is the Multi-National Security Transition Command-Iraq, or MNSTC-I.

The author graduating from West Point, June 8, 1977.

The author as a lieutenant assigned to A "Alpha" Company (Airborne), 3rd Battalion, 5th Infantry, 193rd Infantry Brigade, Fort Kobbe, Canal Zone, Republic of Panama.

The author (right) as a First Classman (senior) at West Point. I am receiving an award from my cadet regimental commander, Ricky Lynch. Ricky is now a 3-star general and the former military spokesman in Iraq, and also a former division commander there. He is now the III Corps Commander at Fort Hood, Texas.

To Mike
With Best Wishes,

The author shaking hands with President George W. Bush when he visited the remote headquarters of the Office of Homeland Security (OHS) in Building #3 on the US Navy's Nebraska Avenue Complex (the "NAC"), across from American University at the intersection of Massachusetts and Nebraska Avenues in northwest Washington, DC. The author was Governor's Ridge's Senior Director for Administration at OHS.

The author and friend with President George W. Bush and his wife, Laura Bush, at the White House Staff Christmas Party, 2002.

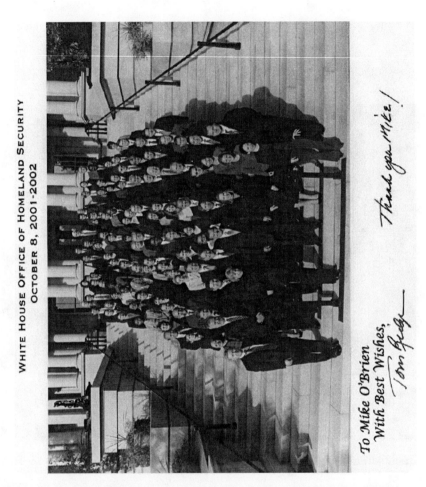

The Office of Homeland Security staff with Governor Tom Ridge on the east steps of the Old Executive Office Building across the driveway from the West Wing of the White House. Governor Ridge (called "Governor" out of respect for when he was the Governor of Pennsylvania before coming to Washington) is front center. The author is standing two rows behind Governor Ridge's left shoulder.

The Kuwait Hilton, Kuwait City, on the Persian Gulf. This is where contractors stayed before they took off for Baghdad. It looks nice, but the accommodations inside the "villas" along the beach were nothing to write home about. They were extremely plain inside, almost dismal. Wealthy Kuwaiti families would rent a villa for a week and hang out with their kids. They had money to burn. The best part was the restaurant, which we were given vouchers for.

Kuwait Hilton beach on the Persian Gulf.

The pool. Replace the guy and things would have been just fine.

Inside a US Air Force C-130 transport, ready to take off from Ali Al Saleem US Air Base in Kuwait for Baghdad. We would sit in these for what seemed like hours, usually baking. If you had to go to the bathroom, you were out of luck, unless you were willing to piss in a tube near the cargo ramp while everyone watched. I learned right at the beginning of my tour that getting anywhere in the Iraqi theater of operations was a complete nightmare. On these flights we were practically sitting on top of each other, and we had to carry everything we had with us.

The author.

The author with my associate.
Everywhere she went Iraqi men would just stare at her.

Col. Craig Agena and the author on board a US Blackhawk helicopter on our way to Diwaniyah, near Hilla, south of Baghdad.

The walkway between Phoenix Base and the Ministry of Defense building, which can be seen in the background. Just beyond the MOD building was the wall separating the IZ (International Zone) from the city. The 12 foot high pre-fabricated concrete "T-walls" were the most common sight in Iraq. They were virtually everywhere the Coalition was. I walked down this sidewalk about three times a day.

Closer down the walkway to the Ministry of Defense building. The Al-Mansour Hotel can be seen in the background. One day a sniper shot a bullet from the hotel through the window of General Babakir's (the Iraqi Chief of Staff) office on the side of the MOD building facing the hotel, a distance of at least 1,500 meters. The sniper not only knew which window was Gen. Babakir's, he was also a very good shot. No one was hurt, and the bullet dropped into a trash can after bouncing off the wall in the office.

Believers Palace, up the road and across the street from the Republican Palace. This was the Ba'ath Party headquarters, with Saddam's bunker underneath. It was destroyed by JDAMS—Joint Direct Attack Munitions, or guided bombs—the opening night of the war. The compound surrounding Believers Palace was called FOB (Forward Operating Base) Blackhawk, where I lived for 14 months. Some of the trailers are visible to the upper right.

My home, Believers Palace.

Believers Palace.

Close-up of the front of Believers Palace. The main hall is just inside. It can be seen through the debris because there is no longer a roof, allowing sunlight in.

Believers Palace.

Just to the left of the front door of Believers Palace. At different times I lived in the two trailers in the center of the photograph, under the front overhang of the palace. The air conditioners would go out all the time due to constant use. When that happened it would be too hot to sleep, so we would have to sleep inside the palace on cots. Inside the palace on the top floor was a private bar for Saddam's parties.

Outside of my trailer at FOB Blackhawk. Sandbags were everywhere, most of them in disrepair and leaking sand all over the place. There was almost more sand outside the bags than in.

A trailer that went up in flames near mine. The Iraqi contractors hired to install all of the trailers for the US personnel on FOB Blackhawk didn't bother to use a ground wire when connecting the electrical power to the trailers. A wire in, a wire out. Who needs a third wire? Where was the US supervision? These were going up all over the place like match sticks. The DFAC (dining facility) on FOB Blackhawk lit up like a candle one night and was completely destroyed, but not from bad wiring. Anti-aircraft flares from a US helicopter landed on its roof and it went up in flames.

Michael M. O'Brien

More.

More.

A sergeant from JASG (Joint Area Support Group, the "Mayor" of the IZ) about to enter the stairway leading to Saddam's bunker complex at Believers Palace. We had to go up a flight of stairs, and then down several flights to get to the bunker.

Inside Believers Palace.

Believers Palace.

The main conference room in Saddam's bunker.

Believers Palace.

Saddam's old communications tower on FOB Blackhawk, next to Believers Palace. This could be seen for miles. All anyone had to do was aim at it and have the right distance, and they could drop rocket and mortar rounds near it all day. I lived 25 feet from where the picture was taken. I complained to JASG about the tower, asking why it couldn't be taken down for our safety at FOB Blackhawk, and was told it wasn't going anywhere.

The Republican Palace in the International Zone, formerly the Green Zone. This was Saddam's main palace and the seat of the government. The far end (the north end), was the US Embassy. The near end (the south end), housed the offices of IRMO (Iraqi Reconstruction Management Office) as well as the MWR, Green Beans coffee bar, and other amenities. Contractors who did not live in trailers on the Embassy compound were barred from getting onto it half way through my tour. The row of cars behind the building, to the far right of the picture, is where the mortar round killed the woman from the KBR housing office. It landed right in front of the white SUV in the middle of the row.

The Republican Palace as seen from a Blackhawk helicopter on final approach into LZ (landing zone) Washington across the street. This is a good view looking north across the Tigris River to the other side of Baghdad and Sadr City. It was on the other side of the Tigris River, in the area shown here, that most of the suicide bombings in the markets happened. The markets were where the insurgents got the highest number of kills.

A little closer to landing. The Sheraton Hotel is the tall building across the river. It is where many of the scenes during the opening days of the war were filmed from, providing an excellent vantage point to watch Baghdad getting blown to pieces by the US Air Force.

Inside the IZ looking toward the Tigris River and Baghdad. The tent-like structure is where the main swimming pool was for the IZ. The pool was built by one of Saddam's sons for his parties. A mortar round landed on the edge of it one afternoon, and it had to be closed for repairs. Sadr City is the farthest part of the picture. It is home of Muqtada al Sadr's "Madhi Army," the biggest anti-American militia in the country.

Trailer park inside the US Embassy (Republican Palace) compound.

The Ministry of Defense in the background with parts of Phoenix Base in the foreground. Phoenix Base was the home of MNSTC-I, and is about a mile north of the Republican Palace. We are about to land at the LZ inside Phoenix Base.

The Ministry of Defense, with Phoenix Base in the foreground.

A good look at the front of the Ministry of Defense building. The United States spent $58 million dollars renovating it. It had no air conditioning for over a year because LTG Dempsey refused to pay $48,000 for a longer cable to connect a brand new generator to the building. The building in the background was the former Iraqi Ministry of Planning.

Iraqi soldiers ready for a parade in front of the Ministry of Defense.

On parade. The Iraqis march like the British, who had a presence there for years.

All of the military in the Iraqi armed forces had to swear an oath to the new government and constitution.

The Iraqi Army Band.

The ziggurat-shaped Council of Ministers Hall that was destroyed the opening night of the invasion on March 20, 2003. This building was seen around the world engulfed in flames.

A closer look at the damage.

A closer look.

Close shot of damage.

Damage to one of the 19 new (and still unoccupied) buildings that MNSTC-I J-7 constructed for the 5th Brigade, 6th Division of the Iraqi army at FOB Honor, located in the IZ. Anywhere within the IZ was an easy target for 122mm mortars fired from anywhere outside the IZ.

A closer look. The damage was minimal only because of where the round hit, and because the building was still empty. All the insurgents had to do was fire off a mortar round and it would hit something.

The Hall of Meetings at FOB Honor destroyed during the invasion. The 5th Brigade of the Iraqi army 6th Division occupies sections of it for living quarters.

The swords at Saddam's parade field in Baghdad. The hands holding the swords were molded from his own. There was a matching pair of swords at the other end of the field. The Iraqi flag has Arabic script in Saddam's handwriting. He even had inscriptions on monuments with ink made from his blood.

Tomb of the Unknown Soldier in Baghdad. Some of the architecture in Baghdad was very impressive.

The Baghdad Sheraton.

The radio tower in Baghdad. This is a good view of Baghdad and how large it is. The weather was always perfect. Great place for a resort!

Camp Victory, west of Baghdad and next to the International Airport. This was a resort built by Saddam—many were built during the "sanctions" after the Gulf War—where he had numerous palaces for himself, members of his family, and guests. The water was stocked with fish for their pleasure. It was taken over by the Coalition (the US) and was the headquarters of MNF-I, the Multi-National Forces-Iraq. General George Casey lived in one of the palaces for two and a half years while Iraq went down the toilet.

Notice the spot where the boat can pull under the roof of the palace. Saddam didn't miss a thing. Only the best.

Flying over Baghdad. Blackhawks always flew in pairs for protection and emergency rescue if one was shot down.

Flying somewhere.

The Tigris River flowing through Baghdad.

The outskirts of Baghdad, with date palm trees marking the line between city and farmland.

Blackhawk helicopter pilot.

Baghdad from the air.

Baghdad from the air.

Saddam-era memorial in Baghdad, with bridge over the Tigris River nearby.

A mosque in the midst of chaos.

Baghdad from the air.

Baghdad

Michael M. O'Brien

Baghdad.

After an explosion, quite possibly a suicide bomber, somewhere in Baghdad. We would hear these explosions all the time, and often feel their concussion. They would be followed by the plume of black smoke afterwards that would last all day.

Baghdad apartment building. Notice the number of dish antennas.

The Al-Askari, or "Golden Mosque" in Samarra, north of Baghdad. It was blown up twice by Sunni extremists. An Iraqi infantry brigade was going to be placed along the highway between Baghdad and Samarra to protect travelers on the way to and from the mosque for worship.

The mosque became a focus of the civil war between the Sunni and Shi'ia, and the new Iraqi government's inability to do anything about it, or to rebuild the mosque.

Close-up.

The Tigris River.

Typical view of the Iraq countryside and one of its thousands of irrigation canals.

The Euphrates River.

Date palms.

The Blackhawk had a machine gun on both sides.

An Iraqi farm.

Iraqi country village.

A wealthy man's house.

Irrigation canal. The water in these was the deepest blue I have ever seen.

The author waiting for the helicopter to be re-fueled. We would have to get off the aircraft and walk 100 feet away from it whenever it re-fueled in case of an explosion.

Notice the "sand funnel" beyond the Blackhawk.

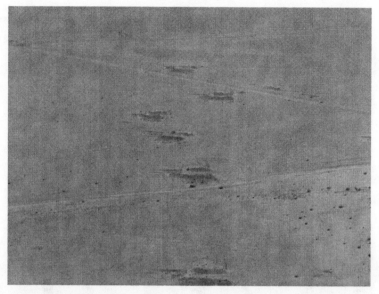

Defensive tank emplacements. A hole is dug and the tank rolled in, while a "berm" of dirt from the hole is built around the tank in the direction of the approaching enemy, shielding it from view. The main gun of the tank sticks out over the berm in the direction of the enemy. This is how all armies set up a tank in a defensive position.

One of thousands of tanks and infantry trenches dug by the Iraqi army during the last war, or possibly the Gulf War. These could be seen everywhere from the air. The trench was designed to allow Iraqi soldiers to move along its length and not be seen, while not being at a parallel or perpendicular angle to an approaching enemy. I doubt its shape had any political significance.

Al Asad Air Base in Anbar province. Built by the Soviets, the air strip is on the plateau, while the hangers for the aircraft are in the sides of the hills that slope down from it. The main base is at the bottom along a waddie.

Hulks of old Iraqi Air Force Soviet-era jets.

In desert camouflage.

The head cook for the Iraqi army brigade headquarters at Al Asad, in his "field kitchen." The Iraqi unit was at the far end of Al Asad, while the Marines occupied the main part of the base with all of the buildings and roads.

The kitchen and staff.

Preparing dinner.

The "field stove," which has multiple uses. It can also be used as a mattress spring, after it cools down.

Dinner with the Iraqi Brigade at Al Asad. I loved the bread.

The Iraqi "PX," or post exchange, at Al Asad.

Old farm house on the corner of the base at Al Asad. J-7 was building a new camp for the Iraqis on this spot. Of course the entire base belonged to the Iraqis, but not according to the Marine major who thought the camp belonged to him and his Marines.

The oasis at Al Asad. Legend has it Abraham stopped here to rest on his journey across the desert.

An archaeologist's dream.

The author and his roommate, the retired US Army colonel who thought the culture of the Iraqi people didn't mean a thing. He retired from the Army with one month's notice to go to Iraq and make the big bucks. This is hardly any notice after serving 29 years on active duty.

8

MNSTC-I

THE MULTI-NATIONAL SECURITY TRANSITION COMMAND-IRAQ (or MNSTC-I, pronounced "min-sticky"), is the only other element commanded by a US Army 3-star general in the country. It is at the same command level as MNC-I. It is responsible for "standing up" the Iraqi Ministry of Defense (MOD) and Ministry of Interior (MOI), in effect getting these two Iraqi ministries started, essentially from nothing, to the point where they can stand on their own and protect and defend the entire country without any outside assistance. This is not possible for reasons I shall explain in detail. Paul Bremer disbanded these same two ministries when he was in charge of the Coalition Provisional Authority. Logic follows that the sole reason for the existence of MNSTC-I is to reverse the very thing that Bremer did. Instead of just "de-Ba'athification" of the senior generals in both the Iraqi army and the national police, and then training and promoting the next senior officers in line who had been vetted and their loyalty to the new Iraqi constitution verified, Bremer fired everyone. If he had left the core institutions, with their mid-level managers and commanders in place, there would have been an Iraqi army and national police the Coalition could have worked with and trained to defend and secure their country. Instead, Bremer left Iraq with no security forces of its own, and the Coalition with nothing to help it protect the country or to mold into an effective fighting army and police force. It fell on MNSTC-I to do all of this.

Before MNSTC-I was fully in place to take on these roles and duties, a "food fight" had occurred between the US Department of State and the Department of Defense, long time institutional enemies and rivals. To begin, State is a liberal and pacifist agency, while Defense is more hawkish. State is about the use diplomacy, while Defense is about the use of force (or at least it's supposed to be). From their very cultures disputes arise every day. These disputes fall over into budget battles, and it is usually up to the President to resolve them. If the President is a hawk, such as Reagan was, Defense will get the lion's share of the money. If the President is a dove, like Bill Clinton was, State will get it. However, under George W. Bush, especially with Colin Powell as Secretary of State and Donald Rumsfeld as Secretary of Defense, the fight became far more intense. Both men had the President's ear and respect, and the country's attention and admiration. Yet, after 9/11 it was Rumsfeld who prevailed, while Powell took a back seat, which he had not bargained for. This is understandable in light of the attacks of 9/11, whereby national defense and the protection of our country was paramount on everyone's mind. Rumsfeld had an easy argument to prove. This is probably why Powell went to the UN, even though he must have known the case for war (e.g., WMD) was weak. He went there because he still wanted to be a player on the world and domestic scene. His days in Washington, however, were soon over. He was not in the mainstream of the administration that wanted to preemptively go after anyone who opposed the United States, and he had completely blown his reputation and his credibility with his bogus and futile UN appearance. Now he stumps for Barack Hussein Obama.

It is said that what goes around comes around. If Colin Powell had done what he should have done during, and at the end of, the Gulf War he would have been the hero of the age, along with the first President Bush and General Schwarzkopf. Instead, he ended up being a dupe for the second President Bush and his hatchet man, Rumsfeld. Powell is out of the limelight now, and the country doesn't have to worry about his lousy advice any more, at least not in an official capacity.

After the initial phases of Operation Iraqi Freedom (OIF) ended in the Fall of 2003, it was left to the State Department to assist the CPA in sorting out the new Iraqi government and drafting its new constitution.

The State Department created the Iraqi Reconstruction Management Office, IRMO, which will be discussed in more detail below. The task of IRMO is to advise, train and equip the new Iraqi government and its respective cabinet ministries. It all sounds good on paper, but it doesn't work in Iraq. Instead of a smooth transition to a democratically-elected government, the effort has been a disaster. The primary reason is because we want the Iraqis to do things the way we do them, which is simply not possible. That is not going to happen—not today, not tomorrow, never. They are Iraqi, they are Middle Easterners, and we aren't. We can't expect Iraqis to do anything the way we do it, to include going to the bathroom. (Westerners go to the bathroom sitting on a toilet. Iraqis, and all other Middle Easterners (and most of the world, for that matter) squat over a hole in the ground or in the floor. I once saw footprints on a toilet seat. This was because the Iraqi who had used the commode before me stood on the seat because it was above the hole in the floor. Of course the commode was there so he could sit on it, but he didn't know that, so he squatted on the seat instead, about a foot and a half higher than he normally squatted. He may have gotten altitude sickness, but he was certainly in the right place for it.)

The IRMO plan could have worked if the insurgency hadn't happened. Its job was for State and the other US Cabinet departments to advise their new Iraqi counterpart ministries. However, the insurgency that began in 2004-2005 between the Sunnis and the Shi'ites turned all that around. Much of this insurgency was fueled by the Shi'ia from Iran to the east, and the Sunni from Syria and Saudi Arabia (where most of the 9/11 hijackers were from) to the west. But now, without its army or national police, and with a skeleton US Army to defend the country, who was there to protect the people and the country whose dictator was in prison awaiting execution? (The trial was a formality, everyone knew Saddam was not long for this world.) The State Department was ill-equipped to deal with Iraq's two "security ministries," as their Ministry of Interior and Defense were now being called, so our Defense Department stepped in and said it wanted the job. State still wanted to keep it, but Defense won out and created MNSTC-I to do it, which it is still doing to this day.

The first commander of MNSTC-I was none other than David Patraeus, who was a 2-star general at the time, not yet having gone back to the States to take over Fort Leavenworth and get his third star. From all accounts I heard when I was in Iraq, General Patraeus did a decent job running MNSTC-I and made a lot of progress. More will be discussed about this later. That is about the best that can be said for his command, and for the organization itself. MNSTC-I is the most convoluted and dysfunctional organization, military or otherwise, I have ever been associated with. I know because I served as a member of its staff for 14 months. Everyone joked about it constantly and talked about how bad it was. This included retired military people, as most of the civilian contractors were. The only ones who didn't were the senior ranking officers there, who would never say anything about the organization, or its dysfunction, for fear of getting into trouble. Speaking one's mind the higher one goes in the military is not going to happen, so fresh ideas and new ways of doing things never get to the table, and never get implemented. It is only the contractors who didn't have the fear of not getting their next promotion who had the courage to say anything. But if they did they got fired and sent home on the first flight out and had to look for another job. This is because the firms they work for want to continue getting government contracts, and the only way to continue getting these is to say nothing and do what the military wants, and keep their mouths shut. Also, 99% of the managers of these companies are retired military officers themselves, so they just continue with the same behavior. Employees of these companies who speak their minds are let go and then replaced by new people who are encouraged by the company to keep their mouths shut when they get to Iraq. This way the firm can continue to be hired by the military to support it. To prove the point my employer in Iraq has a form it asks all of its employees to sign. The form is a waiver of our rights to say or write anything that we have seen or heard while in Iraq after we return. I was asked to sign the form the day before I left, and refused. Why would I sign something that, in effect, says it's OK for my former employer to sue me if I do anything when I get back that they don't like. I wanted to write this book, so of course I didn't sign it. I would be sued by them if I did. The problem is, everything I am writing here is true, and they don't like that because the truth makes them look bad, as well as their client, the US Department of Defense.

When I arrived in Iraq in July of 2006, MNSTC-I was commanded by Lieutenant General (3-star) Martin Dempsey, a 1974 graduate of West Point. General Dempsey is a very likable guy, and takes pride in his signing voice, which he took any opportunity to show off. He sang at the West Point "Founders Day" dinner at Camp Blackhawk, one of the several camps, or FOBs, inside the International Zone in Baghdad. The West Point Founder's Day dinner is held on the anniversary of the founding of West Point in 1802. It is held in cities around the world, in every location and military installation where West Point graduates are located. It is a great opportunity for gathering together and telling "war stories," but mostly to reminisce about Cadet life. It's a great time for everyone.

One of the limitations of life in Iraq was *General Order #1*, which stipulates there will be absolutely no drinking by any Americans in the CENTCOM theater of operations, (e.g., Iraq and Afghanistan), also no pornography, adultery, etc. It is a standing order from the CENTCOM Commander—who is located in Tampa, Florida! It's a joke. No one adheres to it or follows it at all. But it is an order just the same, and if one doesn't follow it and gets caught, they can be subject to disciplinary action and even court martial if they are military. If they are civilians they can be sent home. The State Department, specifically the US Embassy and the staff in the IZ, being the arrogant people that they are, feel they don't have to adhere to General Order #1, so they don't. State Department employees could be seen drinking in front of military personnel all the time, and not giving a hoot about the consequences. The US Ambassador, Zalmay Kahlilzad, didn't enforce General Order #1. He didn't have to because it was issued by the CENTCOM Commander and not the Secretary of State.

There has always been a dispute over who is the higher ranking US official in a foreign country, the US Ambassador or the US Commanding General if he is a full 4-star general. Usually they split the difference and say they are equally in charge and everyone is happy. But in the case of General Order #1, the State Department employees were not going to follow to it at all because that would mean they couldn't drink and screw around. I would imagine they raised all hell with the Ambassador at the time the order was issued, and threatened mass resignations if he made them adhere to it. The result was the military and all its civilian contractors were subject to it, while the State Department staff and all its contractors weren't. The latter were all happy, while the military and its contractors couldn't stand it. One Air Force Captain I knew at MNSTC-I, who was an absolute alcoholic, had gotten drunk and ran into a barricade driving behind the wheel of a Ford Explorer. He was going to be either court martialled or given a lesser punishment, an Article 15 issued by a US Air Force general. Either way his career was over. While he was waiting outside the office of the general who was going to level his punishment, the office being located in the Republican Palace where the US Embassy was, a couple of young female Embassy staffers walked by him talking about the party they had the night before and that everyone had gotten drunk out of their skulls. Nothing was going to happen to them, but this poor slob was going to be kicked out of the Air Force with nearly 15 years of active duty under his belt. He had a serious drinking problem though, and maybe that was the best thing that could have happened to him. Maybe it steered him toward getting some help, who knows.

But the DoD people with alcohol or drug problems didn't bother going crazy because of General Order #1. They simply defied the order and drank and/or drugged anyway. The problem with the US Air Force captain I just mentioned was that he got caught. Many a person, both military and civilian, was sent home because their drinking got out of control. I heard a story of a reserve Army lieutenant colonel during the initial phases of OIF. While on the way back to the States for R&R (rest and relaxation), he got so drunk on the commercial flight the plane was forced to make an emergency landing because the crew thought he had gotten sick. When the incident got back to his military command he was discharged from the Army Reserves. Because he was in the reserves he had a regular full time job. And what was his job when not serving in uniform? He was a social worker specializing in addiction treatment.

I would walk into IRMO offices in the Embassy building and see full blown bars set up. The staff in the office would walk to the free deli downstairs and load up with as many sodas as they could carry to use as mixers for the after-work party in their offices at the end of the day, which could be any time they felt the day was over. This went on all the time because there wasn't anything else to do, unless one had a sex partner. There are many heavy drinkers in Iraq who can get away with it because their spouses aren't around. Many contractors are in Iraq today because they are free to drink (and do drugs) without their spouse coming down on them. If someone had a drinking problem before they went to Iraq, they had a bigger one by the time they left. Of this I have no doubt at all. The situation there is simply too perfect an atmosphere for this type of thing. As for extra-marital sex, that was all the Catholic chaplain talked about during his sermons at Mass on Sunday. Obviously, he was doing a lot of counseling in that area and knew it was going on all the time. A lot of contractors stayed in Iraq for two, three and four years, and in a few cases even five, because they enjoyed the freedom of drinking away from their spouses, and probably the sex too. Of course, the money was fabulous. So if someone has an alcohol or drug issue, and wants to screw around outside of their marriage, and get paid great money all at the same time, Iraq is the place to be.

There was one place that my fellow employees would go because they (and everyone else who knew about it) figured that General Order #1 didn't apply, and that was the British Embassy. The first time I went there I couldn't believe how nice it was. The swimming pool was on par with any four or five-star hotel, with a full bar right next door to it on the "veranda." When I got there for one particular function, I saw US Army officers, to include Major General Kenneth Hunzeker, the chief of CPATT, drinking like it was no big deal, while he was in uniform. What got me was watching the general. Even though it was the British Embassy, it wasn't outside the "intent" of General Order #1, which applied to the entire CENTCOM theater of operations. The order didn't say it was OK to drink at a foreign embassy. I know, I read it. I'm sure MG Hunzeker did too. People like him were splitting hairs with the order just like Embassy staffers were, only using different excuses. He should have been above that. If US Army soldiers or contractors see a general drink at the British Embassy, they are certainly going to drink as well. Why shouldn't they. If they do it there, they will do it in other places too. Where does it stop?

(MG Hunzeker has since been promoted to 3-star general. For much of his 1-year tour he was back in the States for medical treatment. If he was medically unable to perform his duties how did he get promoted? The Army is a tough life, and I know guys who were discharged for the slightest ailment. But once a person has been "picked" for promotion, it doesn't matter if they can do their job or not, they'll still get it. There are many general officers who didn't serve in Iraq, and I would bet most of them didn't get their next star. But if one was sent to Iraq it was tantamount to being promoted. Iraq was simply a rubber stamp on their resume. Once MG Hunzeker was assigned to Iraq, he had 3-star general in the bag. I do hope his health is better. I will say one thing I found very impressive about MG Hunzeker. He was the only general officer I saw in Iraq who rode in a HUMVEE and not a Suburban, and the only one protected by US Army soldiers and not PSD's. See PSD's below.)

My manager for the US company I worked for would get upset because he couldn't believe people would not follow General Order #1, simply because it had been issued by a 4-star general. He was the biggest blowhard I've ever met in my life. I told him once that if someone wanted to drink they were going to drink no matter what the stupid order said, and no order from a general in Tampa, Florida was going to stop them from doing so. He was trying to be righteous and show how much he followed orders. He was a buffoon and would have walked off a cliff if a general told him to. I was told by colleagues who saw him do it that General Dempsey would drink at the British Embassy too. That's likely why General Hunzeker did it. He probably knew Dempsey wouldn't mind, and Dempsey was his commander. I was very disappointed when I heard this. How could a general who drank at the British Embassy enforce General Order #1 against a soldier who had gotten smashed, but not at the British Embassy? I guess these generals had no problem with this double standard. If the generals, or anyone else, wanted to drink that bad why couldn't they just do it in the privacy of their room and not in front of the people who worked for them? It's just another example of the arrogance of high ranking officers who think, because they have risen to the level they have, that they can get away with anything. Well, if you look at Tommy Franks letting his wife sit in on classified briefings and getting away with it, then it's easy to see why they think this way. It happens every day. But don't let the soldier get caught doing the exact same thing. He's screwed. Generals who drank, no matter where they did it, were not only violating General Order #1, they were thumbing their noses at their 4-star commander in Florida, right in front of everyone else, soldier and civilian. Great examples of leadership. Both Generals Hunzeker and Dempsey have been promoted to the next higher rank of 3- and 4-star general, respectively.

The mission of MNSTC-I was to get the Iraqi Ministry of Defense and Ministry of Interior up and running. Defense was responsible for the Iraqi army, navy and air force (its national protection), while Interior was responsible for the national police (its internal protection). When Paul Bremer disbanded both he created the void in security that has been mentioned, added to the minimum number of US forces Rumsfeld and Franks sent there to invade and later secure the country. Bremer's disbanding of the two Iraqi security ministries created a huge pool of newly unemployed soldiers and policemen, many armed with their issued weapons, who became potential recruits for the insurgency. After the Defense-State battle, MNSTC-I was tasked with the mission of getting these two ministries started again, essentially from nothing, thanks to Paul Bremer.

MNSTC-I was made up of so many organizations that it took the average person months just to figure out all its different parts. I would try to explain it all to new people who I was going to be working with, only to see their eyes glaze over because it was simply too complicated for them to follow and figure out right away. I realized it was better to just let them figure it out on their own. The MNSTC-I organization consisted of its own staff, called the "J" staff due to its level within the US Army hierarchy. For example, all the staff sections in a battalion are called the "S" staffs, with the "S-1" being the Personnel Officer, the "S-2" the Intelligence Officer, the "S-3" the Operations Officer, and so on. As the levels of command go higher, the letter designations of these same staff functions change. Because MNSTC-I is commanded by an Army 3-star general, the staff functions all begin with the letter "J."

The various "J" staff sections of MNSTC-I performed a variety of missions, mostly for the Iraqi Ministry of Defense and Interior, and to a lesser degree for the benefit of MNSTC-I itself. It was as if MNSTC-I was the de facto headquarters staff of MOD and MOI. The staff section I had the most dealing with by far was J-7, the Construction Branch of MNSTC-I.

The J-7 section of MNSTC-I, the Construction Branch, didn't build facilities needed by MNSTC-I. Instead, J-7 built facilities needed by the Ministry of Defense and the Ministry of Interior. The other parts of the MNSTC-I staff actually performed staff functions needed by MNSTC-I, as well as the Iraqi Ministries of Defense and Interior. However, regarding construction of any facilities, J-7 did this just for the Iraqi ministries, and not for MNSTC-I at all. J-7 was, in effect, the construction branch of the Iraqi Ministry of Defense and Ministry of Interior. J-7 was totally responsible for the physical infrastructure of the security ministries of Iraq. This was a huge responsibility that I will describe in a separate chapter.

The organizational role of MNSTC-I is critical. It was as though MNSTC-I was itself a part of these two Iraqi ministries, an extension of them. But because of the dysfunctional way MNSTC-I did business, and the lack of coordination and control of its various primary staff elements, the Iraqi Ministry of Defense and Ministry of Interior are years away from being able to stand on their own.

But there were more parts to MNSTC-I than just its primary staff sections. MNSTC-I was made up of many other functional areas, all under the command of its 3-star general, yet all having different missions. The organization was hard, if not impossible, to make any sense of. It was also impossible to effectively manage. In addition to its primary staff areas described above, MNSTC-I was also made up of transition teams, or TT's, that addressed the different parts of the Iraqi Ministry of Defense and Ministry of Interior. MNSTC-I's other parts consisted of: the Ministry of Defense Transition Team (MODTT); the Ministry of Interior Transition Team (MOITT); the Coalition Police Advisory Transition Team (CPATT); the Joint Headquarters Transition Team (JHQTT); M-4-TT, which was part of JHQTT; the Health Affairs Transition Team (HATT); the Coalition Military Advisory Transition Team (CMATT); and the Coalition Air Force Transition Team (CAFTT). Needless to say, the workings of these various staff elements proved difficult at best. The worst thing, however, was getting any of this make sense to the Iraqis we were supposed to advise.

From MNF-I down, the entire organizational structure of the Coalition is dysfunctional and impossible to make sense of to the Iraqis we are supposed to advise and help get on their feet. We can't even figure it all out ourselves and make it work, so how can it be made to work for them? But nowhere is MNF-I more dysfunctional than MNSTC-I, an organization of around 2,500 people including American military, Coalition (non-American) military, American civilian contractors and advisors, and non-American contractors and advisors. The relationship between the US military and the US civilian contractors was terrible. The military didn't want the contractors there, primarily because they were jealous of the money we were making, but also because we had a lot of experience in the areas we advised. In most cases we were not only advising the Iraqis, but were also keeping tabs on the MNSTC-I staff who were doing work for the Ministries of Defense and Interior we were advisors to, and making sure that work was done right. The last thing the MNSTC-I military staffs wanted was for us contractors to comment in any way about the how they were doing their business, or the quality of the work they were doing. This is where I got into trouble.

Just as the US Department of Defense has two sides to it, the military and the civilian, so does the Iraqi Ministry of Defense, mostly because we have designed it that way. In the US Department of Defense the military side is comprised of the Joint Chiefs of Staff. The civilian side is comprised of the various Under Secretaries and Assistant Secretaries for Personnel, Logistics, Finance, etc. These functions serve to provide support to the military side of the department, thereby allowing our military to wage war. The same basic structure exists in the Iraqi Ministry of Defense, where I was an advisor. MOD had the military side, the Joint Headquarters Staff, and the civilian side, the Directors General, the equivalent of our Assistant and Under Secretaries in the Department of Defense.

I worked on the Ministry of Defense Transition Team (MODTT), an organization of about 50 civilian advisors. Our job was to advise the civilian side of the Iraqi Ministry of Defense. There was also the Joint Headquarters Transition Team (JHQTT), whose job it was to advise the military side of the Ministry of Defense. It all made sense in theory, but in reality it didn't work at all. Because of the emphasis on "Coalition building," the head of my team was a British civil servant from his own Ministry of Defense in London. A nice fellow, he had no business running a team made up almost completely of Americans, especially when the United States is paying the freight and sending the bulk of the troops to Iraq. But because of the "politically correct" attitude of the Bush administration, there are non-Americans running key parts of the MNSTC-I organization. They're all over the place. The British and Australians even have to take "cultural awareness" training before they leave for Iraq to learn how to deal with Americans! And because the head of my team was British, his main concern was for the Commonwealth members of his staff, and not the Americans. The Joint Headquarters Transition Team was headed up by an Australian Brigadier General. Whenever these people would rotate out and go home, they would be replaced by another person of the same rank or civilian grade from their country. When the head of MODTT, David Murtagh, left Iraq he was replaced by John Cochrane, who came from the British Ministry of Defense as well.

I was hired to be the Real Estate Advisor to the Iraqi Ministry of Defense. I was employed by a firm in Alexandria, Virginia, which is a division of a major US corporation. More often than not, whenever I told someone what my job was, they would ask me what I was doing selling houses in Iraq. Or, if they did have an idea of what I might be doing over there, they would ask me what real estate had to do with the war. The paradox about real estate is when most people see or think of the words "real estate," all that comes to mind is the "FOR SALE" sign on the lawn in front of their house. Most people have no idea there is a distinct difference between residential (houses) and commercial (buildings and other non-residential) real estate. And most people have no idea what I mean when I say that I'm in "commercial real estate." The average person only thinks of selling their house when the term "real estate" comes up. Unless they are in the business, most people don't have a clue what commercial real estate is. Essentially, commercial real estate is any real estate other then someone's house. It's everything other than residential real estate. Needless to say, it covers a lot. My job was to advise the Iraqi Ministry of Defense about everything that had to do with its land and buildings, to include all its military installations. That's what my job had to do with the war.

The staff sections of MNSTC-I were not working for MNSTC-I itself as much as they were working for the Ministry of Defense (MOD) and the Ministry of Interior (MOI), augmenting the staffs at these two ministries. More than any other MNSTC-I staff section, the one that did this the most was J-7, the Construction Branch of MNSTC-I. The entire mission of the J-7 staff was to perform the construction functions of the MOD and MOI. J-7 was responsible for the construction of all new Iraqi military camps and installations across the country, as well as police and frontier border stations.

When I arrived in Iraq J-7 was headed up by an active duty US Navy Captain, the equivalent of an Army full colonel. The man holding this job headed a staff of dozens of military personnel, most of them reservists. His deputy was an Army Lieutenant Colonel, a reservist from Mississippi whose full time civilian job was teaching high school. All of the construction for the entire Iraqi military and national police was being supervised by a single active duty navy captain who had been in the Pentagon for five years before coming to Iraq. By his own admission, at his going away party before leaving Iraq, the captain said he had never been responsible for any construction project over $12 million dollars in his entire career. This is the financial equivalent of a one-car garage compared to the Bellagio Resort in Las Vegas. Yet in Iraq he was the sole person responsible for the oversight of billions of dollars worth of construction for these two Iraqi ministries. And most of his senior staff were reservists who hadn't put on a uniform in years, other than one weekend a month and a couple of weeks during the summer. The results of this poorly staffed and poorly run organization showed. The captain never made any effort to determine who owned the land that every new Iraqi army camp was located on that he was building, or the land any new national police station or border station was located on either. I asked him once if he would build a house on land he didn't own back in the states, and he just grunted. He simply didn't care, and he certainly wasn't going to listen to some civilian contractor like me. I would get this same type of treatment the entire time I was in Iraq, to include getting it from the captain's replacement, another US Navy Captain, and his deputy, a US Navy Commander.

I went to my boss, David Murtagh, the British Ministry of Defense civil servant, and told him what was going on. He couldn't have cared less. At one point I asked to have a meeting with both he and the captain to discuss the issue. The meeting began with the captain talking directly to David Murtagh, leaving me completely out of the conversation, when I was the one who had asked for the meeting in the first place. I wanted to discuss ways to better determine the ownership of land where the captain was building Iraqi military camps, so he wouldn't be in any land title trouble. He wouldn't hear anything I had to say. The problem was getting around the country to visit the Land Registration Office in each province where all the land records were kept. The only way we could determine who owned land the captain wanted to build camps on was to get to these offices. I had previously given him the complete list of these offices, which he didn't even know existed until I gave it to him, in order to locate the owners of the properties and compensate them for their land. The captain had staff out in the countryside who could get to these offices, and who were going there already, but the people who really needed to get there were the real estate staff from the Ministry of Defense, who the captain was building these camps for. After I finally got a chance to speak, I said all of this to the captain and David Murtagh. I explained the problem the Coalition was creating by violating the private property rights of Iraqi citizens when their land was taken and a military installation (and police or border station) was built on it. I asked the captain for his help to get the Iraqi Ministry of Defense real estate staff to the land registration offices because they had absolutely no way of travelling to these locations themselves. I got nowhere with him. David Murtagh started talking about "geopolitics." The meeting ended with nothing resolved, and the captain pissed off at me.

I was trying to prevent a situation where the Iraqi Ministry of Defense, and the United States Government, could quite possibly be held responsible for taking private property in Iraq without the owner's permission, and building an army camp on it. But no one cared. The captain was there to build Iraqi military camps, all with US money, and that was what he was going to do. The consequences of his actions meant absolutely nothing to him. And if I got in his way I could just get out of it or be mowed over. That's exactly what happened. My boss, David Murtagh, just watched because he, like everyone else there, was not about to go against the US military. It didn't matter that I was sent there to do a job, and that my client was the Iraqi Ministry of Defense, and that the captain was violating private property rights of Iraqi citizens in the effort to construct camps for my client. It was my problem, and I could just shove it.

During the initial phases of Operation Iraqi Freedom (OIF), the US military (on behalf of the entire Coalition) was taking land anywhere it was needed to construct Forward Operating Bases, or FOBs. The taking of land where and when it was needed by the Coalition was understandable during the exigencies of combat. The US Army Corps of Engineers Gulf Region District (GRD) made the effort to lease land or purchase it from Iraqi land owners for these FOBs. The Corps was honoring the private property rights of Iraqi citizens, with fair compensation for the "taking" of private property paid by the Corps for the basing needs of the Coalition. It was after the main combat efforts subsided and the Coalition was in the progress of "transitioning" the responsibility for the security of their country over to the Iraqis that the situation I have described began. We said we wanted the Iraqi Ministries of Defense and Interior to take on the responsibility for their country's security, and we would assist by constructing their bases and police and border stations for them. When "transition" kicked in under LTG Dempsey, J-7 had complete responsibility for building all Iraqi military camps and police and border stations. Under J-7 all pretence of proper title and land taking went out the window. LTG Dempsey knew of this but did nothing. David Murtagh couldn't have given a damn. The Corps of Engineers, being professionals in real estate and land issues, did it right when we were in the opening stages of the war. But the US Naval officers commanding J-7 didn't have a clue about land rights and clear title, or if they did they simply didn't care. Hell, it's Iraq. They didn't have to worry about that. By its actions J-7 (and MNSTC-I), was telling Iraqi land owners to pound sand if they thought they were going to be paid rent or a fee for their property.

As time went by many of the old FOBs built during the initial phases of OIF were no longer needed by the Coalition, and it wanted to turn them over to the Iraqi government to occupy and use. When I arrived in Iraq there was no system in place to do this. I heard of FOBs being left vacant by Coalition units, with no prior coordination with the Ministry of Defense to have an Iraqi army unit move in and occupy it. How could this happen, especially when these FOBs cost the US government tens of millions of dollars each to build? The reason was very simple, and it was the cause for 99% of the problems in Iraq—no one told the Iraqis what was going on, in this case that a FOB was going to be vacated and available for them to move into. So when the Coalition left, the local population who lived near the FOB came in and completely gutted everything in sight. Losses in the millions occurred every time this happened.

I asked the basing and facilities staff from both MNF-I and MNC-I, the ones who occupied these FOBs, to let me know when they planned to vacate them. Only two times was I told of a pending FOB transfer, for the transfers of FOB Sommerall and FOB Arlington, both of which were near Bayji, the oil refining center north of Tikrit. I tried to coordinate their transfer from the Coalition to MOD with the US advisors at JHQTT so that an Iraqi army unit could occupy them, but this effort went nowhere. I'm not sure if an Iraqi army unit ever moved in, but I do know the Ministry of Defense's Director General for Infrastructure and the Director of the Real Estate Division never played a role in these two transfers, never knew what happened, never placed them in their inventory, and were ignored by both the Coalition as well as the Iraqi Joint Headquarters Staff. Other than these two locations, I was never informed of any FOB transfer so I could coordinate its turnover to the MOD, with the Real Estate Director and his staff assisting their military counterparts at the JHQ. There were dozens of FOBs released and vacated by the Coalition, but the MOD staff section that existed to deal with these property turnovers was never involved. If a local Iraqi army unit was stationed nearby it could just move in if the commander had the backbone to do it. But if there wasn't an Iraqi military unit around, the FOB was left empty to be gutted by the locals. MNSTC-I's dysfunction made sure it turned out that way. Instead, all we heard

General Dempsey talk about was transition, and General Casey telling everyone the Iraqis were ready to step up and take over any time they wanted to. To make matters worse, the Iraqis had absolutely no travel capability beyond their personal vehicles in Baghdad. Even if they knew that a FOB was going to be vacated, and they were going to be given it for free from the US government, the Coalition refused to provide transportation for the Iraqis to the location to inspect and accept it. Instead, the Coalition wanted the Iraqis to accept and sign for FOBs and other facilities without seeing them at all, which they refused to do. Who could blame them?

It became clear to me that nothing was going to change the way the Coalition (e.g., the US military) was going to conduct the business of land acquisition, basing of Iraqi military units, or the transfer of former Coalition FOBs to Iraqi control. I arrived in Iraq with over 20 years of experience in real estate, which included commercial real estate in both the US Federal government and in private industry. I was a licensed real estate agent in three states. I had spent nearly 10 years working for the US General Services Administration in Washington, DC. I had been a warranted Contracting Officer for the US Government. I knew a little of what I was talking about. But I realized the dilemma of being a contractor in Iraq. I was just a warm body who was a source of revenue for my company to collect fees off the US government. That was it, and nothing more. No one cared at all if I accomplished a thing, or if I had years of experience to offer the Coalition and the Iraqis in my specific field. The US military actually didn't want me to do anything if it was going to run counter to what they wanted to do, were planning to do, or were going to do, regardless of whether I was the real estate "subject matter expert" who they had hired through my firm. The irony was that my position was created by two officers who had been on the J-7 staff before the arrival of the Navy captain who was in charge when I got there. They knew the importance of land ownership in Iraq, but they were both long gone. The captain wouldn't listen to a thing I had to say about a field he knew nothing about, but should have cared a lot about. The question for me became—why am I here?

The firm I worked for was started about 20 years ago by a group of retired US Army lieutenant colonels who began getting Army contracts running rifle ranges. Not glamorous work by any stretch of the imagination. But during the conflict in Bosnia the company got its start in consulting and advisory work for DoD. A former US Army Chief of Staff took over the reins of the firm about ten years ago, and his #2 man is another retired 4-star general. Great officers, but the real reason for their being in the job is to rub shoulders with current Army brass to get these contracts awarded to their company. If a retired 4-star general walks into the office of an active duty 3- or 4-star general and asks for business, what is the active duty general going to say? Even in retirement a 4-star general carries a huge amount of clout, and no one is going to make him wait outside their office.

My firm started to get these consulting contracts, but when Operation Iraqi Freedom happened the barn doors flew open. The amount of money the company made in Afghanistan and Iraq from 2003 to 2007 has been one billion dollars. It is everywhere the US military is, especially the US Army, to include Africa. It has even received a large contract to support the US Centers for Disease Control in Atlanta, Georgia, assisting CDC in its preparation for the outbreak of the avian flu because it was able to sell its management expertise to the CDC Director. That's great for the firm, but it sure doesn't say much for the CDC staff's ability to run an epidemic.

All of this would be great if the company's management would allow its staff to do the things they were actually hired to do by the client paying the bill. In my case I was hired by the US military to advise the Iraqi Ministry of Defense on its real estate issues, which also included getting its real estate staff up and running. But when I saw what was going on, such as J-7 ignoring the private property rights of Iraqi citizens, anything I said about it was ignored. So I turned to the company I worked for and told my manager in Baghdad. I have never met a more incompetent person in my life. A retired US Army lieutenant colonel, he was responsible for the contract I worked on. He never did anything except sit at his desk all day staring at his computer. If anyone had a question or a problem, he would start talking about anything that popped in his mind, like the two or three months he spent in Vietnam, or when he was with our firm in Afghanistan, or anything other than the issue you dropped by to discuss with him. (He got to Vietnam as the war was winding down and had nothing to do, so he went around trying to find work and get a "command." He commanded a company in Vietnam for about one month, but that's all he ever talked about. I heard he commanded a battalion in the 82nd Airborne Division, which I found difficult to believe.) So inept was this person that if you really had an issue with something, he simply refused to discuss it, and on occasion he threw people out of his office. The folks at our company headquarters knew all about this, but refused to fire him. People quit because of him, yet the firm did nothing. He must have been in someone's back pocket. He was probably a junior officer under one of the 4-star generals who ran our company when they were battalion commanders earlier in their careers.

Once I went to this clown with a leave request to go to Jordan for a few days. The leave policy at our firm for those of us in Iraq was pretty good. They didn't count days of travel to get to or from your destination. For example, if I wanted to fly back home to the States, I had two days of travel at either end of my trip that didn't count against my vacation as long as I flew via Kuwait. If I flew via another route, such as Jordan, I got one free day of travel at either end of the trip. I wasn't aware of the distinction between two days and one day when I made my request. I filled out my leave request with two days at either end of the trip, and turned it in to my manager. He asked me what the request was for, when it was obvious it was for a vacation to Jordan. He went nuts, telling me to fill the request out again, but not because I had the travel days wrong. He was actually pissed off that I would have the nerve to request a vacation to Jordan, and not to the United States. He said vacations were for going home to the States, which was complete nonsense. I told him that he was wrong, that vacation was mine to use any way I wanted to, and that others on his contract had travelled to countries like Italy and Switzerland for their vacations. He went through the ceiling and told me to return the next day with the revised leave request, talking to me like I was one of his screwball soldiers from the 82nd. I went back and filled out the vacation request again, researching the company policy and discovering the distinction on the travel days. I went back and gave him my revised request, this time bringing with me the company's policy on travel days. My revised request was totally accurate, and I had accrued the days that I wanted to use for the leave. I handed him the company policy and he looked at it for about half a second and then threw it on the floor. He then started to berate me about my "attitude," at which I commented that must be the real reason he was putting me through this. Then he kicked me out of his office. I never took that vacation because it wasn't worth the hassle, but I began to see the writing on the wall. He didn't like me because he couldn't handle me questioning his decisions and his judgment, both of which were as lame as he was, and he knew it. I wasn't questioning his authority, I was questioning his lack of professionalism and lack of knowledge of company policy (he had no idea of the travel policy of our firm, yet he was the contract manager), and most of all his abuse of his position. He was the same manager who couldn't believe people would actually drink alcohol when they were precluded from doing so by General Order #1. He was incompetent, yet the company would do nothing about him.

It was sinking in that my place was not to advise the Iraqis as I had been hired to do by the US military, through my firm. It was not to bring issues or problems to people's attention. It was not to try and get things done correctly. My job was to continue breathing and keep my mouth shut, so that my company could continue to collect fees off of my being over there, alive and in one piece and not in a pine box. If I was not there, then my position was not filled, and the company made no money. Not good for my company, especially for its publically traded parent. And that was the real rub. I have an MBA in finance. Having a little knowledge about these things I know that at companies like mine, a publically traded corporation, the only thing that matters to its management and the management of its subsidiaries is shareholder value. It is certainly not the happiness or job satisfaction of its employees who are deployed into a combat zone. Who cares about them? Needless to say, I was not able to do nearly the amount of work I could have done for the Iraqi people and their Ministry of Defense. In order to do that I would have had to get cooperation from the Coalition military staff who were constructing all of these facilities for MOD, and that was certainly not going to happen as long as the Navy captain was around. And I certainly wasn't going to get any help from my manager, who was not going to do a thing he thought might upset a US military officer, even if that officer didn't know what he was doing. And David Murtagh, my British supervisor at MODTT, just cared about getting his civilian award from DoD and LTG Dempsey, and a promotion back at the British Ministry of Defense in London. He was the same as my manager, only with a lot more class.

What of the other MNSTC-I staff sections? On the Ministry of Interior side of MNSTC-I there was CPATT, for Coalition Police Advisory Transition Team, and MOITT, for Ministry of Interior Transition Team. CPATT was led by a US Army 2-star general, while MOITT was led by a British Brigadier (1-star). When I first arrived in Iraq CPATT was commanded by Major General Joseph Peterson, who was later replaced about half way through my tour by Major General Kenneth Hunzeker, the guy who used to drink at the British Embassy. MOITT was led by British Brigadier Rob Weighill, who will be mentioned again later.

MOITT was responsible for mentoring and advising the Iraqi Ministry of Interior, similar to MODTT for the Ministry of Defense. It worked on a daily basis with the civilian side of that ministry. CPATT, on the other hand, worked closely with the uniformed side of the Ministry of Interior, the national police, which actually mirrored in many ways a military organization and was staffed like the Iraqi army. They wore military uniforms like the army, only theirs were blue camouflage, where the army's was standard desert brown. I didn't work on the Ministry of Interior side of MNSTC-I, but I spoke with my military and civilian colleagues who worked there every day. We worked in the same building on Phoenix Base, the walled compound within the International Zone that was the headquarters of MNSTC-I. Many MOITT advisors also worked at the Ministry of Interior building on the other side of the Tigris River, in one of the worst sections of Baghdad. Regardless of its location, however, all of my MOITT colleagues preferred to work there because it was "away from the flag pole," meaning it was away from MNSTC-I headquarters at Phoenix Base in the IZ, and the accompanying rat race. Many American military and civilian police advisors assigned to CPATT have been killed or wounded while serving in Iraq. It is very much a combat assignment, as these advisors are with their Iraqi police counterparts every day in the middle of the cities and towns throughout the country. There is a hallway inside the building where we worked with pictures of those who had been killed-in-action as CPATT police advisors, the majority of them civilians, most of them retired police officers.

On the Ministry of Defense side I had much more knowledge of the other sections besides the one I was assigned to, MODTT. The JHQTT advised the military side of the Ministry of Defense, the Joint Headquarters Staff. The Iraqi Joint Headquarters Chief of Staff is General (4-star) Babakir, and the Deputy is General (also 4-star) Abadi, whose son is a foreign exchange student at the US Air Force Academy. General Abadi is an Iraqi Air Force officer, although today the country's entire air force consists of about a dozen helicopters and a few C-130 transport aircraft. The Iraqi Navy consists of a half dozen Italian-made patrol boats in the mouth of the Tigris River at the north end of the Persian Gulf (called the Gulf of Arabia by Iraqis). The entire Iraqi coast at the northern tip of the Gulf is only a few miles long. The Tigris River flows into the Gulf at the Al Faw peninsula. The Iraqi army is about 98% of the country's entire military structure.

CAFTT, the Coalition Air Force Transition Team, was first commanded by Brigadier General Stephen Hoog, and later commanded by US Air Force Brigadier General Robert Allardice. The mission of CAFTT was to transition the new Iraqi Air Force into an effective military unit. There was no Iraqi "Air Force." We had destroyed everything the Iraqis had that flew during both the Gulf War in 1991, and again during this conflict. The new Iraqi Air Force was going to consist of nothing but transport aircraft, both fixed wing and helicopter. But there was one incident I will never forget. One day I was sitting in a meeting with some MNSTC-I staff, mostly officers. General Allardice was the ranking officer at the meeting. At one point he was in a discussion over manning strength of the Iraqi military with a US Army full colonel. It got down to raw numbers, and how many Iraqi army personnel were needed versus air force personnel. General Allardice, a real piece of work, said to the colonel: "one Air Force person is worth at least 60 Army people." He was referring to the US Air Force and the US Army. The US Army colonel just looked at him. I think the colonel thought he was joking. But General Allardice was dead serious. He meant exactly what he said. In his mind a US Army soldier wasn't worth a thing next to a US Air Force airman. This clown just doesn't get it. His Air Force supports the Army, not the other way around. He wouldn't know which end of a rifle was which, and he probably couldn't care less. That's what a US Air Force general thought of his sister service, and actually had the nerve to say to a US Army full colonel, in public. He obviously looked down on the Army, the guys who have boots on the ground and take the bulk of the casualties. Brigadier General Allardice's comment brings disgrace to the US Air Force. Of the US military who have died in Iraq since 2003, how many have been Army and how many Air Force? It's about a 20/1 ratio Army/Air Force. But what does that matter to BG Allardice? What does matter is that senior ranking US military officers can say things like that—and get away with it. General Allardice has since been promoted to Major (2-star) General. The different branches of the service are all supposed to get along in the new "joint force" structure of today's modern US military. That's a joke. And if he can treat a full colonel without any respect, imagine how guys like him feel about contractors.

If General Allardice felt this way about our own army, how did he feel about the Iraqi's? What made his comment so ridiculous was the Iraqi army was probably 98% of its military strength. I don't know what General Allardice did while he was in Iraq, because there wasn't an Iraqi "Air Force" to advise. He probably thought the Iraqi Army should be scrapped and its Air Force could defend the entire country with a half dozen C-130 transports, a dozen old Huey's, a few Bell Jet Rangers, and a handful of Mi-17's. General Allardice was one of the senior military advisors on MNSTC-I staff. If his opinion was being given any merit, which it had to be based on his rank, Iraq would never be able to defend itself. But he was assigned to Iraq, so his second star was on its way.

The Ministry of Defense is supposed to be a balance between the military and the civilian sides, with the latter supporting the military in its mission of defending the country. It is also led by "civilians," just like ours. But the reality of it is far different. All of the senior civilians at MOD were either retired generals, or active duty generals wearing suits. Because Iraq was run by a military dictator for so long, who wore civilian clothes most of the time, the military side runs the show. The Minister of Defense (a former general) has a lot of power and runs the Ministry, but he can't do anything if the Joint Headquarters Staff does not want to go along. The Ministry of Defense was constantly in a state of flux. It was constantly changing. After I had been in Iraq for about 6 months, we came into work one morning and the Minister of Defense, Abdul Qadir, had decided to completely reorganize the entire Ministry, from top to bottom. So out of touch was LTG Dempsey, the senior US military advisor to the Minister of Defense, and MNSTC-I commander, he didn't even know this was going to happen. Nor did David Murtagh, the senior civilian advisor to the Minister of Defense and my MODTT boss. LTG Dempsey never included the Iraqis in on anything, so why should they let him in on what they were going to do. What goes around comes around. The entire Joint Headquarters Staff, as well as the civilian side of the Ministry of Defense, was reorganized, and no one at MNSTC-I knew it was even going to happen until the day it was announced. The Ministry went through a reorganization that lasted nearly six months, and it was still going through the tail end of it when I left 8 months after the reorganization was first announced. LTG Dempsey still got his 4th star though.

There was another part of the MNSTC-I organization called CMATT, for Coalition Military Assistance Transition Team. CMATT was led by a US Army Brigadier General named Terry Wolff, a 1979 graduate of West Point who looks like he's about 19 years old. At first General Wolff seemed to be a straight talker and a straight shooter. But as my experience with the CMATT staff progressed I realized that it didn't really do much at all. It never seemed to get anything accomplished. It was CMATT's job to train and equip Iraqi military units in the field, very similar to what CPATT did with the Iraqi national police, only far safer. Instead of being embedded with Iraqi police forces in the middle of cities and towns like CPATT, CMATT advisors lived and worked in the middle of large Coalition camps, safe from harm's way. I knew of no CMATT advisors who were killed in Iraq. Their job was very cushy and safe. Its advisors were there to run training classes for the Iraq military forces. They would do this by getting in their armored vehicles and driving with armed convoy escorts down the road from the safety of the Coalition camp where they lived, which had amenities like Pizza Hut, Subway, Burger King and a Starbucks-like coffee emporium called

Green Beans. They would drive from this to the squalor of the nearby Iraqi camp where the Iraqi troops they advised were based, living like animals.

CMATT was also responsible for working with the Iraqi Joint Headquarters Staff as well as JHQTT and MODTT. This is one of the many examples of overlapping responsibilities that existed throughout the MNSTC-I organization that we had to work with and try to overcome. It caused nothing but problems. Each staff section at MNSTC-I did its own thing, and rarely communicated what it was doing with the others, even though their coordination would have helped the two Iraqi ministries that it was MNSTC-I's mission to stand up. No one at MNSTC-I was really held responsible for something if another part of the organization was also involved. It not only caused confusion, it was a great way to deal with failure or inaction where no one was held entirely responsible for anything. It was as if MNSTC-I was designed that way. Of course everyone wanted to take credit when things went well, but that rarely happened. In a way MNSTC-I operated a lot like MOD itself—confusion, overlapping responsibilities, no accountability, and complete lack of coordination. It was truly an example of the blind leading the blind.

A good example of the dysfunction of MNSTC-I was the construction of Iraqi army bases. J-7 was responsible for the construction of new bases and facilities for the Iraqi military. JHQTT was responsible for working side-by-side with the Iraqi Joint Headquarters military staff, CMATT worked with the Iraqi Joint Headquarters Staff also. When I arrived in Iraq I was told there was a strategic plan to have 85 permanent Iraqi garrisons (camps and installations) that would house and maintain all the forces of the Iraqi Army, Navy and Air Force for years into the future, sort of a "master plan" for Iraq's military installations. These garrisons were divided into groups arranged by their size. The five largest ones were the Regional Support Units, or RSU's, and the smaller ones were the Garrison Support Units, or GSU's. The Garrison Support Units would each be capable of providing support for their own camp, to include low-level vehicle and weapons maintenance, and feeding the soldiers and storing bulk supplies. The Regional Support Units would be much larger and capable of doing what the Garrison Support Units beneath them could not do, such as higher levels of maintenance, more storage capacity, etc.. On paper the layout and organization of the RSU's and the GSU's looked much like an organizational chart for a military unit, which in effect it was. There were the five RSU's across the top of the chart, and the numerous GSU's within their regions underneath them, with the GSU's relying on the RSU's above them for their higher level logistical and other major support.

I started to hear more about the RSU's and GSU's, and what they were supposed to do. Because these bases would need land to be constructed on, they would be included in the real estate inventory the MOD Real Estate Branch was supposed to be responsible for acquiring and managing. The real estate staff also needed the experience and responsibility of locating the best sites for these bases. None of this happened, nor was it going to change regardless of what I tried to do. I realized CMATT was selecting all the locations for these camps on its own, with minimal input from the Ministry of Defense. Neither the Joint Headquarters Staff nor the civilian staff of the Infrastructure Directorate (which was responsible for the real estate, construction, and basing of all Iraqi military units that belonged to the Joint Headquarters Staff) were involved. The only section of the Iraqi Ministry of Defense that had anything to do with these new camps was Base Management, under the command of Major General (2-star) Saad, whose limited involvement will be discussed shortly.

What was interesting was that JHQTT and CMATT did all the planning for this, but never included MODTT. Just as within MOD itself, the military advisory teams within MNSTC-I completely ignored the civilian advisory teams. Why should the Iraqis on the military side of MOD, the Joint Headquarters Staff, include in any planning the civilian side of MOD, the Directors General, when they saw the US military at MNSTC-I doing the same thing to their civilian counterparts? MNSTC-I was so dysfunctional, it was incapable of advising or helping in any tangible way the Ministry of Defense. We had nothing to say about how messed up that Iraqi ministry was, when we were just as bad. And we were under the command of a United States Army 3-star general who couldn't even hold a monthly meeting, whose sole purpose was to discuss the status of transition from Coalition to Iraqi control of both its military and national police, and invite the Iraqis to it. That was the single most important part of his job. He's now a 4-star general.

The function of the civilian side of our Department of Defense is to support the military side, the Joint Chiefs of Staff. It is the civilian side, the Under and Assistant Secretaries, that support the military and provide them with what they need to fight wars. The Iraqi Ministry of Defense is supposed to be set up the same way. That is why there are advisory teams at MNSTC-I to help the military and civilian staff at that ministry. But when MNSTC-I's advisory teams can't work together, to the point of the military teams totally ignoring the civilian, how can the two sides of MOD be expected to behave differently? It was directly due to the poor coordination within the advisory teams at MNSCT-I that MOD was operating in the same dysfunctional way. LTG Dempsey let the Iraqi Ministry of Defense down by allowing this abysmal staff coordination within MNSTC-I to exist, and failed to do anything about it. It was beyond his control. Just as General Casey sat on his hands while the insurgency got out of control, General Dempsey sat on his while the Iraqi Ministry of Defense and Ministry of Interior spun around and got nothing done when they should have been moving forward. One general failed to use the forces under his command to defend Iraq, while the other failed to use his command authority to run a well organized staff and get these two Iraqi ministries on their feet.

Iraq is full of political, diplomatic and intelligence failure by Bush, Cheney, Rumsfeld, Tenant and Bremer, military failure by Franks, Sanchez and Casey, and transition failure by Patraeus and Dempsey. There is no good news to report.

I tried to make my presence known to CMATT because I wanted the MOD Real Estate Branch to play a role in the RSU/GSU initiative. CMATT worked just across the way in another building on Phoenix Base, but they ignored me because I was a civilian, and they didn't talk to civilians. On more than one occasion I was chewed out and treated like crap by one of their staff, a reserve lieutenant colonel who thought he was George Patton because he was wearing a uniform. His job in real life back in the States was with the Minnesota Highway Department. But he was wearing a uniform and I wasn't, and that was all that mattered.

I found out after being in Iraq for nearly 10 months that the RSU/GSU concept hadn't been accepted by the Iraqi Joint Headquarters Staff. Even though CMATT had RSU and GSU advisors located at Coalition camps around the country to "advise" the Iraqi army, the Iraqis never formally agreed with the plan or the concept. This meant the Coalition, MNSTC-I, and CMATT in particular, were doing this completely on their own, with no approval or buy-in from the Iraqis they were doing it for. It never officially got beyond being a concept, a plan. RSU's and GSU's were just organizations on paper, with no Iraqi concurrence to make them reality, even though the entire ten months I had been in Iraq before finding this out CMATT talked like they were the real thing, with US Army lieutenant colonels working on them every day. What did they spend their time doing if the Iraqis never bought into the plan? That the Iraqi Joint Headquarters Staff hadn't formally approved this plan, after all the time CMATT had been working on it, blew my mind. What was BG Wolff doing all that time? He left for his next assignment in Washington, DC, to be on the National Security Council, without the RSU/GSU plan approved and accepted by the Iraqis until practically the day he left. And this was one of the primary missions of CMATT which was under his command.

I once found out through the grapevine (which was usually how I found out about anything) that there was going to be a meeting concerning the RSU's and GSU's. This happened to be prior to my knowledge about the Iraqis having not yet approving the plan. The meeting was going to be the next day, and was going to be chaired by BG Wolff's CMATT Deputy Commander, a Norwegian Navy Admiral. What was a Norwegian Admiral doing as the Deputy Commander of CMATT, the MNSTC-I staff section responsible for assisting the Iraqi Joint Headquarters Staff with equipping and training the Iraqi military forces, 98% of which is the army? This was another example of the ridiculous staffing that we saw every day under the Coalition concept. It was a mixing bowl of every nationality, title, rank and uniform one could imagine, like the bar scene in Star Wars. It was laughable. Because of the "Coalition of the Willing," the US had to work with military from all over the world, which would have been a good thing for PR, except they were placed in key positions on the MNSTC-I staff. Needless to say it didn't help.

I attended the meeting, which was held using interpreter headsets like they use in the United Nations. These were actually quite effective. The Norwegian Admiral, who didn't know what was going on, started the meeting and immediately handed it over to Major General Saad, the Iraqi officer in charge of Base Management at MOD. General Saad was a very distinguished fellow. Like most Iraqi men, he always had his prayer beads in his hand and would constantly flip them one after another with his thumb. I always wondered what benefit Iraqis got out of doing this, but it did seem to calm them and help their concentration. He started to discuss the RSU's and GSU's, and eventually got to the point of saying that he didn't think there was a need for 85 of them, which had been shown on the plan all along by CMATT. For a year CMATT had been doing its own thing by planning for these camps, and when the Iraqis were finally invited to a meeting to discuss them, to discuss camps that were for them, they had a completely different opinion about the entire concept. As the discussion went on the number was lowered to 80, with the same five Regional Support Units, and 75 Garrison Support Units. That was the last I heard of the RSU/GSU plan for several months. No one asked me if the MOD Real Estate Branch could assist, nor did I have any idea of more meetings on the subject.

About three months later I discovered the total number had changed again, from 80 to around 35! I had no idea of this change, but then again no one from CMATT would ever tell me anything, even though I constantly asked them to keep me informed. How could I advise the Ministry of Defense real estate staff if I had no idea what MNSTC-I was doing—that directly involved the Ministry of Defense's real estate staff? But I wasn't alone in this treatment. The MNSTC-I military staff who advised the Iraqi Joint Headquarters Staff never told their MNSTC-I civilian counterparts anything, and they were there to advise the Iraqi civilian staff of MOD. Everyone was kept in the dark. The MNSTC-I military had nothing to do with the MNSTC-I civilians, primarily because the military (the vast majority civilians themselves in real life) disdained the civilians. The MNSTC-I military didn't want civilian contractors around, were jealous of the money they made, and in general had a pompous and arrogant attitude about everything. The civilian side was not kept informed nearly to the level it should have been, and could have been, by the military side. We Americans were just as bad, really we were worse, than the Iraqi military who we always complained about as being backward, arrogant and pompous. I never knew what the MNSTC-I military staff involved in land and basing of Iraqi units was doing. This specifically involved J-5, J-7 and JHQTT. I was always trying to find out what MNSTC-I was up to that affected Ministry of Defense land and basing issues. Usually the best I could do was sit in on a meeting and take notes, or pipe in when I could, most of the time finding out about the meeting right before it was starting, usually by accident when I overheard someone talking about it. I was never kept in the loop beyond sitting in on the occasional meeting that I nearly always found out about on my own, at the last minute, and by pure coincidence.

I was hired to assist the Iraqi Ministry of Defense real estate staff, yet was only able to do a fraction of what I could have because I had to fight for every bit of information I needed from our own US military staff at MNSTC-I. Just as the Iraqi military didn't keep their civilian counterparts informed because of their pro-military culture, the MNSTC-I military didn't keep their civilian counterparts informed either, and for the exact same reason. The US military at MNSTC-I would work with the Iraqi military at MOD, and they would both exclude their own civilian counterparts. But our problem was far worse because we had billions of US dollars to spend, and we should have known better. I sincerely feel that a lot of this dysfunction, bad feeling, and poor communication within MNSTC-I was due to the vast majority of MNSTC-I staff who were reservists, and really civilians themselves. This led to two problems. Now that these people were wearing uniforms their power went to their heads and all civilians (which they were themselves before being deployed to Iraq) were considered scum. And because they weren't full-time career military, they didn't know how to work and interact with civilians who support the military, which occurs every day throughout the US military around the world.

We at MNSTC-I were supposed to be "rebuilding" Iraq, so we should have been working together far better than we did. The MNSTC-I civilian contractors were hired by the MNSTC-I military, yet we were treated like dirt by the same people we were hired to help. Neither I, nor any of my civilian contractor friends, would have been in Iraq if we hadn't been hired by MNSTC-I and the US Defense Department in order to support them.

So why were we there, much less treated this way? General Patraeus didn't want us there, nor did General Dubik who took over MNSTC-I from General Dempsey. I know this from friends who heard them say it. If they felt this way, it is highly likely they did because their predecessors, Generals Casey and Dempsey, felt the same way and passed it on to their successors, which is common in any bureaucracy. They both said they disliked contractors, specifically my firm, in front of people who were there and heard them say it, and they told me. If they didn't want us or my firm around, how did it get these contracts? That's why two retired 4-star generals were working there. They were there to walk around DoD and schmooze their buddies and get these contracts to send people like me to Iraq, to get treated like crap by the military who had nothing to do with awarding the contracts in the first place, and who didn't want us there. It was a "Catch-22." The generals in the Pentagon don't care what their commanders in Iraq feel about having my firm and other contractors around. The commanders in the field don't want us there, but their higher headquarters cut a deal with the two generals who run my company and over we go. It's a different world between the Pentagon and Iraq. They walk in, get the contracts, and send guys like me to Iraq to be treated like unwanted guests by the US military who had nothing to do with awarding our contract. But firms like mine and the stockholders of major corporations that own them make a ton of money. That's what it's all about. And, of course, promising jobs at my firm when they retire for the active duty generals in the Pentagon who awarded the contracts.

DoD contracts worth literally billions of dollars are being spent on firms like mine to send guys like me over to Iraq to do nothing, because the US military we are hired to support don't even want us there. We would always complain about how narrow focused and military-centric the Iraqis were yet the Coalition, MNSTC-I especially, was exactly the same. We would talk about this in our weekly MODTT "all hands" staff meetings with David Murtagh, and then with his successor John

Cochrane, but they wouldn't say anything to Generals Dempsey or Dubik for fear of pissing them off. And why should they say anything? They were both high ranking British civil servants there to punch their tickets, get a civilian medal from Dempsey or Dubik when they left, and then a promotion and a big fat job in the British Ministry of Defense when they got back to London. On the other hand, at least 80% of the MODTT staff were Americans like me, so why should Murtagh or Cochrane do squat for us. That was how the Coalition worked. It was all nonsense. If I had a problem with the MNSTC-I military not listening to me, or not letting me in on what they were doing that affected the MOD real estate staff, I was on my own because David Murtagh was a Brit and didn't want to upset the same US military people who were blowing me off. His successor, John Cochrane, wasn't much better.

When I left Iraq in September of 2007 the Iraqi Ministry of Defense, specifically the Joint Headquarters Staff, had finally approved the CMATT concept plan for the Regional and Garrison Support Unit locations, and the staffing of them. But not a thing had actually been done to implement the plan. I was there for 14 months, and from the time I arrived until the time I left not one single RSU or GSU facility had been built, not one RSU or GSU military unit had been staffed or manned, and not one RSU or GSU camp actually existed to support any Iraqi military units. This was after 14 months that I was in Iraq, and the RSU/GSU plan had existed long before I got there. This was CMATT's "baby." The main thing CMATT was working on never even got off the paper that it was written on. This shows minimal accomplishment on the part of Brigadier General Wolff, and a lack of competence on the part of the two Norwegian Admirals, his two successive deputies who had no business being in that job in the first place. But it also shows how the "Coalition concept" was far more important than getting anything accomplished or helping the Iraqis. If the Coalition couldn't get this done for the Iraqis, what could it get done? General Wolff is now in Washington as the Senior Military Advisor on the National Security Council in the White House. I'm sure he'll be getting his second star soon, if he hasn't gotten it already. After all, he was assigned to Iraq.

To say MNSTC-I was dysfunctional would be an understatement. It had so many parts that no one knew who was responsible for what, who was doing what, and in most cases there was more than one staff section working on the same thing. The example of the Regional and Garrison Support Units shows how there were at least four different functional groups involved within MNSTC-I: CMATT, JHQTT, J-7, and MODTT. Yet no one shared information with anyone else, certainly no one spoke to me about anything they were planning regarding the locations and basing of Iraqi military camps, or the transfer to the Ministry of Defense of Coalition Forward Operating Bases. Yet I was the real estate advisor to the Ministry of Defense, the Iraqi ministry that MNSTC-I existed to support. And if this was happening in the area of land and facilities, where else was it happening within MNSTC-I? It's safe to assume it was this way with everything.

When it was decided to construct a camp for the Iraqi military, in most cases the Iraqis weren't even involved in the decision. If they were it was more a formality than anything else, and only involved the military side of MOD. The Coalition military did everything, only including the Iraqi military in on what they planned to do, and that was it. Neither Coalition or MOD civilians had any idea what was going on beyond a scant knowledge, at best. The camp was located without the Real Estate Division on the civilian side of the Iraqi Ministry of Defense having any idea what was going on. It was constructed by J-7, without the Director General for Infrastructure having any involvement in the design or the construction of the installation, and the Iraqi army occupied it without any involvement of the civilian side of the Iraqi Ministry of Defense. The only part of MOD that was involved was the JHQ, the military side of the Ministry, and that was minimal at best. Our military only worked with the Iraqi military, barring the civilians, both Iraqi and Coalition advisors, from playing any role. And the Iraqi military was involved only a fraction of what it should have been. In short, the US military was doing everything for the Iraqis, even though General Casey had been blowing smoke up the President's backside that the Iraqis could take over any time and start doing everything themselves. There were too many parts of the MNSTC-I and MOD organizations that had a role to play, but didn't have any say in what was done. Whatever MNSTC-I did was copied at MOD. If the Coalition did it, why couldn't the Iraqis too? The worst part was the Iraqis saw the dysfunction and confusion within MNSTC-I, yet we were supposed to know what we were doing and show them how things got done right. Instead, we were showing them how things were done wrong. They would sometimes say to me "You Americans can put a man on the moon, so why can't you get these simple things accomplished?" It was hard to come up with an answer.

The paradox was that the US was trying to form an Iraqi Ministry of Defense similar to our own DoD, whereby the civilian leadership had heavy sway in the running of MOD like at our own Pentagon. We were sure doing a lousy job of it. Where was the senior US civilian advisor to the Ministry of Defense, who was the counterpart of LTG Dempsey, and who was there to make sure the civilian leadership of the MOD was doing its job of running the ministry? He didn't exist. The closest we had was a Brit named David Murtagh, who wouldn't say shit to LTG Dempsey because he was intimidated by him. If we had had a strong American civilian advisor there, who wasn't afraid of LTG Dempsey and his uniform, the entire situation at MNSTC-I would have been completely different. But that's what happened when DoD won the food fight with State. Not that State would have done any better. But the result was the extreme scenario we ended up with, where there was no civilian leadership at all advising MOD and MOI. If we had a senior American civilian advisor to the Minister of Defense much of these problems would not have occurred. My colleagues and I would have had someone to go to who might have listened.

There was one project that was handled differently than any other construction being done for the Iraqi army—the SIB's, the Security Infrastructure Battalions. The SIB's battalions were intended to have platoon and company sized units at intervals along the county's pipelines and power lines. This would involve constructing small camps every few hundred meters or so. I was never brought into the full scope of what was being done with these, and exactly who was building them. The SIB's units went up to battalion size. This was a huge undertaking. The only involvement I had was sitting in on a couple of meetings for my associate while she was away on leave. One of these was held in the office of General Abadi, the Vice Chief of Staff of the Iraqi Joint Headquarters Staff. A bunch of Coalition officers and advisors gathered around his office while he talked about a few other issues before he got into the situation with the SIB's units. Then he began to talk about them, and like it was no big deal he said the JHQ didn't know if it would guard the country's oil lines or its electrical grid first! Everyone nearly fell out of their chairs. I didn't know much about SIB's, but hearing him say this I almost fell out of my chair too. This single decision was monumental, for it was the entire direction of which part of the nation's power infrastructure it would guard first, and which one would be left exposed. My associate was handling this on her own, and she never included me in on it at all until she went away on vacation. But it dealt with land, regardless of who was constructing the facilities or camps, and I should have been involved more.

The best story of the dysfunction within MNSTC-I was the "warehouse project." I had just returned to Iraq from vacation back to the States in December of 2006. On my first day back at work my associate told me the Ministry of Defense was going to have warehouses built at bases around the country. For the first time I was being asked to assist in locating sites for Iraqi army installations. The Iraqi Joint Headquarters staff, with Major General Saad of Base Management and Major General Jawdat of M-4 (who couldn't stand each other and refused to be in the same room together), wanted the Iraqi army to have logistics locations around the country for storage and food preparation. 23 warehouse complexes would be located at 22 Iraqi bases (there would be two of these warehouse located at Taji, north of Baghdad) to provide support to the Iraqi Army, Navy and Air Force. The plan called for "life support" warehouses that would store everything from uniforms to dry goods, and have mess facilities and bakeries to feed the Iraqi troops in the geographic areas served by these new facilities.

The job originally began under the auspices of the JHQTT staff, specifically the M-4-TT, which was the MNSTC-I staff section that advised the Iraqi M-4 Logistics staff section within MOD. But right from the beginning there were problems. If our M-4-TT was assisting and advising the Iraqi Joint Headquarters M-4 staff, under the command of Major General Jawdat, and the Iraqi Base Management staff under Major General Saad, then what about the Coalition Military Assistance Transition Team (CMATT), which was also advising the same MOD staff sections? CMATT was responsible for equipping and training the

Iraqi armed forces, and it was also responsible for working with Major General Saad and Major General Jawdat in setting up the Regional and Garrison Support Units (RSU's and GSU's) described above. CMATT was also responsible for working with the rest of the Iraqi JHQ, and so were the other parts of MNSTC-I. When the project was first conceived (presumably by both the Iraqis and MNSTC-I), it was given to M-4-TT to implement. My associate was told about it by a US Army Major on the M-4-TT staff. The major was originally from Vietnam, and his family had left on a boat when he was an infant and settled in Los Angeles. He was an extremely friendly fellow, but his English was so bad I couldn't understand a word he said. He had lived in the US for over 25 years.

The major came to see me after my associate told me of the project, and he handed me a list of the 22 bases where these warehouses were going to be located. It was going to be my job to coordinate the travel to these locations and find sites for them. I was all over it. This would involve bringing Iraqis from the MOD Infrastructure Directorate with me on every trip to find sites on the bases to locate the warehouses, with each site requiring a large plot of land 400 x 400 meters in area. The major and I went over the list and began to prioritize the locations, starting with those in the Baghdad area, and then going farther out from there. We decided to travel to Taji, about 20 miles north of Baghdad, for our first trip. We went on a US Army UH-60 Blackhawk helicopter. Probably 90% of all air travel in Iraq is on these aircraft, which has a crew of four and can sit up to 12 passengers. We flew to Taji, and conducted our site inspection, and then returned that same day. It looked like things would go smoothly. We were very badly mistaken.

As time went by it became harder and harder to make these trips, not because of the distances involved, but because of the nearly impossible task of coordinating the US military air transport. About the same time our trips began, the insurgents started shooting down US helicopters, which were doing most of their flying during the day because the air had been relatively safe for a long time. The month we started the warehouse project the first US helicopter in a series of attacks was shot down, killing all 16 passengers and crew on board. One of them was a West Point classmate of my younger brother. To the best of my knowledge the Army has never made a formal declaration of what caused the crash, but it doesn't take a genius to figure out it was from enemy fire. Why the Army couldn't make an announcement on the cause of this crash is beyond reason, but it wouldn't do so. Did it want everyone to think things were better than they really were by not admitting this aircraft was shot down? For over four years the administration has played down just how bad things really are in Iraq, why not do so here? As the weeks went by more aircraft would get shot down, so daylight flights came to a swift halt.

One of the aircraft that went down around this time was an observation helicopter owned by a security firm. The company operated two or three McDonnell Douglass MD-500 helicopters that flew out of LZ (landing zone) Washington, across Haifa Street from the Republican Palace. This is the same model as the helicopter on the TV show "Magnum PI." They're very fast and maneuverable aircraft, and we would watch them flying all the time over Baghdad. The pilots would fly them so low and fast, I often wondered how they could observe anything. It would be like trying to observe something while riding in a NASCAR race. They would cut the sharpest banked turns I've ever seen helicopters do, almost like they were putting on an aerobatic show. Two observers would be in the back with their legs dangling over the sides, carrying their weapons like they were riding shotgun on a stagecoach. I was at Phoenix Base one day when one of them flew right over my head toward downtown Baghdad. It was typical for them to fly the same route, often going right over Phoenix Base to the sector of Baghdad north of the IZ and on the west side of the Tigris River. About two hours later we heard the helicopter had gone down. It had been hit by weapons fired from a building it flew past, hit some power lines and then crash landed onto the street. Witnesses confirmed the pilot and three crew members were still alive. Insurgents were seen running out of the building and over to the aircraft. They then shot each one of the crew in the head.

From this point onward all flights would be made in the middle of the night. This caused tremendous hardship and loss of sleep, as we had to work all day prior to our departure and then fly at night. But that's exactly what the insurgents wanted to happen.

What made matters worse, to the point of impossible, was when we had to fly anywhere into Anbar Province, which we had to do when we made our site inspection at Al Asad. Al Asad had been a major Iraqi Air Force base before the US wiped out the Iraqi Air Force. The base had been built by Russian engineers, with the airstrip on a plateau, and the hangers built into the sides of the hills that sloped away from it. The taxiways from the airstrip to the hangers were actually roads that wound down the sides of the hills from the plateau to the flat lowland below, where the main part of the base was located, most of it along a waddi. I had been to Al Asad before on US Army aircraft, but now the Marines would not allow the Army to fly there. So much for interservice cooperation. But the MNF-I Commander, LTG Odierno, let the Marines get away with this nonsense. It took us 2-3 days just to get to Al Asad on Marine aircraft, and 2-3 days to get back, when the entire amount of time needed to get the inspection completed was about five hours. This would become the norm for anything involving Marine air support.

When we arrived at Al Asad we had to get rooms to sleep because we would have to stay for a couple of days due to the flight arrangements. Our trip there was coordinated through the CPATT Garrison Support Unit chief at Al Asad, a US Army Reserve lieutenant colonel who was about as sharp as a door knob. He had two people working for him, a US Air Force Captain and an Air Force sergeant. They had a small office at Al Asad, but I have no idea what they did because there was no Iraqi army "Garrison Support Unit" in existence there. The Iraqis had never approved of the RSU/GSU plan. The lieutenant colonel and his staff referred to themselves as the "GSU," but all they were was a team of CMATT guys hanging out at Al Asad waiting for the actual RSU/GSU concept to be adopted by the Iraqis so they would actually have something to do. What they did their entire time in Iraq is beyond me, but what a great way to spend their tour and make up war stories.

The most interesting part of the trip was when we dropped by the Marine Base Commander's office at Al Asad. I asked the lieutenant colonel if we could visit the base commander, a full colonel, while we were there as a courtesy to say hello and tell him about our mission. Al Asad is a huge base by Iraq standards, and we could have come and gone without him ever knowing we had been there, so I wanted to make sure he knew about our trip. We went to the base command building and the lieutenant colonel walked inside to announce our arrival. We waited outside for at least 20 minutes and I went in to see what was going on. He was in the middle of a long conversation with a Marine colonel when I walked up to them and said hello. When they saw me the colonel said he had to get going to a meeting, but would give us a few minutes of his time, most of which had been used up by the lieutenant colonel. We went into an office off the main hallway where there were several drafting tables and maps on the walls. This was a good place to have our short meeting, as we could use the maps to describe to the Base Commander what our plans were for the warehouse. There were about 10 people standing around a drafting table and another half dozen or so who worked in the room listening to us. At one point during the meeting, a Marine major turned to me and asked me question, and was about to say something else when he caught himself and said he would ask me after the meeting. I answered his question as best I could and didn't think anything more of it. The meeting ended and the Base Commander, the full colonel, was very gracious and said he would help us any way he could, and then left. Most everyone was gone, leaving the Marine major, the lieutenant colonel and me standing at the drafting table, with the people who worked in the office still there. The Marine major turned to me and the Army lieutenant colonel from CMATT and started blasting us for not informing him of our presence on the base and our mission there. He berated me and the lieutenant colonel for not keeping him informed of the plans we had for "my [his] base." He said if he had known we were on Al Asad and had plans to use part of the land there, "I would kick you out the door."

    I stood there and bit my lip as hard as I could. I looked at the lieutenant colonel, who looked like he was a punching bag but finally mustered some courage to stand up to this insubordination from a junior officer. He told the major he had called and spoken to him the previous day, and had told him we were going to be there, and that he (the major) needed to cool down. The major did not cool down at all, and was so belligerent toward me and the lieutenant colonel I couldn't believe what I was hearing. I knew the Marines were pompous and arrogant, but this went way beyond that. The major was a complete ass, and the lieutenant colonel should have locked his heels and ordered him to shut up, but he never did. The lieutenant colonel was as shocked as I was, but he was also afraid to stand up to this jerk, which he had every right to do and which he should have done because the major was speaking disrespectfully toward a superior officer.

The craziest part of the entire thing was the comment about "my base" made by the Marine major. Al Asad was being used by the Marines as an air base to support their troops in Anbar Province. It wasn't a Forward Operating Base built from raw land by the US Army Corps of Engineers just for the Marines to occupy. It was not "their base." The Marines are using it with the "permission" of the Iraqis. But that's the problem. The Marines, the US and the Coalition don't really give a damn what belongs to the Iraqis, who we invaded but are now there to protect. If we need it, we take it. If the Iraqis decided they wanted the base to use themselves the Marines would be gone in a week (maybe), but that was unlikely to ever happen. If it had, it would be another land issue that I would have to work on with the Iraqis in the real estate office at the Ministry of Defense—if I was even informed about it.

If this scene wasn't bad enough, the Iraqis were soon going to occupy a camp in a far corner of Al Asad anyway, near the oasis where legend says Abraham stayed during his journey across the desert. That's where the warehouse was going to be located. The Marines were "letting" the Iraqis occupy a corner of their own base. How nice. The major was berating us and making a fool of himself for absolutely no reason other than to show us (and the others in the room) that he was a tough Marine badass, and to tell us that nothing happens on "my base" without him knowing about it. Jerks like him give the Marines a bad name.

We were checking off more bases and making some progress getting to them, even though it was a huge effort. But then we hit a road block when we made our attempt to get north to "K-1," the base at Kirkuk. We tried to fly up there twice, me and the Iraqis who were travelling with me, but both times we only got as far as Balad, about 60 miles north of Baghdad. Getting to Kirkuk was just about impossible. We never made it there, but used up two or three days doing nothing each time we tried.

After trying to get around to these camps for about three months, we took a break from the trips after the second attempt to K-1. The Iraqis were getting tired of the wasted time and wanted to be with their families. With all the air resources the US had over there, it was like pulling teeth to get anywhere. I spent half a day on several occasions trying to get from Camp Victory at Baghdad International Airport to the International Zone, a distance of about five miles. The only way to make that trip was by road convoy at around 3:00 in the morning in armored buses called "Rhinos," or by helicopter. It would take up to 12 hours just to make this five mile trip. And that was just in Baghdad. Trying to get up to a place like K-1 was impossible. There was one base I heard of that was so hard to get in and out of that people would spend days waiting by the helipad listening for the sound of the in-coming helicopters (they always flew in pairs), like the opening credit scene from the TV show M*A*S*H, and would beg to be let on the aircraft. So we took a few weeks off. That's when things started to get interesting with this project, but in a different way.

The Army major from Vietnam had rotated back to the States after completing his 6-month tour. He was so anxious to leave that he told me he couldn't take any more trips because he had to get ready to go home, but he had a month and a half left in Iraq. He handed the project off to another US Army major who was a pleasure to work with, and 100 pounds overweight. I was gaining weight in Iraq too (the food was great, but meant for a 19 year old), but the new major had to be over the Army's weight limit by a country mile. But he was a great guy just the same. Soon he had to leave as well, as his one year tour in Iraq was ending. So the person from M-4-TT chosen to replace him was a young female Air Force First Lieutenant.

The lieutenant was permanently assigned to an Air Force base in Germany, and had been told she was going to Iraq with less than two weeks notice. When she arrived she was assigned to the M-4-TT staff under a US Marine full colonel who was one of the nicest people I had the pleasure to work with the entire time I was in Iraq. Before the colonel left he, the Air Force lieutenant and I had a talk about keeping her busy. She had complained to him that she didn't have anything to do. (I found out she would sit at her desk playing on the internet and talking to her boyfriend in Germany all day, which didn't help her reputation very much. I later found out her boyfriend, another US Air Force officer, was on his way to Baghdad too. The lieutenant would have plenty to keep her occupied once he arrived.) I told the colonel I would keep the lieutenant as occupied as I could on the warehouse project, and the meeting ended.

But the Air Force lieutenant did not work for me, she worked for the Marine colonel. I was helping him by trying to keep one of his staff busy, but it was his job to keep her occupied, not mine. Because he was leaving in a matter of weeks, and was also leaving the service when he got home, the colonel probably had a lot on his mind and was looking for me to help him keep one of the younger and less experienced officers occupied. I was happy to help, and I needed the help from the lieutenant on these trips. I looked at it as a win-win situation. The project had started with the Army major on the colonel's staff whose English I couldn't understand. The entire project belonged to the Marine colonel, not me. Besides, as a civilian I could have no official responsibility for anything. But I was glad to be involved in a land and facilities project for the Iraqi army. When I got involved, at the request of the major, I became the de facto guy in charge. How could this happen? I wasn't on the M-4-TT staff, but on MODTT. But I wanted to help in any way I could, and be as useful as possible. I was a contractor and I was the only one still around on the project who knew anything about it, so it was being handed over to me little by little as each military person rotated out. This was typical. The contractors stuck around, mostly because of the pay, but also because all of us were there for at least a year. But not the US military. They, on the other hand, left as fast as they could. The Air Force lieutenant was the third person from M-4-TT assigned to the project, and by the time she got there the guy in charge of that office, the Marine colonel, didn't really care about it. The US military were on 90 day to 12 month tours of duty in Iraq, depending on which branch of the service they belonged to, yet all under the same command, so there was inconsistent rotation of forces within MNSTC-I. The contractors were the only ones who were consistently there for any length of time. We were the only institutional knowledge MNSTC-I had, yet the military on its staff treated us like crap. If the MNSTC-I military had treated us as members of their team we could have accomplished a lot more. When the Marine colonel left he was replaced by a reserve US Navy captain who turned out to be the biggest asshole in MNSTC-I. He was the latest arrival in what was becoming a succession of US Navy captains who had nothing better to do than make life miserable for people trying to do their jobs.

The new Navy captain came by my office one day and asked me if I had a few minutes to discuss the warehouse project with him. I said yes and we went over to an empty cubicle to talk. Right away he asked why I had been to so few of the 22 locations on the list of bases that were going to have the warehouses located on them. Then he started in on me for a trip his lieutenant had made a few days before. She and I were going to one of the camps with a couple of the Iraqis from MOD who travelled with us to all the locations. At the last minute we lost one seat on the aircraft, so I let the lieutenant run the trip. She was new and I thought it would be a good experience for her. I was tasked with mentoring her, so I figured this was as good an opportunity as any for her to get her feet wet. But when she and the Iraqis got to the camp things didn't go well at all. The trip just didn't work out.

I could sense the confrontational tone in the captain's voice and figured I was in for an interesting meeting. He and I had spoken on the phone one time, and had never met face-to-face. I didn't know the guy at all. I explained to him the difficulty we were having getting out to these locations, citing examples of the number of times we had attempted to get to some of them, using K-1 as my best example, only to end up never making it there. I told him that of the seven camps we had been to up to that time, we had attempted to get out about 15 times all together. He didn't seem to care a bit for my explanation. All he wanted to do was make me look bad, which became very apparent as the conversation wore on. I explained to him the entire background of the project, which took some time. He then asked me why the Air Force lieutenant was involved in the project, clearly implying that she wasn't doing anything on it and that it was my fault. He was coming across as though I had gotten his staff involved, when his staff had gotten me involved. I told the captain that it was a former member of the M-4-TT staff, the Army major, who had originally started the project, and therefore his staff had been involved all along. It appeared that he and the Marine colonel had not coordinated prior to the latter's departure for the States. But maybe they did, and the captain knew everything that had transpired, and wanted to pin the responsibility for the warehouse project on me. I don't know. I was there to assist the Iraqis, but wanted to help the MNSTC-I staff whenever I could. In addition, the lieutenant did not belong to me, she belonged to the Navy captain. I honestly feel he got off the plane in Baghdad with a bone to pick with contractors, and I was the target of his little Napoleonic ego.

Then he said something I found to be very interesting. He said his office should never have been involved in the warehouse project in the first place, that it was a CMATT issue and not an M-4-TT issue. If that was the case, why was he coming down on me? He was pulling his staff off the project, so what difference did it make to him how it was going? I told him that I agreed and had no problem with this. CMATT was the MNSTC-I staff section responsible for assisting the Iraqi Joint Headquarters Staff in setting up the Regional and Garrison Support Unit camps, and the warehouses were an integral component of them. But as far as I knew CMATT had never been involved in this project, which was clearly in its area of responsibility within MNSTC-I. The captain told me he was going to tell CMATT of his decision, and that his staff was no longer going to be involved (even though it had been the lead on it from the beginning), and that the lieutenant was no longer going to be working on it with me. I said fine.

The next day the lieutenant dropped by my desk and told me she was no longer involved in the project. I told her I had spoken with the captain the day before and was aware of this. We chatted for a few more minutes and then she left. I decided to e-mail the captain to inform him of the conversation I just had with the lieutenant. I asked him if there was anything more we needed to discuss. I also wanted to make sure he had spoken to CMATT. It was a simple e-mail to close the loop on the issue after speaking with the lieutenant. The response I got from him blew me away. He insulted me by indicating I didn't know my job, and if I needed clarification on the warehouse project, or any other issues, I should speak to my associate, the woman I have mentioned previously. His response was totally out of line, insulting, inappropriate, and it was copied to a dozen other people. It was very obvious the captain was on a mission to discredit me and make me look bad to as many other people as possible. We had met face-to-face one time.

If I had any doubt the captain had it in for me, I had no doubt now. I didn't know him at all, had only spoken to him twice, and had exchanged one e-mail, yet he was blasting me in an e-mail and copying everyone he could think of. I had done nothing to deserve the shit I was getting dished out from this creep. He had been in Iraq for maybe a month. There was now a cabal of Navy captains at MNSTC-I that he was the newest member of, among them the two successive Navy captains who ran J-7. I knew the J-7 ones wanted me gone. Now they could send one of their little pals on "ops" (military "operations") to screw with me.

Thus began the road leading to the end of my stay in Iraq.

I have tried to figure this Navy captain out. Months prior to his arrival, the J-7 staff had been hinting about taking over the functions of the civilian advisors to the Ministry of Defense Infrastructure Directorate, specifically myself and my female associate. They even came into our office one day to pick out which of our desks they were each going to take. This was all being done on their own, obviously with the blessing of the first Navy captain in charge of J-7, who didn't want us around. J-7 wanted to be the only entity involved in Iraqi Ministry of Defense real estate and construction projects, even though they didn't have a clue about real estate, land, facilities or construction, which was my area of expertise. Out of the blue my associate and I found out that another US Navy captain was coming to the MODTT staff (not the captain who had replaced the Marine colonel) and this person was going to be part of the MOD Infrastructure advisory team along with us (in addition to my associate and I, we had on our small team an Iraqi expatriate whose family had left Iraq after the Gulf War). This US Navy captain showed up, and in no time at all we found out that he was going to be our boss.

The Chief of Staff of MODTT was a US Army lieutenant colonel. He was a Signal Corps officer, which meant he was involved in communications his entire career. About a week after he arrived in Iraq I was walking past him and said hello. I was just trying to make casual conversation and happened to ask where he had come from before coming to Iraq. With that he began what ended up being a 20 minute monologue about how he had spent his entire career at the global communications level, how he was not a field soldier, how the only thing he cared about in the world was his family, how he couldn't stand being in Iraq, how he couldn't wait to get the hell out of there and back home—all this from the mouth of a career US Army officer (he was not in the reserves) who was my number #2 supervisor under David Murtagh. He had just arrived in Iraq, and was supposed to be setting a leadership example.

I told the MODTT Chief of Staff, the US Army Signal Corps lieutenant colonel, that I had not come to Iraq as a civilian advisor on a civilian advisory team only to end up working for a Navy captain who, we had found, didn't have any idea what he was doing with regard to real estate, construction or infrastructure. I was convinced the Navy captain had been put in his job by the captain in charge of J-7, with the acquiescence of the MODTT Chief of Staff. I was proven correct later. My associate, our Iraqi ex-pat and I prevailed with the Chief of Staff, but it was short lived. What we did succeed in doing was pissing off J-7, who we found out had planned on the new Navy captain being our boss so they could control us and push us off to the side, to marginalize us. About two weeks after this coup almost succeeded, the new Navy captain (who was a nice guy but had to go along with his Navy captain buddies) told me he was sent to MODTT to be our boss, and when it didn't happen because my associate, the ex-pat and I pushed back, the new Navy captain in charge of J-7 was all pissed off. Right when our Navy captain showed up, the one in charge of J-7 passed by my associate one day with a big grin on his face and said, "Hey, I hear you're getting a new boss." This was before we temporarily derailed their plan when we spoke to the MODTT Chief of Staff. The captain in charge of J-7 let the cat out of the bag that the other captain was sent there to be our boss, and he himself confirmed it after the plan backfired on them. But we didn't get away with it for long because these four US Navy Captains (the first J-7 chief, the second, the one who replaced the marine colonel from M-4-TT, and now this one), weren't about to be outflanked by a couple of contractors.

Just when the new Navy captain didn't get the job as our boss, the one who replaced the Marine colonel showed up in charge of the M-4-

TT section of MNSTC-I. This new bumper crop of US Navy Captains all stuck together like glue. The Marine's replacement would come over to our building every day and stand next to our new boss' desk and just watch him like he was his older brother. It was ridiculous watching two US Navy captains acting like a couple of old ladies. That was when the one who replaced the Marine colonel started to bust my balls over the warehouse project. He had something to bite onto that he could twist the facts of, for the purpose of making me look bad and pumping up his little reserve Navy ego. Because he was a Navy captain and I was a civilian, he would win and I would lose, and he knew it. The fact that he had just put on his uniform a month before didn't mean a thing to him. Suffice it to say, the warehouse project was a mess from the beginning due to our inability to travel anywhere, and the total lack of coordination between CMATT and M-4-TT. It ended up being an example of senior US military officers lying and making every attempt to discredit civilians who were there to do a job, which included helping them. This Navy captain didn't know what he was talking about. Prior to his arrival his own staff had begun the warehouse project, and he had only been in Iraqi about a month when he started screwing with me about a project I was pulled into by his staff. It wasn't even my responsibility. So much for trying to be of assistance to another section within MNSTC-I. Nothing was done about it by my own managers, specifically by the MODTT leadership of John Cochrane and the MODTT Chief of Staff, the US Army lieutenant colonel. He was getting ready to depart (having served less than his full year in Iraq) around the time the Navy captain who replaced the marine colonel started to play his stupid games, and he was replaced by another US Army lieutenant colonel, a female Army fixed wing (airplane) pilot, who would take it upon herself to end my stay in Iraq.

On August 6, 2007, an article appeared in the Washington Post about nearly 200,000 missing AK-47's and 9 millimeter semi-automatic pistols that had disappeared in Iraq. The US Army had purchased the weapons for issue to the Iraqi army and national police, part of $2.8 billion the United States had spent to train and equip the Iraqi security forces up to that time, but there was no record of where the weapons ended up or who had them. They were gone. The article went on to describe the background behind these weapons and came to the conclusion that no one knew where they were or in whose hands they ended up. The US Government Accountability Office (GAO) had discovered this little mistake, and that's when it hit the papers.

What amazed me as I read the article at my desk at Phoenix Base in the IZ in Baghdad, was the command responsible for arming and equipping the Iraqi armed forces and the national police, the same entity that purchased and then lost these missing weapons, was none other than MNSTC-I, the very same unit I was assigned to. The other thing that amazed me was when the disappearance of these weapons occurred. It happened in 2004 and 2005, when MNSTC-I was under the command of the first Multi-National Forces-Iraq Commander, the newly promoted 4-star general, David Patraeus. It was when he was the first commander of MNSTC-I that these 200,000 weapons were purchased for issue to the Iraqi army and national police, and then disappeared. Yet nothing occurred as a result. The fact that these weapons could end up missing is disgraceful, but the fact that the general who was in command of the unit that lost them could get promoted from 2-star, which he was at the time this screw up happened, to 4-star general, was beyond my comprehension. Isn't that what the word "command" means? He was in command, therefore he was responsible. But you wouldn't know it by looking for any effect it had on his career. Not only did General Casey screw up and get promoted to US Army Chief of Staff, General Patraeus was getting the same royal treatment too. And the worse thing of it all is where those weapons probably ended up. They are very possibly in the hands of insurgents and being used to kill American soldiers. But Patraeus got his 4th star. Where's the "personal responsibility" Bush talked about during his 2000 campaign? The same place it was after 9/11 with George Tenant—nowhere.

9

J-7

My job was to advise the Iraqi Ministry of Defense about everything that had to do with its real estate. This included its land and all "improvements thereon," meaning buildings and facilities. I was the advisor to the MOD on all issues pertaining to land, construction, buildings and installations. I was responsible for advising the real estate staff of the Ministry which, when I arrived in Baghdad, consisted of about a dozen people whose chief was a former mail clerk, but whose brother was the head of the Infrastructure Directorate for the Ministry. The Real Estate Chief was out sick when I arrived, and his deputy was the acting chief. I never saw the full-time head of the office for nine months, when he decided it was time to come back to work. He continued to get paid, however, because of his brother's position.

I wasn't in Iraq long when I realized that MNSTC-I was responsible for the construction of all Iraqi military camps—being built with US tax dollars. With MNSTC-I responsible for the construction of all Iraqi military camps, bases, police stations, border stations, hospitals, schools, and everything else needed by the Iraqi security ministries (the Ministries of Defense and Interior), a huge weight had to be carried by its construction section, the J-7. Much has been discussed about J-7 already, but its role is so important to the reconstruction of Iraq, its future and that of the Iraqi people, that a separate chapter is deserved.

Because J-7 was responsible for all this work, it was also responsible for awarding the contracts to get it all done.

Imagine one entity responsible for the construction of every Iraqi military installation, every Iraqi police station, and every Iraqi border station, all in the midst of a war for the internal security of a country, and a war for the national security and sovereignty of a nation? Needless to say, J-7 has a daunting task. But it is not up to that task, as I will describe.

To begin, it is not properly staffed with active duty US Army Corps of Engineer officers, who are adept at construction of land-based military installations and the facilities on them. Nor does it have civilians on its staff who know construction and real estate acquisition, and who do this work for a living. The two chiefs of this section while I was in Iraq were not US Army officers; they were both US Navy civil engineering officers who were not equipped, trained or experienced to deal with a land warfare situation, nor with the expertise to construct facilities of the type needed to house police and army units. What the J-7 staff should have been made up of were US Army engineers, as well as army civilians used to building such facilities. To make matters worse, nearly all the rest of the staff of the J-7 under these two chiefs were reserve officers who hadn't constructed a building in years, if ever. Just because someone is a reserve officer in civil engineering, that does not mean he or she has the slightest clue how to do this type of work in real life, especially in a combat environment. This is not an island in the Pacific during World War II. The Seabees have no business building an Iraqi army camp in the middle of a desert country. This is not a naval war. It's a land warfare theater. It's an army thing. Do these people train by constructing buildings on their one weekend every month and two weeks in the summer? They show up for "drill," which is what these weekends are called, hang out, go to lunch, and then leave at the end of the day, in many cases staying at a nearby hotel and drinking in the bars all night. Most don't construct buildings for a living. The Deputy J-7 taught high school in Mississippi. What did he know about building a military camp in a desert half way around the world in the middle of a war?

Who actually built these camps? It wasn't the J-7 staff themselves, for all they did was manage projects and track the spending of US tax dollars. But they still needed expertise in how to construct these camps. The construction was actually done by US contractors, all of whom have made a fortune doing this work in Iraq. They were hired to do this work by the US Air Force Center for Environmental Excellence, or AFCEE, which is a politically correct title for the Air Force's equivalent of the US Army Corps of Engineers. So, the entire infrastructure of the Iraqi military, 98% of which is their army, is being done by people who build docks and aircraft hangers. How nice. AFCEE was the contracting arm, or contracting mechanism, that J-7 used to get its projects built by these US construction companies. But then these companies only acted as the General Contractors, turning the projects over to local Iraqi companies and labor to do the actual work. The money that is being spent on these projects is staggering.

It wasn't just camps and installations that J-7 had constructed by these American companies. It was also hundreds of individual buildings—both renovations of existing structures as well as new construction from the ground up throughout the country, both on military camps and off. J-7 built not only for the Ministry of Defense, but also for the Ministry of Interior, so the combined total number of individual construction projects (each building was considered its own project with its own tracking number and budget) was about three thousand projects, with hundreds more planned. All of these were being built with US taxpayer dollars for the Iraqi Ministry of Defense and Ministry of Interior. The tracking of the budgets for these projects was one of the single most important financial exercises in Iraq. When I arrived I was told by J-7 these projects had to be "closed out." This meant that, because all of these projects were being paid with US Treasury money, and even though they were being given to the Iraqi government as a gift by the American people, they still had to be accounted for.

Shortly after first arriving in Iraq I was told by an officer within J-7, who turned out to be a good friend, that these construction projects had to be accounted for. What J-7 was attempting to do was have the Iraqis accept each individual project, which meant signing for each building that had been constructed for them and was being given to them as a gift by the American government. This was a mandatory requirement by the US Government. It couldn't be waived. J-7 was under orders to get these projects signed for by the Iraqi government so it could "close the books" on each one of these construction projects, on each individual building. Even though all of these projects were going to be given to the Iraqi government at no cost, the United States Treasury still needed to account for the expenditure of the funds that paid for the gift. It's simple: when money leaves the US Treasury to pay for something, you have to account for what it was spent on.

I was told the number of completed projects done for the Ministry of Defense was several hundred, and over two thousand for the Ministry of Interior. (The reason for the large number of MOI projects—individual buildings—was because this ministry had all of the police stations and frontier border stations throughout the country, obviously a very large number of individual facilities.) I told the lieutenant colonel I would help in any way I could, and would try to get the buildings inspected and the documents signed for transfer over to the Ministry of Defense. What I envisioned was having the Real Estate Branch that I advised, along with engineers from the Infrastructure Directorate of the Ministry, inspect these facilities and accept them, and then sign the paperwork to close out the files for J-7. Not a big deal. That's the job of the MOD Infrastructure Directorate staff, or at least it would be if J-7 let them do it. Not a hard concept to grasp. How wrong I was. Not only did J-7 never take me up on my offer to get the Ministry of Defense Real Estate Branch and Infrastructure Directorate involved, I found out after I had been in Iraq for a year that J-7 hadn't even gotten the documents prepared for the Iraqis to sign, yet was going on about how important this was.

J-7 had been constructing buildings for the two ministries since 2004, and hadn't gotten a fraction of them signed for and accepted by the Iraqi Government, as required by the US Government, and now it was 2006-2007. The US taxpayer was paying for all of these projects, with J-7 having the responsibility to act as the steward for these funds and for their proper expenditure. And J-7 hadn't even gotten the documents put together for the Iraqis to sign. Whenever a military commander takes over a unit, they always want to leave their mark. While I was in Iraq J-7 was run by two US Navy captains. When the first one took over J-7 he had his "mark" staring him in the face, and that was to close the books on all the projects started by his predecessors. He had two tasks when he took his position. The first was to continue building (legally) facilities for the Iraqi military, in other words to carry on with the mission at hand. And the second was to close out the project files to account for the money that had been spent the preceding three years. He did a lousy job on the first, and failed the second task miserably.

When I asked my friend, the lieutenant colonel, why J-7 hadn't gotten these documents put together yet he told me they couldn't get the documents from the US contractors that were doing the work on J-7's behalf. Every contractor working for J-7 should have been called in on the carpet for not getting that paperwork submitted. These contractors were making huge amounts of money, yet they couldn't even provide J-7 with the documentation needed for the Iraqis to sign. These contractors all worked for his boss, the Navy captain. Why couldn't he get this done? The US taxpayer has paid the freight on all of these projects without the documentation to account for them.

The packages with the documents for each individual construction project finally started to trickle in for the Iraqis to sign. But many of the facilities had been built going back three or more years. J-7's failure to get the paperwork together for its projects, and then get the Iraqis to sign it all, created a whole new problem. J-7 wanted the Iraqis to sign for all of these buildings even though the Iraqi army had been occupying some of them for that entire amount of time. By now the buildings had been completely trashed by the Iraqi army, whose concept of cleanliness and trash removal is non-existent.

J-7 wanted these buildings signed for, and I offered to assist, even though getting this done wasn't my responsibility. It was 100% the responsibility of J-7, but I wanted to help. Not only did the Navy captain do nothing to get the documentation from his contractors for the entire year he was in charge of J-7, he also made no attempt to take me up on my offer of assistance to have the Iraqis inspect the facilities so they would feel comfortable signing for them, thereby helping him close out the projects. So much for cooperation between MNSTC-I military staff and its civilian contractors. And when I asked the captain for his help getting me and the Iraqis from the Real Estate Branch to locations around the country, in order to check out the land records so his staff would not be building camps on property the Ministry of Defense didn't own, I got the same response—nothing. I was asking J-7 for help so the Ministry of Defense real estate staff, who I advised, could help J-7 do its job of supporting the Iraqi Ministry of Defense. Isn't that why we were all there? Isn't that why J-7 was there? The Navy captain couldn't have cared less for my offer to help him or my request for his help, nor did my boss, David Murtagh. I was just making noise as far as they were concerned.

As time went by and these facilities were not getting signed for by the Iraqis, the J-7 Navy captain was replaced by another Navy captain and civil engineer. He quickly assumed the same personality and attitude as his predecessor. He would send his staff directly to the Ministry of Defense to talk to the Iraqis themselves, the Iraqis I advised. But they were affecting me and the Ministry by circumventing an already existing civilian MOD advisory team—MODTT—that I worked for. Not only were they brushing me off to the side, they were also doing the same to my counterpart, the female associate I worked with who had served in Iraq as an activated National Guardsman for 15 months, and had come back to Iraq as a contractor for another 3 years. In all, she was in Iraq over four years by the time I left in September 2007. J-7 wanted her out of the way too. They had no idea what they are doing, or the expertise they were blowing off. But that was the culture of MNSTC-I and its military staff.

When the new Navy captain first took over J-7, I asked if I could give him a run-down of the Ministry of Defense's real estate and facilities program. We were in his office and I was drawing the MOD organization on a white board with his deputy, a US Navy commander, listening off to the side. I thought this would help him, as he was new to the job and MOD was a very confusing place. About 10 minutes into the discussion the captain's phone rang and he took the call, leaving me to stand there for about 15 minutes until he finished. This was typical. We had other conversations like this, but the one that sticks out in my memory was when we were talking about getting the Iraqis to sign for the hundreds of buildings J-7 had constructed for the Ministry of Defense, as I have mentioned above. I told him they would not accept these facilities without inspecting them first, and he replied it was their problem. I asked him if he would buy a house he had never seen, and of course he said no. I asked him if there was any way he could provide transportation for the Ministry's representatives to go to these locations and inspect the facilities, so they would sign for them. I knew they would because they had told me so. I will never forget his response. He said he would not do that, and the Iraqis could travel to these locations themselves, which was impossible for them to do, and he knew it. They didn't have the resources to travel anywhere outside of Baghdad, and he knew this. I told him this would not work, and it was only after several weeks he agreed to try to transport the Iraqis to these bases, if he could. In the case of land title I couldn't get any cooperation from the first Navy captain, and in the case of facility inspections I couldn't get any cooperation from the second one, and in both cases I was trying to help them do their jobs.

This was another example of the many impasses I encountered dealing with our own US military. Near the end of my time in Iraq, J-7 started making overt attempts to take over my function and that of my associate. Simply put, J-7 wanted us out of their way. I knew the last thing J-7 wanted was me bringing up the issue of its building camps for the Iraqis, with US money, on land they had taken without any attempt to address legal ownership. Nor had J-7 made any attempt to get the land placed in the name (title) of the Ministry of Defense. In effect, J-7 was illegally constructing bases in Iraq with US money. Not only did J-7 want me and my associate out of their way so they could continue to do this without the whistle being blown on them, they also wanted to be the construction branch of the Ministry of Defense itself. But the Coalition was supposed to be "transitioning" control of the Iraqi's destiny over to them, not holding onto it. Back then, and even today, whenever I hear that the Iraqis are going to take over and run their own show and defend themselves, I know it's nonsense because we won't let them. We say we are trying to get them to take control of their own country, refusing to occupy it ourselves, yet we won't let the Iraqi's do anything on their own. They have the money, but we won't let them spend it their way because we insist they follow our contracting procedures, which for them is impossible. J-7 never involved the Iraqis in the design and construction of their own camps and facilities, when they could have done it if we had given them the opportunity, whether it was with their own money or ours. We could have supervised the expenditure of US money and made sure they built quality facilities with it as a free gift from the American people. Instead, we designed their facilities, built them with American contractors, let the Iraqis move in and trash them, and then expected them to sign for the facilities three years later. The Iraqis acknowledged they had moved into the buildings, and they even acknowledged that their soldiers had trashed them, but they were not going to sign for them now without at least having an MOD representative inspect them first. If we weren't going to let the Iraqis do these things on their own because we were afraid of the waste of money that might result, we sure did a lousy job of preventing this waste ourselves.

Near the end of my stay I was in a meeting with staff from J-7 and the new Director of Real Estate in his office at the Ministry of Defense. The J-7 staff wanted the head of Real Estate, a 2-star general who had been on death row for insulting one of Saddam's sons, to sign for hundreds of buildings he had never seen. The J-7 people said that many of the buildings had already been occupied by the Iraqi army, so the general should sign for them. The general said if the Americans wanted the Iraqis to sign for these buildings, then they should have had the paperwork ready at the time they were completed and handed over, following a complete inspection. The J-7 staff officer just sat there. There was nothing he could say. The Iraqi general was right, and he knew it. He wasn't going to be pushed around by some reserve US Army officer who just got off the plane.

The only time I thought the process might work was when J-7 finally arranged for a trip to the Iraqi army camp called Q-West, near the town of Qayyarah West, about 20 miles south of Mosul. The camp had been built at the order of J-7 by one of the American companies contracted by AFCEE. J-7 asked the construction company if it's security contractor, a firm called SafeNet, could fly a group of us to the airstrip at Q-West in its own twin-engine aircraft. We arrived and inspected the 12 new buildings J-7 had constructed, and at the end of the inspection we all gathered in the mess hall ready for the Iraqis to sign the acceptance and transfer documents. The Iraqis would not sign the paperwork because they said they didn't have the authority. They said they would make the recommendation to their superior, the 2-star general, to sign them. This satisfied everyone present, and we all thought we had broken new ground. But the Project Manager from the construction company, the J-7 contractor who knew we were coming a week before, didn't have the paperwork ready for us to take back to Baghdad. I couldn't believe he didn't have this when we had gone through all the trouble to get up there. We were assured by the Project Manager the paperwork would be in Baghdad within two days for the Iraqis to sign. A week went by and the paperwork hadn't shown up yet. Then one day I was told it had arrived—signed. I asked who signed the documents, but was never given a clear answer. It wasn't anyone at the Ministry of Defense. I'm convinced the documents were signed by someone who did not have the authority to, so that J-7 could close the books on its projects without having to deal with the MOD Infrastructure Directorate.

When the new head of J-7 told me he would not provide transportation for the Iraqis from the Ministry of Defense to travel to the locations where J-7 had constructed facilities for them, I told him that travel for the Iraqis should be part of the construction budget for each project. He would hear none of this. But what was wrong with this suggestion? I thought it was a great idea. But because he had no concept of creative thinking about construction in the real world, he thought the idea was crazy. When I asked his predecessor for assistance in helping the Iraqis travel to the Provincial Land Registration Offices to determine the ownership of land he planned to construct Iraqi military camps on, he blew me off. So did my own boss, David Murtagh. Now the new captain was doing the same thing.

About the time the Minister of Defense, Abdul Qadir, decided overnight to overhaul MOD (without General Dempsey even knowing about his plan), Iraqi Prime Minister Maliki enacted an initiative to add more units to the Iraqi armed forces. This was called the "Prime Minister's Initiative," and was a huge deal for everyone. This was going to add another army division to the ten already in existence, and at least another brigade to the three brigades already in each division, and in some cases two more. In addition, it created the Samarra Brigade, an Iraqi army unit that was going to be spread along Route 1 between Baghdad and Samarra to protect travelers on their pilgrimage to the Al

Askari Mosque (also known as the "Golden Mosque") that had been all but destroyed by Sunni rebels. The "PMI," as it became known, would require more basing and facilities for the Iraqi army. One would have thought that now J-7 would use all the help it could get. Not quite. J-7 completely ignored me and MODTT. But it also ignored the MOD Real Estate Division responsible for acquiring the land, with its legal title, for these new facilities. J-7 being what it was, what did it care about land title? It just went out and grabbed what it needed and started building. J-7 (and also J-5, see below) started making its own trips, selecting locations for the Iraqis' new camps without the input or the participation of the people responsible for the portfolio of real estate and installations of the Ministry of Defense—the Real Estate Directorate and the DG for Infrastructure.

In addition to the J-7 staff, there was another MNSTC-I section called J-5 Plans. A lieutenant colonel on its staff personally took on the responsibility of determining where these new "Prime Minister's Initiative" camps would be located, to include the Samarra Brigade. I honestly believe he had nothing to do and decided on his own to take on this duty. Prior to the lieutenant colonel's arrival at J-5, a junior US Air Force captain was in the role as the real estate coordinator for the J-5 staff. This involved working with J-7 on Iraqi basing. The Air Force captain was very sharp and knew what he was doing, but he was too junior an officer to have the amount of responsibility that had been placed on him. However, it would make absolutely no sense for a lieutenant colonel, on the list for promotion to full colonel (albeit in the reserves, which compared to the active Army doesn't really count), to take over a job held by a junior captain unless he had nothing else to do, regardless of what the job was.

I had no idea these new camps were required for the PMI, because no one ever told me, yet I was advising the Ministry of Defense real estate staff. I was a contractor, so in the opinion of the MNSTC-I military staff why should I have a need to know anything. But MNSTC-I was not supposed to operate in a vacuum. Everything it did was "supposed" to be for the Ministry of Defense and Ministry of Interior. As previously mentioned MNSTC-I did everything on its own, with minimal input or involvement of MOD, its client on whose behalf it existed. The newly promoted J-5 colonel started to take a couple of Iraqi officers from the Joint Headquarters Logistics staff, the M-4, with him around the country to locate sites for these new camps. Because of the MOD reorganization, the officers he took with him worked in an office that was being merged into the Real Estate Directorate that I advised, and he knew this. He knew that anything he did with these other officers, without including anyone from the staff I advised, would create confusion later on because the Real Estate Directorate wouldn't know what had been newly included in its own portfolio. I told him this, but he ignored it. The MOD real estate and infrastructure staff should have been involved in what he was doing, completely on his own, so it could coordinate the acquisition of new sites and secure their title before J-7 started construction of new camps on the land. But MNSTC-I, while saying it was there to help the Iraqis "transition" and be responsible for their own security, went right on doing everything itself, sometimes taking a couple of Iraqis along for the ride because the colonel from J-5 had become friends with them. Countless times I asked him to include me and the real estate and infrastructure staff on his site selection trips. He did this twice, only after being asked to do so by the Air Force captain, whose job the colonel had taken. But on the rest of his trips he left us sitting back in Baghdad not having any idea what he was doing. As expected, after the reserve colonel from J-5 left for the States, most of the locations he selected for these new "Prime Minister's Initiatives" camps wouldn't work because of issues he had failed to consider because he didn't have expertise in this area, where I and the real estate staff at the Ministry did. That's why I was brought to Iraq. But I was a contractor, so why should he include me? If he had included me and the Iraqi real estate and engineering staff on his trips these problems would have been greatly reduced, if not avoided completely.

I can not close this discussion of MNSTC-I and its construction branch, J-7, without relating the story of the Iraqi army camp next to the ancient city of Ur. One of my trips to select a site for the Iraqi army warehouses was to the army camp near this ancient Iraqi city, famous for being the home of Abraham. Ur is about 20 miles north of the northern tip of the Persian Gulf. At one point in time the Gulf actually went as far north as Ur itself, which is why it was located there, having once been on the water. The gulf has since receded the 20 or so miles. The land in between the Gulf and Ur is all lowlands of marsh and saw grass now.

We flew to Ur on a US Army twin-engine fixed-wing aircraft called a "Sherpa." It's a flying boxcar that is actually very nice inside, and is flown by the pilots at treetop level in most areas of Iraq so it can't be seen and shot down. We flew to Ur at 250 miles per hour, 100 feet off the ground. When we landed at Ur we stayed at the Coalition camp 10 miles to the south, at Tallil. This was originally and Italian army camp, named after its commander. After several Italian soldiers were killed by a suicide bomber in November 2003, Italy began to withdraw its forces from the "Coalition of the Willing." Of course, soldiers can get killed, that's a risk of the job. But when they actually did, the Italians pulled out. They wanted no more part of Operation Iraqi Freedom. I suppose they thought none of their soldiers would die when they sent them into a combat zone. Call it "Italian logic." It is now an Australian Army camp, with CMATT advisors who convoyed twice a week to the camp at Ur to train the Iraqi soldiers there. We waited a day for the next convoy to take us to the camp, riding in the Australian Army "Bushmaster" armored personnel carrier. This is the Australian home-grown and designed armored vehicle that is being adopted for use by the US Army in Iraq because of its V-shaped hull, which deflects IED's (improvised explosive devices), and especially EFP's (explosively formed penetrators), from blasting through the undercarriage of the vehicle and killings it occupants. (The US had sent its initial attack forces to Iraq in the spring of 2003 with no armor plating on their HUMVEE's. Many of our soldiers were killed as a direct result, yet Donald Rumsfeld refused to take any action to correct this terrible problem until a soldier had the balls to confront him during his famous visit to the troops in Iraq in December 2004. The question, and Rumsfeld's response, were broadcast around the world, making Rumsfeld look like a complete fool.) The driver sits on the right in British style, and the remote machine gunner on the left with pistol grips and a TV camera that he uses to automatically control the mini-gun mounted on the roof. Staying with the Australians was great, but it wasn't the blow-out party that we all hear about. We all had work to do, and things were serious but very friendly.

We convoyed to the camp at Ur, going straight to the camp commander's office for chi (tea), which is the Iraqi custom. We then set out to inspect the camp for the warehouse site. Once this was done we toured the rest of the camp, and that was when I saw something I'll never forget. The camp had been built by J-7 for the Iraqi army, using an American construction company as the General Contractor, with local labor. This was how J-7 constructed all of the camps for the Iraqi army. The buildings were all made with white sheet metal skin on the outside, similar to a "butler building" in the States. The insides were all concrete stucco and tile, which is very typical in Iraq. But what got my attention was the condition of the facilities. I have mentioned how the Iraqis trash their buildings, but I wasn't prepared for this. Their concept of "barracks police" and basic cleanliness does not exist. But Ur raised this to a whole new level. Urine and feces were all over the latrine floors. Not even the holes in the floors they used for commodes worked. The basic condition of the facilities was terrible. The plumbing didn't work, water was leaking everywhere, tiles were popping up off the floors and walls, and windows were falling out of their frames onto the ground outside. The lack of trash cleanup was one thing, but the condition of the physical facilities was another. The place was so poorly built it was completely falling apart. Cleanliness would have helped, but superficially at best. The construction of the buildings at Camp Ur was the worst I've ever seen. The condition of this camp was so incredible I took pictures, and have included them in this story.

The Iraqis have no concept of maintenance or cleanliness, except in their own homes. Outside of their homes they don't care. This is a cultural thing. But J-7 never included a budget for facility maintenance in its construction of these camps, nor did it include any training of the Iraqi Base Engineer at each camp on how to keep the facilities under his charge running efficiently for any length of time. J-7 just went in and built these places on land the Ministry of Defense didn't own, and then walked away. Not only did it fail to get the Iraqis to accept and sign for the work, it failed to get any useful life out of the facilities it built by providing a budget for training and follow-on maintenance. Anyone who knows anything about commercial facilities knows these things. Of course, it also failed to budget for transportation of MOD representatives to the camps to conduct their inspection before signing for them. I suggested doing all these things to the US Navy captains who ran J-7 during my tour, and they both ignored anything I had to offer.

And what of the cost for these facilities at Ur? Based on the amount of construction and the type, I thought maybe $5 to $10 million dollars. When I asked the Project Manager from the American construction company he gave me a very direct answer—$118 million! Not only is this amount of money incredible, it also points to the very real possibility of fraud. It's difficult to come to any other conclusion.

If MNSTC-I did not care about the American civilian contractors on its own staff, or the Iraqis it was there to support, J-7 most certainly didn't. The colonel from the J-5 staff didn't either, as shown by him leaving the Ministry of Defense real estate and infrastructure staff completely out of what he was doing. The truly amazing thing about it all was the fact that MNSTC-I's sole mission was to assist the Iraqi Ministry of Defense and Ministry of Interior to stand on their own. When I arrived in Iraq General Dempsey's buzzword, his mantra, was "transition." We heard it every day. But as time went by, as it became clear the Iraqis weren't getting anything done (I wonder why), he changed course and ordered his entire staff to do everything for the Iraqis just to get things done. General Dempsey may have just been following the orders of his superior, the Joint Forces Commander, General Casey. But he was a very powerful 3-star general, and had a lot of his own authority. General Dempsey was one of only two 3-star general officers in Iraq under General Casey. The other was General Odierno, the commander of MNC-I. General Dempsey could have done anything he wanted to. All he needed to do was justify why. He commanded a 3-star unit in combat, so if he couldn't make his own decisions, then what's a person doing at that level job in the first place? If General Dempsey wanted to, he could have let the Iraqis do it all themselves and watch, observe, advise, and correct where needed. But neither he, nor the entire US effort in Iraqi, ever gave the Iraqis a chance to learn to do things for themselves. Whenever they would try, the Coalition would just talk about how stupid and backward they were, instead of helping them get on their feet. Instead, MNSTC-I did everything for the Iraqis, like building the camp at Ur. For the US money that was spent, the Iraqis would have been better off in tents.

We constantly heard of how inept the Iraqis were. They would have to be because they've never been allowed to do a thing by themselves, in their own way, since we "liberated" them. They are forced by the Americans in control (but we're not "occupiers") to do everything our way, which they are culturally unable to do. We simply don't understand that, or can't accept that, or refuse to accept that. Yet we are there to help them. What sort of help are we giving them if the offer to help is extended only it if they do things our way? But that is exactly the way it is. They don't need our money. They have enough oil revenue to buy whatever they want. But they can't buy anything with their own money because we force them to contract for goods and services the American way, which they will never grasp or understand, and then we say the Iraqis are inept. Who's inept here? The US won't let Iraq spend its own money as it wants to and knows how to, yet we got rid of Saddam because he was a tyrant. I guess that makes us "nice tyrants."

10

IRMO

THE US STATE DEPARTMENT OCCUPIES Saddam's former Republican Palace, located in the center of the International Zone, inside a bend on the west bank of the Tigris River in central Baghdad. It is a beautiful building, as many of the buildings in central Baghdad are. The palace is long, with large wings at either end, two stories above ground, and has a huge rotunda in the center with a ceramic blue dome on top. The bright blue dome, typical of Iraqi architecture, can be seen for miles from the air, and is the landmark the helicopter pilots use in daylight to land at LZ (landing zone) Washington across the street.

The entity that was put in place by the State Department to staff up and advise the non-security ministries of the newly democratic Iraqi government was called IRMO, for Iraqi Reconstruction Management Office. The name changed just as I was departing Iraq for the States, but the mission remains very much the same. IRMO was the entity responsible for getting the non-security Iraqi ministries on their feet, which is another way of saying it had all the money. The amount of money IRMO had to dish out to the Iraqi government must have been staggering, and was very likely in the tens, if not hundreds, of billions of US dollars since the Iraqi conflict began in the spring of 2003.

When Paul Bremer disbanded the Iraqi Ministry of Defense and the Ministry of Interior, basically leaving the country totally defenseless, he opened the door for every terrorist group to come in and set up shop, and he did all this with Bush's approval. He also took all the real property (e.g., land and buildings) owned by these ministries and turned it over to the newly created Iraqi Ministry of Finance. I was told the reason he did this was as a control measure to gather all assets of financial value under one ministry. In theory this made a lot of sense. It was prudent to collect all Iraqi government-owned assets at the Ministry of Finance, in order to come up with a determination of their value for borrowing power on the world financial markets. But Paul Bremer had to do this for another reason as well: he had disbanded the Ministry of Defense, so how could it hold onto the land it once owned if it didn't exist any more? However, Bremer left this door open a crack by enacting one of his many CPA (Coalition Provisional Authority) regulations, CPA Regulation Number 67.

CPA #67 stated, in effect, that all old Ministry of Defense real property would revert over to the new Ministry of Defense assuming, of course, that Iraq would someday have one. I discovered this regulation shortly after I arrived in Iraq. At first I believed this to be the solution to the issue of whether the Ministry of Defense still owned its former bases and camps. But this was where I got into the Iraqi culture and its peoples' knack for complete inaction. When I first asked the real estate staff at the Ministry of Defense to show me a list of all the properties it owned, I was told "we don't own anything, Mr. Bremer gave it all to the Ministry of Finance." Well, this wasn't entirely true. He did give it all to the Ministry of Finance, but CPA #67 gave it all back. It would be months before I could get a solid legal opinion from anyone on this issue, specifically the validity of CPA #67. Only when the MODTT legal advisor arrived at MNSTC-I half way through my tour did I get this. He did the legal research and determined that CPA #67 had the force and effect of law in Iraq, and that all old Ministry of Defense land and real property did indeed belong to the new Ministry of Defense. The problem with Ministry of Defense real property ownership finally got resolved, but it took far longer than it should have.

But what of privately owned land? As I have stated in the previous chapters, MNSTC-I's J-7 branch was taking any land it needed, without permission of the owner, to construct a military camp, a police station or a border station. J-7 simply didn't care. If the land had been a former

Iraqi military camp, J-7 would go in and renovate the existing buildings, or construct new ones. Based on the authority granted by CPA #67, the land reverted over to the Ministry of Defense. Of course, J-7 didn't know this until I brought it to their attention. But what about land that wasn't previously used by the Ministry of Defense as a military camp, or land that hadn't been previously used as a police station? To the best of my knowledge there was not a similar CPA regulation pertaining to former Ministry of Interior real property like there was for former Ministry of Defense real property, as addressed in CPA #67. I only worked on the MOD side of the house. Therefore, I'm not sure if old Ministry of Interior police and border stations reverted over to the new Ministry of Interior. However, I do know that whenever J-7 constructed new military camps, police or border stations, in every case it was on land owned by someone or some entity **other** than the two security ministries it was building the installations for. J-7 was doing nothing to secure clear title, or acquire long-term leases, for the land needed to construct these facilities. The result was hundreds of land claims from people stating that a police station, border station, or military camp had been built on land that they owned. I was informed by the IRMO advisor to the Iraqi Ministry of Justice that as of late 2006 there were 125,000 real estate claims in Iraq. This is a staggering number, and I would say that much of it was caused by the actions of the US military, specifically J-7. But when I tried to bring this to the attention of the US Navy captain running J-7, or later his successor, or my British boss David Murtagh, I got nowhere.

Prior to the MODTT legal advisor providing a determination about CPA #67, I tried to see if there was another way to address the issue of real property being turned over to the Iraqi Ministry of Finance by Paul Bremer. One day I looked up the name of the IRMO advisor to the Iraq Ministry of Finance. I wanted to meet with him and talk about the whole issue of real property in Iraq, specifically Paul Bremer's decision to give all real property owned by the former Iraqi government ministries over to the new Ministry of Finance. I thought a meeting was a good idea. It would be a chance to meet the guy who advised the Ministry of Finance, a chance to talk about the overall strategic issue of real property ownership in Iraq, and most important a way to resolve land ownership issues throughout the country for the Ministry of Defense (and the Ministry of Interior if it would help). He refused to meet me. I e-mailed him half a dozen times and all I got were excuses why he couldn't meet, usually saying he was busy or travelling. Or I got no response at all. The guy simply would not meet with me, and I wanted to discuss real estate and its implications for the Iraqi people, specifically as this related to the defense of their country. Yet this guy wouldn't even give me a minute of his time. I spent months working on land ownership and title issues, most of which could have been resolved in a matter of days if not hours, if this pompous jerk would have met with me.

All that IRMO was responsible for, I don't know. What I do know is it had all the money for the Iraqi Ministries, other than MOD and MOI, to exist and to operate. As a result IRMO had the clout to do whatever it wanted. It could get things done. I had already been treated like a second class citizen by the US military in Iraq. But when the advisor to the Ministry of Finance refused to meet with me I really began to see the true dysfunction of the US involvement in Iraq in the post-Operation Iraqi Freedom period. The fact was that our own State and Defense departments hated each other (sort of like the Army and the Marines) and refused to work together at all.

I told David Murtagh about the difficulty I was having getting a meeting with this guy. Finally, David told me he was going to be in a conference with him the following day and would specifically bring up my request for a meeting. The conference was going to be in General Dempsey's office, so it was a big deal. The following day I saw David and asked him if he had any luck with the guy, specifically if and when I could expect to meet with him. David looked at me and shook his head. He told me what the guy said in the conference, when asked about meeting with me, he couldn't even repeat. I never did find out what the guy said to David Murtagh. I was told by two good friends of mine who worked at IRMO, one of them very closely with the guy, that he was the most arrogant asshole either of them had ever met. I'm not at all surprised. But I do know that I never met the man, and the real estate issues I was trying to resolve went on for months. So much for working together as a team to help the Iraqi people.

One day I ran into a guy from ITAO (by now IRMO had changed its name to the "Iraq Transition Assistance Office," or ITAO—why the name change?). He needed to get in touch with my associate regarding the SIB's battalions. I told him I would pass along his business card to her, but that she was away on vacation. We started to talk about SIB's, and as the conversation went along it came out that this guy held all the US money to pay for the SIB's construction projects—all the camps along the power lines (or oil pipelines, whichever the Iraqis had decided to do). I asked him if he was attending the weekly SIB's planning meetings, because I knew my associate attended these, and he said he had no knowledge of them. When I ran into my associate upon her return from vacation I gave her this fellow's business card, which showed that he was from ITAO. She said she would contact him, but when I told her about him holding all the money, she acted as though she couldn't have cared less. It didn't make any sense to me, but nothing around there did. I never heard anything more about him, or what role he played in the SIB's initiative. But here was a guy running around the IZ saying he had all the SIB's money, who didn't know about the SIB's planning meetings, and had never met my associate. It was just another example of the complete lack of coordination between all the players in Iraq. There were so many people and organizations involved in different things, sometimes the same things, walking around with tons of US money for various projects, and no one really knew who was involved in what and who was responsible for what. We were probably double-paying for the same projects with different pots of money, all coming from the same location (the US Treasury), but being handed out by different components of the US in Iraq. We would complain when we heard of an Iraqi taking off with a suitcase full of US money. We were creating the problem ourselves with the sheer volume of money we were handing out without any controls. What else could we expect?

The US Embassy was located in the north wing of the Republican Place, while IRMO was in the south wing. I was trying to get maps of Iraq and discovered the National Geospatial-Intelligence Agency, or NGA, had an office in the Embassy. (NGA has changed its name so many times it's hard to know what it is called from one day to the next. It has also been called the Army Map Service, the Defense Mapping

Agency, and the National Imaging and Mapping Agency.) I was able to get the maps I needed, made by NGA, but couldn't find any old maps of Iraqi military installations. No one had any old maps of Iraq. Everyone I asked about old Iraqi maps said the same thing, that they had all been destroyed when the mapping and surveying facility on the outskirts of Baghdad was bombed by the US during the opening days of the invasion. I did some digging and met an Iraqi ex-pat working in one of the offices at IRMO, in the south wing of the palace, who told me he knew of an Iraqi general who had maps in his house he had taken with him during the US invasion in 2003. He told me the officer would produce his maps if he could get a job. Sure enough, one day an Iraqi brigadier general showed up at MOD as the new Deputy Director of the Real Estate Division under the Iraqi 2-star I advised. It turned out he was a friend of the general, which is how he got his job. He brought with him two huge folders with large maps of the entire country, with every old Iraqi army camp marked in red grease pencil. I felt like I had hit the mother lode. I took these to the NGA folks at the Embassy and, after a very long wait, they were able to scan each map sheet and create a digital copy of the general's maps, showing where every former Iraqi army installation had been located. With this we could tell J-7 where old Iraqi camps were, and also load the information into the database of the Real Estate Division at MOD. If J-7 would even use this information was another matter. Once in a while something positive got done.

11

THE IRAQI MINISTRY OF DEFENSE

FOR NEARLY THREE YEARS, FROM 2003 to 2006, all we heard in the American media was how great the Iraqis were doing, all during the height of the insurgency. But in 2007 things started to change. By then the American people were getting tired of the same old story, and reality began to set in that the Iraqis may not be in such great shape after all. What people don't know, and what the media never reports, is the fact that the Iraqis are never going to be able to defend themselves with any degree of success, not after we destroyed their economy and removed their two security ministries. These institutions will take years, maybe decades, to rebuild. But it only took days for us to destroy them. How could anyone in their right mind think Iraq would be capable of defending itself when it has no economy and no security, when it is sandwiched in between Shi'ia to the east and Sunni to the west, and everyone hates each other. And of course there is the autonomous region of Kurdistan to the north that Iraq, Iran and Turkey all want their hands on because of its oil reserves.

The United States took away Iraqi's ability to defend itself when Paul Bremer disbanded its defense infrastructure—when he disbanded the Iraqi army and national police, when he fired every member of its armed forces and police down to the simple private and crossing guard. Then he fired everyone in Iraq who was a member of Saddam's Ba'ath Party, so there wasn't anyone around who knew how to do anything. They have all left the country with the money they grabbed as the Americans were rolling up the road into Baghdad. The ones who remain don't have enough money to pay the $70,000 entry fee charged by Jordan to cross its border. They have nowhere left to go.

Although Saddam Hussein may have been a scumbag, and although he had slaughtered his own people, that didn't mean every private in the army was also a scumbag and a mass murderer too. On the contrary, the Iraqi soldier was just a simple guy who wanted a job, just like our own soldiers do. There is no difference between their soldiers and ours, only they are from different countries. But within the ranks of the thousands of Iraqi soldiers and policemen that Bremer fired, with their AK-47 rifles and ammunition, there was an existing framework upon which the Coalition (the US) could have built a new army and national police force that was loyal to the new Iraqi Constitution. When Bremer disbanded everything, he also disbanded Iraq's ability to do even the most rudimentary things necessary to defend itself. Now, like the adult child still dependent on its parents, Iraq is becoming a country that can't do anything for itself. It depends on the United States for everything, even its defense, when it has oil revenue in the tens of billions that it could spend for this very purpose. It had an army and national police that it could have been equipping and training, with our help, for the past five years as well. But now it can't spend its own money because we haven't allowed it to, due to our extremely complicated contracting and procurement methods that we have trouble doing ourselves. We are forcing the Iraqi government to contract for goods and services the same way we do it here in the States. They can't do this because they simply don't grasp the concept of open competition like we do. I was there and saw it myself. The United States' policies in Iraq have not only dissolved its entire security infrastructure, it has also built into the new Iraqi government obstacles that make it impossible for the Iraqis to get anything done, to include spending its own money to defend itself.

I was an advisor to the Iraqi Ministry of Defense for 14 months. The things that I witnessed astounded me, not only those things related to the Iraqis I advised, but also the way the Coalition, the Americans, were doing things for the Iraqis. We designed the new Iraqi Ministry of

Defense to be structured just like our own Department of Defense, with a military side and a civilian side. That was the beginning of the problem. We never stopped to look at the Iraqi culture, to observe how they do things in their own country. They are so different than we are, there is no possible way they can run a ministry like we run one of our cabinet departments. We would complain all the time about how backward the Iraqis were, yet we never realized that their intelligence is not the issue, it's their culture. Trying to get Iraqis to run a ministry like we run one of ours is like me trying to herd a flock of goats. I don't know how, and I don't really care to learn.

My first roommate in Iraq had just retired from the US Army as a full colonel, after serving 29 years. He retired by giving the Army a month notice that he was leaving, so he could get his job in Iraq with our company to make the big bucks. He was a Medical Service Corps officer, which is not a doctor but a health care administrator. One day I was talking with him about the Iraqi people and their culture and all the issues the Coalition was having with this. He strongly disagreed, which he did about anything anyone said to him—he was the most argumentative individual I ever met. He replied, saying, "Their culture has nothing to do with it!" That was the assessment of a retired US Army full colonel who supposedly had years of training in how to deal with people and cultures—and potential enemies—around the world. If he thought like this, it's safe to say most US military officers do too.

Long before the declaration of "Mission Accomplished!" by President Bush on the deck of the aircraft carrier the Coalition Provisional Authority, first under LTG Jay Garner and then Paul Bremer, began to set up the new Iraqi government. This made sense then, and makes a lot of sense today. This was needed to establish a caretaker government at the conclusion of the initial round of fighting. But what is at issue is how we went about doing this. We took over the day-to-day operation of Iraq, and then started to create a new government, placing Iraqis in key positions throughout, but under the American model of our own Executive Branch. Even this may have been pulled off successfully, but when we started to put into place processes and methods of doing things in this new government that mirror our ways of doing things in the States, we lost them. Iraqis are not capable of doing things the way we do them, certainly not in the time frame needed to accomplish anything. But in most cases what we want them to do they simply don't see the need to do in the first place. On top of everything, we expect them to change the way they govern themselves in the middle of a war.

As mentioned previously, the United States designed the new Iraqi government based on our own, and the new Ministry of Defense (MOD) based on our own Department of Defense (DoD). Like our DoD, the Iraqi MOD has a military side and a civilian side. The military side is called the "Joint Headquarters Staff," or JHQ. The civilian side is made up of branches, each lead by a "Director General," or DG, similar to our own Under and Assistant Secretaries. These branches were simply referred to as the "DG's." There was the "DG for Personnel," the "DG for Armament and Supply," and the one that I advised, the "DG for Acquisition, Logistics and Infrastructure," or AL&I. This DG would later be broken up into smaller parts. The DG for AL&I was the civilian branch of the Ministry of Defense responsible for all purchases and acquisitions, supplies and infrastructure for the Iraqi armed forces. It was huge. Like all the civilian DG's, it was headed up by a retired (sometimes active) Iraqi army general who was given the job by his old buddy, Minister of Defense Abdul Qadir, himself a retired Iraqi army general. There are no qualified civilian executive men in Iraq to take these jobs. They are all gone. They have either been killed, have fled the country or, in most cases, they can't work because Paul Bremer banned them from serving their new government because they belonged to Saddam's Ba'ath Party. If they are still alive, every capable and educated man who could have taken one of these jobs has left the country, either after the Gulf War in the early 1990's, but certainly within the past four years. (There are no women in any positions in the Iraqi Ministry of Defense above the level of secretary, translator, or the occasional soldier. I knew the senior ranking woman in the Iraqi army. She was a major who worked in the Surgeon General's office in the Ministry of Defense.)

The DG for AL&I had immense responsibility, yet never got anything done. None of the DG's in the Ministry ever got anything done. Yet MNSTC-I staff complained about how inept the Iraqis were, instead of doing something about it. (At the same time General Casey was telling everyone how great the Iraqis were doing.) One of the responsibilities of the DG for AL&I was contracting for supplies and services for the Iraqi army. When the Americans recreated the new Ministry of Defense, based on the likeness to our own DoD, we also established new ways for the Iraqis to contract for things. As if we were still in the United States, MNSTC-I forced the new Iraqi Ministry of Defense to use our methods of contracting and procurement for ordering supplies and services, which included enforcing competition to get the "best quality and the best price," just like in the Good 'ol USA. This doesn't quite work in Iraq. As it has been done for a few thousand years, in Iraq you buy from your friend, your cousin, or whoever you want to buy from. Being a Director General in an Iraqi cabinet ministry only means that you have even more authority and latitude to buy from more of your friends, from more of your relatives, and from whoever else you want to buy from. But the way the United States has created the "new and improved" Iraqi Ministry of Defense, with competition and everything else the Iraqis don't understand, nothing gets done. When MOD wants to purchase something, it has to use a "Form 53," designed in true American bureaucratic fashion, which requires as many as 19 signatures for completion. But I can't place all the blame on the US. The Iraqis share in it too. The form, requiring all these signatures, also brings into play another key aspect of the Iraqi culture, of the Iraqi mind—the shear genius by which they avoid taking responsibility for anything.

Under the Saddam regime, in Middle Eastern feudal fashion, everything was done for the people by the government. This follows the Middle Eastern tribal tradition of having the leader run the show, while the rest follow. Saddam was that leader, and the Iraqis allowed themselves to be led. There is absolutely no initiative on the part of the individual. It is also the Middle Eastern way to let things go until another day, true procrastination. Why do anything today that can wait until tomorrow? In America we think the exact opposite. If it has to get done, it may as well be done now to get it out of the way. Also, because something else might come up that could get in the way of getting the thing done, it should be taken care of now. This makes sense to us, but not to an Iraqi. If they can do it later, then what's the problem? Form 53 was the answer.

Form 53 may not have required as many as 19 signatures when it was originally created, but by the time the Iraqis got through with it they needed everyone's signature short of the dog catcher. By requiring so many signatures no single person could be blamed if things went wrong. The whole group would have to take the hit, which would be too hard to prove and too difficult to punish. The Iraqis raised bureaucracy (i.e., inefficiency) to new levels, to new heights that an American bureaucracy can only dream of. By requiring so many signatures, not only did the Form 53 literally take months to get completed so things could be ordered and purchased, but there was no way any individual could get blamed for anything that went wrong. The only problem with this system was that nothing ever got ordered for the Iraqi army. But bureaucrats working in the Ministry of Defense could sleep soundly at night knowing they wouldn't get in trouble for being responsible for something that might not work out as planned. It was far better to get nothing done at all. Their job was to be present, at their desks, and collect a paycheck so they could feed their families. But MNSTC-I enabled this inefficiency by doing everything for the Iraqis at MOD. So why should they do anything on their own? Sort of like welfare. Of course the US allowed all this to happen instead of training the Iraqis, including the senior managers at the Ministry, to get things done and take on more responsibility. We were really too afraid of offending their sensibilities. We just let it go on the way it always did, which meant getting nothing done, yet "talked" a lot about how well the transition was going. We never helped them change at all.

The shear inability to complete anything, repeat **anything**, by the Iraqis was astounding. We would shake our heads constantly over the ineptitude of the Iraqis. To a very large extent this was their own fault. But the title of this book tells another side of the story. Where were the Americans in all this tale of woe? We were right down the street from the Iraqis we were supposed to be helping. MNSTC-I has dumped billions into the Iraqi Ministry of Defense and Ministry of Interior, yet the rate of progress from these two agencies is abysmal. It stinks. There isn't any progress, no matter what US generals say at the press briefings. General Dempsey was paying the freight for everything at MOD and MOI, even though the Iraqi treasury is awash in oil revenue. If that is the case, why can't the US just let the Iraqis order supplies for the Iraqi army *with their own money and in their own way*, and be done with it? Even though we want the Iraqis to do it for themselves, which is a good thing, we're forcing them to do business using our US Government procurement methods, which they don't understand. It's that simple. If the United States would let Iraq spend its own oil revenue, and purchase things the way they do it, there would be no issue at all with the Iraqi armed forces manning and equipping themselves. None. They can't do this, not because they are inept or have no money. They can't because the Unites States is forcing Iraq to procure goods and services using our extremely complicated Federal Acquisition Regulations—Iraqi style. It's a joke.

The Coalition (US) should have occupied Iraq. We should be there to provide security only, and let the Iraqis run their own country, with their own money, and with guidance and assistance from the United States. Instead, we invaded with a fraction of the troops needed to fight an enemy we didn't know was there, not enough troops to secure the country when the main fighting ended, we disbanded their own security infrastructure (army and national police), and then we told them to run their country "on their own," using our systems and processes that they will never understand. It's a complete mess. The billions that Iraq has in oil revenue is not able to be spent in part because of their corruption, but mostly because we are forcing them to procure goods and services our way. We are forcing the Iraqis to procure these things using American "competitive" systems, which they simply don't know how to do because their cultural makeup doesn't allow them to grasp the concept.

We invaded, then we disbanded their military, then we formed a new defense ministry, then we told them how to order supplies for their new army but in ways they don't understand, that are not the way they have done it for centuries, then we called them inept, then we got mad that they couldn't get anything done, and then they got pissed off at us and left their country if they had the money. It's the same all over Iraq. If we invaded, then we should have taken on the responsibility of occupying the country for the few years that would be needed to provide safety and stability. We are not helping Iraq by telling them in the midst of a civil war, that we essentially created, to do it themselves but to do it our way. It goes around and around.

All of this goes full circle back to the terrible planning for the war in the first place. If Tommy Franks and Donald Rumsfeld had brains, or if they simply chose not to use them but just listened to General Shinseki, we would have gone in with enough troops to defeat any enemy, and therefore enough troops to occupy the country when the conflict was over. Then, if we had people in Iraq during its reconstruction who had a clue of the culture, we would let them spend their own money any way they wanted to, ensuring they were doing it toward the development of a free, democratic society. If these things had been done, we would not be having any of the problems we are having in Iraq today. This is not hindsight. The study of warfare, and what happens when the fighting is over, proves it to be the case time and again. It is always those who fail to study history who are doomed to repeat it, as the saying goes. Bush, Franks, Rumsfeld, Tenant, Bremer—they all fail the test of history, regardless of what their memoirs say.

When discussing the Iraqi Ministry of Defense one cannot leave out the Multi-National Security Transition Command-Iraq, MNSTC-I, which I have mentioned. I do not know the amount of money MNSTC-I has spent (or should I say "wasted") setting up the new Iraqi Ministry of Defense and Ministry of Interior. I feel it is safe to say it is tens of billions of dollars. It has to be. At his farewell party, the outgoing head of J-7 told the room how, in his entire career previous to Iraq, he had never been responsible for a construction project over $12 million dollars in value. I was shocked. This is peanuts, yet in Iraq he was responsible for at least $2 billion in construction projects per year. If he was there for one year, and many of his projects were started before his arrival going back to 2004, interpolating from that figure J-7 has probably been responsible for around $5-7 billion in construction projects in Iraq. Yet, J-7 can't close the books on the expenditure of these funds. And this is just one area that MNSTC-I is responsible for.

MNSTC-I does too many things for the Ministry that it should do, and could do, for itself. A good example is J-7 building camps for the Iraqi army. MOD should be constructing these on its own, with its own architects and engineers, and issuing the building contracts using its own procurement methods and its own money. But no, we just can't let them do that, yet it's their country. It could be said that in this regard the Coalition is indeed doing what an occupying force would do. But this gives a false picture. If the Coalition was truly an occupying force, it would protect the Iraqi people so they could live their lives in some type of peace. It would have allowed them to keep the institutions they had, only purging them of pro-Saddam (Ba'ath Party) loyalists at the highest levels. With enough of our forces on the ground no insurgency would have been able to gain traction, and by leaving the Ministry of Defense and the Ministry of Interior in place there would have been a security infrastructure to protect the country and its people. All this while the Coalition—through MNSTC-I, MNC-I and MNF-I—was protecting the country and training and equipping the two Iraqi security ministries that had been left in place, instead of being disbanded by Paul Bremer. The Iraqis could have paid for it all with their oil revenues. None of this happened.

Today the Coalition does not have the forces to protect the country, so it wants the Iraqis to do it themselves, with a brand new army that has to be created from scratch since Paul Bremer disbanded the one that had been around for decades. So, being caught between the proverbial rock and a hard place, the Iraqis are foundering. With its old army gone, the new Iraqi Ministry of Defense is trying to build a brand new army the way we want them to do it. Ordering of supplies is just one example. If we got out of their way, the Iraqis would order supplies all day long, just not the way we want them to. They would pay the bribes and purchase without competition. But why not, it's their money. And why should we care, it's their country. We want them to follow procurement integrity rules like we do in the United States, and they look at us like we're crazy. As a result nothing gets ordered. They get 19 signatures on a single purchasing document so if it ever gets ordered and something goes wrong they won't get blamed for the mistake. We're promoting inefficiency in Iraq, not stopping it. Why won't we let them order supplies from their cousin Mohammed? Why won't we let them purchase food from their friend Amir? Why won't we let them contract with their uncle Rashid to construct the new army camp? Because we won't let them spend their own money the way they know how to, and because they can't do things the way they are used to doing them, nothing gets done. Even though Iraqis may do things in ways we think are corrupt or backward, how do we think they will do things after we leave? We should let them do things their own way, supervising them while we're there until they are able to defend themselves. What does it matter how they do it? On one hand we can't protect them, and on the other we won't let them protect themselves in their own way.

We want the Iraqis to defend themselves, yet we disbanded their army and national police. We want the Iraqis to equip their army, yet we want them to use our procurement methods and processes when they can't. We want them to take over their own country, yet we were instrumental in creating a civil war that has killed hundreds of thousands of their citizens when we should have had enough troops on the ground to protect them. We invaded their country. We should have taken on the responsibility for defending it afterwards, but instead we've dropped that little task in their lap. And we won't let them spend their own money, in their own way, to do it. And all the while President Bush has been telling us everything is going great.

When I arrived in Baghdad in July 2006, it was 120 degrees. My associate walked me over to the Ministry of Defense building next to Phoenix Base and introduced me to the Iraqis I would be working with for the next year. The building had been the former home of the Iraqi Parliament, and had been badly damaged by US bombs the opening night of the invasion, as most of the government buildings had been. The United States spent $58 million dollars renovating this building. It was a dump. But the most noticeable thing was the lack of air conditioning. It felt like an oven inside the Ministry of Defense building that first day I went there. One day I was walking down the hallway when one of the senior advisors employed by my company in Baghdad walked past me. He was the advisor to the DG for A,L&I. He had a very important job. As he walked by, alongside his DG and his entourage, he yelled at me, "Where's your tie!" It was an oven inside the building, yet this clown was yelling at me for not wearing a tie. We had to wear our 35 pound armor-plated vest and 10 pound Kevlar ballistic helmet everywhere we went. I had just taken these off when this guy made his comment to me, in a sneer as he passed me in the hallway. Whenever I took off my vest I would be soaking wet with sweat. It looked like I had just gotten out of the shower. I had been told to dress the same as the person (i.e., man) I advised, which I was doing, but this advisor just wasn't happy with that. He wanted me to wear a tie like him, so he took it out on me in front of the DG he advised, to put me in my place. It was just like being in the military again, only we weren't wearing uniforms. In the military this happens all the time. It should if a person isn't wearing their uniform properly. But as civilians in Iraq, what's the point? The fact is, 99% of the contractors were ex-military and some, like this guy, still wanted to swing their dicks around. I went to my incompetent manager and asked him if our company had a dress code for Iraq, and he did what he always did, he referred me to the company website. There I found the company dress code all right, for employees who work at the company headquarters in Alexandria, Virginia. I went back and told my manager this. As the Program Manager he was in charge of all the firm's staff in Baghdad. He said he had no idea what the dress code was and then stared at me like I was from another planet. I asked him if he would enact a dress code. Like he always did he said he would "check with corporate" in Alexandria. I never heard another thing about a dress code in Iraq. I started to wear a tie.

As I said, there was no air conditioning in the MOD building the day I arrived and was introduced to my new Iraqi friends, as they would soon become. The days went by, and then the weeks. In Iraq there are seasons just like in the States, only at much higher temperatures. The winter months coincide with ours here, but the temperatures are in the 50s at night. In the summer things get dicey. On the hottest day it can get up to 130 degrees without a problem. This is in July and August. It was at this time I arrived and found there was no air conditioning in a building the United States had spent $58 million dollars to renovate. One day I found out why. The Iraqi expatriate from New Zealand who sat next to me in my MNSTC-I office was an electrical engineer. He told me there was a brand new 1.5 KVA Caterpillar generator behind the MOD building to power the air conditioning and the rest of the electricity for building. The building was on the Baghdad power grid, which provided power about 3-4 hours a day, and the rest of the time the power was provided by a smaller generator that was crapping out, hence the brand new Caterpillar generator out back. All of Baghdad was powered the same way. The city provided power a few hours during the daytime, while everyone had to provide their own power the rest of the day with small generators. The fuel for these generators was the key. It was almost impossible to get fuel most of the time. Only people who were connected got it. Without fuel people sweated during their sleep all night long because they had no air conditioning, and in the morning no hot shower—if they had running water. After all this, those who worked at MOD would then risk their lives coming to work.

I asked the Iraqi ex-pat why there was no air conditioning with a brand new generator. That's when he told me about the power cable. When the Caterpillar vendor from Kuwait installed the generator, he placed it on a concrete slab that he poured behind the MOD building, in the best location he felt was available. But when the vendor went to connect the generator to the building the cable wasn't long enough. The generator came with a standard length cable, but it wasn't long enough to reach the building from the location out back where it had been placed by the contractor. The contractor probably knew this all along, and wanted to make more money by selling MOD the longer cable, typical of any Middle Eastern businessman. Screw the client in order to make more money now. Forget about getting any follow-on business, get all the money you can today. The Ministry of Defense, who had purchased the generator with much fanfare because it was actually able to get the contract awarded, refused to pay the vendor for a longer cable, saying it was the contractor's fault the cable wouldn't reach the building. The longer cable cost $48,000. The contractor said he would not pay for the longer cable because he had performed the contract to its specifications, which did not say anything about where to place the generator. (Needless to say, we made the Iraqis use our procurement procedures, but we never trained them how to write a valid legal contract, which would have prevented this oversight from occurring. I was a Contracting Officer with the US General Services Administration. We took dozens of courses over several years to be issued our "warrant" as Contracting Officers. Things like this would be studied inside and out. And if we were there to help the Iraqis, where was the US oversight to check on the length of the cable—just in case—when the generator was placed on the concrete slab?) Of course, the contractor also took no responsibility for failing to check the length of the cable before laying the concrete slab and then dropping the generator on top of it, too far from the building for the cable to be connected to it. In addition, the contractor had not received his initial partial payment, which was due when the generator was first delivered. He said he would provide the longer cable when he received this payment. This went on for months. The MOD Inspector General, the office responsible for investigating fraud, got involved and said that nothing could be done until an investigation was completed. The IG himself wanted the contract for the generator to go to his friend, and when it didn't he delayed the investigation for months.

The summer came and went, and then the winter. Most of the time half the lights in the hallways of the MOD building were out, because the only power was either from the city or the smaller generator that was constantly breaking down. Finally, the contractor agreed to install the longer cable, still not having received any money from the Ministry of Defense a year after he had first delivered the generator. The new generator was finally connected to the building but only ran a short while. It failed to run due to the Iraqi concept of preventive maintenance. Iraqis have no concept of maintaining mechanical equipment. Even though half the men were engineers and would brag about this every time they opened their mouths, everything would break down. I don't know what kind of engineering degrees they get over there, but actually performing any kind of maintenance is "beneath" them, so it never gets done. Generators require tremendous amounts of maintenance, especially in the dusty environment of Iraq. Without maintenance they go down all the time. The contractor refused to come and maintain the new generator, which was required of his contract, because he still had not been paid a single dinar (Iraqi currency). But MOD wouldn't pay him unless he came out and provided maintenance on the generator. Another Catch-22. Finally, around the time I left Iraq in September 2007, the generator was up and running. It had been delivered and installed behind the MOD building prior to my arrival in July 2006, and was finally up and running when I left in September 2007, fourteen months later. I worked in this building every day, unless I was travelling to another part of the country.

This story brings to light many things about the Iraqis and about the Coalition. The United States spent $58 million dollars renovating the old Parliament building for use by the new Ministry of Defense. If it spent this kind of money, why couldn't LTG Dempsey drop another $48,000 for the longer generator cable so we could all have air conditioning? I asked this question dozens of times while I was watching this fiasco transpire, and every time I walked into the oven that they called the MOD building. The answer was that General Dempsey, trying to "play tough" with the Iraqis, was forcing them to fix the problem themselves, and pay for it. Instead of paying for everything, one day Dempsey stopped paying for anything. This resulted in the Iraqis being left to pay for things they really needed, which resulted in the disaster of them trying to purchase things on their own but using our competitive—but impossible—contracting procedures. With the Iraqis responsible for buying what they needed, everything came to a halt and nothing was purchased at all, resulting in their refusal to pay the vendor for a generator that had already been delivered, and for a longer cable that cost $48,000. MNSTC-I probably dropped billions a year on MOD, but couldn't spend another $48,000 to help us through the 120 degree heat. And the jerk from my firm was yelling at me to wear a tie.

We all went to work every day at the MOD building in these conditions, while General Dempsey sat in his beautiful air conditioned office on Phoenix Base in the lap of luxury. So much for "leadership by example." He lived like royalty. Of course the Minister of Defense, Abdul Qadir, had separate air conditioning units for his office too. But their worker bees sucked it up, both American and Iraqi.

What could have been done, what should have been done, was that MNSTC-I could have paid for the stupid generator, both its delivery and its installation. That would have been the end of it. But General Dempsey wanted to show the Iraqis how tough he was, so he stopped paying for anything just around the time the generator was delivered. As a result, nothing got done. Did the Iraqis "learn their lesson" and straighten up? Of course not, because they aren't going to snap to and change overnight because a US general wants them to.

The paradox of our situation in Iraq is this: we either do everything for them, or we do nothing. If we want to get anything done our way, security being at the top, we have to do it ourselves. If we have to do everything ourselves, then we need to have the troops strength there to do it, which we don't have. But if we want them to do everything for themselves, then we need to get out of their way without forcing them to do things the way we want them to, leaving them alone to spend their own money as they see fit. This includes their security. Either we do it and pay for it all, or we let them do it themselves and pay for it with their oil money. Instead we do neither.

Iraq has become a hybrid of sorts. We don't have enough forces to protect them, so we want them to do it themselves. But they can't because we disbanded their army and national police. We won't send any more forces over beyond the "surge," which is successful but will never achieve what it could because there aren't enough US forces staying in place. Any way you look at the situation the same conclusion is reached. Either we have to do it all, or we pull out and let the Iraqis do it themselves. Instead, we are trying to do both. They protect themselves, but our way. We protect them, but we don't have enough soldiers to do it. They purchase things with their own money, but using our procurement regulations. We purchase everything for them, but then change our mind and stop buying anything, and bake in the heat for a year.

As is often the case, the problem can be traced to money. In the case of the construction projects run by J-7, there is no accountability of where the US money has gone other than IBM Maximo spreadsheets showing how much the projects cost. But the Iraqis rarely signed for anything to prove the projects were accepted because they couldn't get there to inspect them. And J-7 refused to make the effort to get the Iraqi signatures needed to close the books. J-7 couldn't even get its American contractors to provide the paperwork and accompanying documents and plans of what they had built on MOD's behalf. In the case of regular procurement of supplies, the US purchases things for the Iraqis, but there is little if any oversight as to where the products go, such as the 200,000 weapons purchased by General Patraeus. If everything is left to the Iraqis the result will likely be corruption and chaos, much of which was created by the sanctions after the Gulf War. This insecurity and chaos was added to by the disbanding of the Iraqi military and national police by Paul Bremer. Either way, the United States is responsible for the disasters that have befallen Iraq. Now there is open talk of splitting the country into three parts: Shi'ia, Sunni and Kurd. We will not stop until the country we professed to save is destroyed, and half its population is dead or gone, all under the guise of creating a democracy in Iraq modeled after our own.

12

IRAQ

When I was in grade school I remember hearing about the "Land Between the Tigris and the Euphrates Rivers," the "Fertile Crescent," and the "Cradle of Civilization." I never knew my teachers were talking about Iraq. I learned so much about the Iraqi people and their country after I arrived there, it was as if I had known nothing at all before. I really didn't know anything about Iraq.

Iraq is about the size of Texas. It is about the size of the Eastern Seaboard of the United States, from Maine down to South Carolina. It is approximately 850 miles north to south, and about 400 east to west. The western part of the country is desert, from the Persian Gulf (the Iraqis call it the Gulf of Arabia), along the border with Saudi Arabia, Jordan and Syria. To the east and north it is mountainous along the Iranian frontier, and up to the northern border with Turkey. In between the desert and the mountains is the "Fertile Crescent," where the land is suitable for agriculture.

Baghdad is the largest city in Iraq. The center of Baghdad is located on the Tigris River at a sharp bend, where the water slows down, which is likely why it was settled there in the first place. With the water slowing down due to the bend in the river, people could fish and wash their clothes, and use the water for irrigation. On the western edge of Baghdad is the Euphrates River, with the city's western half lying in between the two rivers. Not more than 3 miles away from the rivers, to the east and west of them, is desert, with hardly any land available for farming without the extensive canal system that emanates from the two rivers in all directions. What few trees exist are no more than 20-30 feet tall with a few leaves to provide shade. There are waddies and oases in spots, and when found the vegetation is beautiful and lush. There is hardly any grass in Iraq at all. Of course, there are date palm trees everywhere.

The Iraqi people are very friendly. I say this with all sincerity. They are extremely religious by western standards, probably 98% of them being Muslim. Iraq is a sectarian country. It is not a "Muslim" country like Saudi Arabia, where Islam is the state religion. In Iraq a person can be any religion they want to be, and I was told it was tolerant of all faiths under Saddam. When the subject of religion comes up it is always in the context of Sunni versus Shi'ite Muslim, and the tension between the two sects. I once spoke with the Iraqis I worked with at MOD about being a Catholic and believing Jesus to be the Son of God. Boy, did I get a reaction! Iraqis believe Jesus existed, but he IS NOT the Son of God. I never brought the issue up again.

I was very surprised when I arrived in Baghdad and I heard of the availability of alcohol. I assumed alcohol was banned from the country, but not after I drove by a liquor store inside the International Zone.

Iraqis love their families, and they love to eat. I heard a story that the former Prime Minister of Israel, Golda Meir, once said if a man wanted to eat like a king he should join the Iraqi army. She knew what she was talking about. Meals are considered very special to Iraqis, and they go to great lengths to set up a spread like I had never seen before. I often visited Iraqi army camps to meet with the camp commander. We would be in the middle of a discussion about something that I thought was very important to me and to him, when one of the commander's soldiers would walk in and announce, in Arabic of course, that lunch (or dinner) was ready. That would end our meeting then and there. We would all get up and walk down the hall, or wherever the room was, and sit to a feast. Every time I made one of these visits the camp or unit commander would be in his very beautiful office, sitting at his ornate full-size desk, with flags of Iraq behind him and maps of the country on the wall, with couches and chairs all around the room. Officers on his staff would sit there and not say a word, listening to our conversation. The sign of importance would be the large TV in the office. If someone wanted to look important, they had a TV in their office that was on all the time. The rest of the camp wouldn't be fit for a dog, but not the camp commander's office. He was in charge, and that was that. He would always stop to talk on his cell phone whenever it rang, and I had more than one occasion to watch an Iraqi army general with three cells phones going at once. This was their only means of communication. Where would we be without cell phones!

The conditions of Iraqi army camps were deplorable, but not the meals we ate. We would leave the commander's office and walk down hallways that had rooms on either side with soldiers sitting on cots and bunks that no American would go near, yet when we entered the commander's dining room everything changed. It was a festive atmosphere, with soldiers waiting on all of us, and the commander sitting at the head of a long table, always made up of smaller plastic tables pushed end-to-end. The food was always the same—the main course either chicken, or fish from the local lake, river or canal, with rice, bread and fresh vegetables. The Iraqis would reach for the chicken or fish, which was on platters in the center of the table, and pull it off the bone with their hands. Then they would wrap it in bread with rice. I loved the bread, which was always baked in clay ovens right there on the camp. The vegetables were the freshest I've ever had, and the rice was great. It probably came from China, but I didn't ask. Every meal came with a side dish of dates, which I didn't touch.

I was amazed how the Iraqis would continue to have children in the midst of the war, but they didn't seem to care. It may have been out of fear of losing some of their children, so they wanted to ensure their legacy. I did know of many single Iraqi men I worked with who did not want to get married because of the war. To them it wasn't worth the time, the effort, or the risk. Why bother while the war was going on? But what about the single Iraqi women?

My interpreter was a beautiful, single, 25 year old, which for marriage is very old by Iraqi standards. She told me the only thing her mother ever talked to her about was getting married. To Iraqi women marriage is the single most important event of their lives. It means everything to them, other than having children, of course. It's as if marriage is their sole reason for living. At least it appeared that way. The only thought of an Iraqi mother is when her daughter will get married and start a family. My interpreter's mother was a basket case over it.

But the war is changing all of this. With Iraqi men backing away from marriage, and for good reason, many Iraqi women will never marry during their child-bearing years, if ever. And with half the people leaving the country, the population will continue to drop in the years to come. I feel very sorry for my interpreter. She may never get married, never have children, and grow too old to meet a young man to marry. And her mother will never let her hear the end of it.

There were thousands of Iraqis living inside the walls of the International Zone, and sometimes I would see small children. Once in a while I would see a baby and it would always get my attention, not only for the novelty of it, but because of the life he or she would be living in the years to come. There would of course be young boys hawking for money and selling their "original" Saddam-era Iraqi currency. I bought some for my nieces and nephews back in the States.

Iraqi's are either "traditional" or "western." Because so much of their lives is based on religious belief, Iraqis are either more orthodox in their daily habits of Islamic life, or they are more liberal. For women, the way to tell is how they dress. A traditional Iraqi woman will always wear a scarf wrapped around her head, never letting a man outside of her immediate family see her hair. The only man who will ever see her hair other than her family of origin is her husband. An Iraqi woman of more liberal western views will dress very similar to western women, with jeans and more revealing clothing. I didn't notice much animosity between traditional and western Iraqi women, but it would be hard for me to tell in any case. Because so much of who a woman is can be seen in her clothing, it's far easier to tell a traditional Iraqi woman from one who is western in her lifestyle. Westernized Iraqi women will date a man who is not Muslim or from Iraq, while a traditional Iraqi woman would never even think of dating a westerner, or a non-Muslim, under any circumstance. She would almost commit suicide before she would do such a thing, primarily because of the "shame" it would bring upon her family. She would be considered a "loose" woman, almost like we would think of a prostitute, and that would be the worst fate she could bring upon herself and her family.

But the men are harder to differentiate. One way of doing so is during Ramadan, the yearly month-long period of fasting in Islam. More westernized men will not fast, often having lunch in the middle of the day. The very traditional Iraqi men will never break their fast, under any circumstance. I worked with Iraqi men and women every day in the Ministry of Defense and I was at first surprised at the difference, thinking they were all going to be exactly the same in this area. On the other hand, even a somewhat traditional Iraqi man will break his fast during Ramadan, even drinking alcohol out of sight of his family and friends, and think nothing of it. In general, I got the impression the women who are traditional are far more serious about it than the men.

It is acceptable for a Muslim man to marry outside his faith, another thing I was surprised to see. But it is strictly forbidden for a Muslim woman to marry outside the faith. According to Islamic law, Mohammad declared it would be harder for a woman to be married outside the faith because of all the problems it would create if she did. But there is no mention of any problems if a man marries outside the Muslim faith, the indication being the man will be able to deal with it while the woman won't. A man can have as many as four wives at one time. All he has to do is divorce one and replace her with another, as long as the total never exceeds four. I was very surprised, almost amused, at the incredible double standards in Iraq, and in Islamic society, between men and women. A man can do anything he wants to, while a woman can't do a thing unless her parents, especially her father, approve. Western culture has this to a degree, but nowhere near the degree Islamic culture does. I was surprised at this, but I was also impressed with it at the same time. We often hear of how terrible women are treated in Islamic (Arab) cultures, but like most things it is all relative. They don't have the freedom to do things western women do, but that doesn't mean they are treated badly. On the contrary, women are cherished in Islamic culture, almost to the point of being treated like little girls well into adulthood. This is because their parents, especially their fathers, don't want them to get hurt by a man. This is the reason for their traditional system of the parents (i.e., mother) selecting a mate for marriage. My translator's mother, who just wanted her to get married, was constantly introducing her to young men who were friends of the family. My translator never liked any of the men her parents set her up with, and was facing singlehood as a result. In this regard she reminded me very much of a modern American woman, looking for "Mr. Perfect" but still in the search because she couldn't find him. This showed a degree of snobbery in her, as with many American women who face being single because no man they ever meet is "good enough." I do think the war had a lot to do with her attitude, because she wasn't going to marry the first guy who came along because life was so miserable for her. I think if she married the next guy to walk through the door she would have been unhappy, doing it only because of the war and her mother, searching for a happiness that wasn't within herself. My interpreter was truly searching for something more than that. Unlike the typical American woman of today, who has none of the problems she is dealing with, my interpreter was searching for true love to surmount the lousy life she had. She was far more intelligent than the average Iraqi woman, who would marry the first guy her parents introduced her to rather than risk being single the rest of her life. My interpreter knew of this risk and was not willing to take it. Life was bad enough as it was.

The holy month of Ramadan is a grueling event for everyone who practices it. The beginning of Ramadan shifts each year. Every year it begins ten days earlier than it did the year before. Because it calls for total abstinence from all food and water until sundown every day, the average person isn't worth much by mid-day. In the summer months this is almost torture, as the temperature in the southern part of the country gets up to 130 degrees or more by mid-afternoon. Imagine not being able to even drink water until around 6:00 in the evening every day for a month, especially in the summer, and in the midst of a war. Not a fun thing. However, I heard that Ramadan was an excuse to have some fun. Because it was so hard, Iraqis would "reward" themselves at the end of the day. I never got a clear interpretation of what this meant, but I got the impression it was sex, and maybe even some alcohol too, of course with a lot of food. When Ramadan was over there would be more celebrations, with another celebration called "Eid" at the end. Iraqis love to eat, and Muslims in general love to have religious holidays. They were taking days off for religious holidays all the time. It seemed every time I turned around they had some sort of religious holiday, so everything was shut down.

Then there is the difference between Sunni and Shi'ite. Most of the Iraqis I worked with were Sunni, primarily because the Ministry of Defense was a "Sunni" ministry, while the Ministry of Interior was a "Shi'ite" ministry. The reason was because of the way the new government of Iraq was set up under the direction of Paul Bremer. In his desire to "balance" the government after the fall of the Saddam regime, Bremer forced the Iraqis to practice their own form of segregation, whereby government ministries were staffed based on percentage of religious sects in the population. For example, if the country is 30% Sunni, then roughly 30% of the government must be staffed by Sunni people, and the balance by Shi'ite people. Sunnis and Shi'ites simply don't get along. The Sunnis I worked with at the Ministry of Defense thought the Shi'ites were stupid in their archaic practices, such as whipping themselves as they marched down the streets during some of their religious holidays. To them the Shi'ites were very backward.

The United States Government is forcing the Iraqi government and people to live and do things the way we think they should live, and the way we think they should do things. We have never, since the end of Operation Iraqi Freedom, allowed them to decide their own fate. On the surface it appears they are deciding it, with the purple thumbs and all, but in reality they are not. The hatred between Sunnis and Shi'ia illustrates the point. The only way they will ever be able to coexist is if they work out their own problems by themselves. They will never coexist if the United States gives one ministry to the Sunni and one to the Shi'ia, as we have done. This only created problems because one sect was pissed off it didn't get a particular ministry, and the other sect was pissed off that it got what it did, like segregation in America. People must decide for themselves, as painful as that can be. Segregation is a failure, and Americans know that now. (So is "affirmative action," i.e., reverse discrimination, for that matter.) In Iraq the same holds true. Iraqis themselves need to solve their own problems, not have someone else solve it for them. But how can the Iraqi people solve their own problems when they never had the opportunity to lead themselves under 25 years of rule by a dictator? They can't do this within a short time frame, yet that is exactly what we want them to do, and all this during a civil war between Sunni and Shi'ite, and between the forces of democracy in Iraq and the forces of terrorism coming from outside. It's simply too hard for the Iraqis to do this while they are trying to rebuild their security ministries, but without enough American troops to provide the security the country and the people of Iraq need to solve these problems themselves.

Sunnis and Shi'ites need to understand they are equal, hard as that may be. Their version of Islam is not the same, but it doesn't mean one is better than the other. But putting one ministry in the hands of one sect and another ministry in the hands of the other isn't going to solve the issue of how they coexist. It means Sunnis are responsible for the defense of the country (Ministry of Defense), while Shi'ites are responsible for the defense of the villages, towns, cities and provinces (Ministry of Interior). Separating responsibilities between national defense and domestic security makes sense. But it also means the insurgency is high in Sunni towns and parts of Baghdad because the National Police is pro-Shi'ite and will be more protective of those areas. And it means the level of defense against forces from outside the country are directly related to whether an attack is coming from the Shi'ite east (Iran) or the Sunni west (Saudi Arabia and Syria), because the Ministry of Defense is pro-Sunni. Will this cause the ministry to be weak against defending the western approaches to the country where their kindred Sunni brothers are from? It also means that MOD is run a "Sunni" way, while MOI is run a "Shia" way. But neither ministry is run in an "Iraqi" way. By merging the two sects together at both ministries, each could look over the other's shoulder to avoid these scenarios. But Bremer didn't want to do this because of the tensions that would have resulted in the initial stages. Instead he took the easy route, leaving the mess we have now.

The Iraqi people have suffered incredible hardship and loss since the United States invaded in the spring of 2003. Of course they suffered long before that. But the title of this book is "America's Failure In Iraq," not "Saddam's Failure In Iraq." The terrible things that Saddam Hussein did during his reign of terror could fill volumes, and probably will some day. But Saddam was a scumbag. We aren't. How many Iraqis have died since the United States invaded in the spring of 2003? How many of them would be alive today if we had done things differently, such as plan the war better and with a shred of common sense, none of which was done? The Iraqi people are good, decent human beings. They believe in God, the Prophet Mohammed, they love their families, and they respect their women, almost to the point of treating them like little girls. They love to eat good food, and a lot of it, and they welcome visitors into their homes as if they were family. They practice a faith that most Americans don't understand, but we can understand their love for human life, which I saw every day I was there. They hated Saddam, yet they were powerless to do anything short of a suicide attack to kill him, and even this they could not do because Saddam used look-alike doubles to prevent such an attack. He knew he was hated by most of his own people, so the only way he could rule the country was by shear force, to include torture, prison and murder. We know all of this. But under Saddam, if you didn't get into trouble, if you didn't bring attention to yourself, you got by. If you didn't piss off Saddam or one of his associates, you lived a fairly comfortable life. I was told this many times by the Iraqis I worked with. But after the UN sanctions during the 1990's, after the invasion in 2003 and five years of misery, what does the average Iraqi have? The Iraqi dinar, the staple of the currency, used to be about 3 to the dollar. When I was in Iraq it was around 1350 to the dollar. This is what the United States has done to the Iraqi economy. Was Iraq better off under Saddam? A case could be made that it was. Before the invasion of 2003, a liter of gas was around 20 fils. A fil is 1/1000 of a dinar. This means that a liter of gas was 20/1000 of a dinar. If a dinar was 3 to the dollar, that means a liter of gas was .67 cents, or 1/67 of a cent! It was basically free. Now, gas is nearly impossible to get. Iraq's economy has become a black market.

This is all the direct result of the United States' failure to remove Saddam Hussein from power in 1991, the United Nations' sanctions we had imposed against the Iraqi people after the Gulf War (none of which affected Saddam in the slightest), the disbanding of the Iraqi military and national police, and the failure of the United States to invade with enough forces to provide adequate security for the Iraqi people to begin a new life of their own choosing. All because George W. Bush wanted to kick Saddam's ass and finish what his father should have finished in 1991, and because those advising Bush didn't know what they were doing. Everyone is suffering now—the Iraqi people and the American people. And while all this goes on, Al-Qaeda is licking its chops waiting for its next opportunity.

Michael M. O'Brien

People walk past destroyed buildings in the Sadriyah outdoor market, located in a predominantly Shi'ite area of Baghdad on Sunday, February 4, 2007. The day before, a suicide bomber driving a truck loaded with a ton of explosives obliterated the market, instantly killing at least 135 people while they shopped. The total injured was nearly 350. It was one of the deadliest suicide bombing attacks since the beginning of the U.S. invasion of Iraq in 2003. The following day I saw this picture on the cover of Star and Stripes, the newspaper for US military personnel. I decided then it would be on the cover of this book. (AP Photo/Khalid Mohammed)

The Iraqi army aid station at KMTB (Kirkuk Military Training Base). The LZ where we landed was across the street from the aid station, which had just received about 20 soldiers from a truck accident. One was dead, and the rest seriously injured.

Iraqi Army doctors working on an injured Iraqi soldier. The clinic where the picture was taken was relatively new, but had no medicine. The doctors could only provide bandages for these soldiers, many of whom were in very bad shape. All they could do was wait for the US Army medevac helicopters to take them to Baghdad for treatment by US doctors.

My roommate helps carry one of the injured Iraqis to the US Army medevac helicopter for the flight to the US Army hospital in Baghdad. Without that hospital, thousands of Iraqis soldiers would have died. Once the US leaves Iraq they will.

Two US Army medevac helicopters on the LZ at KMTB.

US Army Apache attack helicopter after landing at KMTB.

The two crew members of an Apache that escorted our aircraft into KMTB. Both are aviators: one flies while the other operates the guns and other equipment.

New Iraqi army recruits at KMTB—just off the street.

New Iraqi army recruits learning how to march. Not quite like my first day at West Point.

Lunch at KMTB.

Ready to fly to Q-West. This was the only time J-7 provided transportation for Ministry of Defense representatives to a camp it had built for the Ministry. The trip lasted five hours and went like clockwork until we realized J-7's contractor didn't have the paperwork for the Iraqis to sign. We flew there on a plane owned by SafeNet, a private security contractor in Iraq who provided escort security for the trip.

Preparing to depart Baghdad International Airport on SafeNet's twin engine plane to inspect the facilities J-7 had built at Q-West, near Mosul.

Q-West. J-7 simply constructed buildings inside old ammunition storage bunkers. Great if they got bombed from the air.

Q-West.

Old Iraqi ammunition at FOB Sommerall, waiting for disposal.

Ammunition waiting to be destroyed.

Waiting for disposal.

An old factory built by the British at FOB Arlington, down the road from FOB Sommerall. Many Iraqi bases were originally built by the British, including this one.

An ammunition storage bunker, built by the French, at FOB Sommerall.

The kitchen for the Iraqi workers at FOB Sommerall.

Major General Saad, Base Management Commander for the Iraqi Armed Forces, speaking to the Iraqi workers at FOB Arlington.

The workers' quarters.

The author trying to make bread without catching on fire.

Making bread.

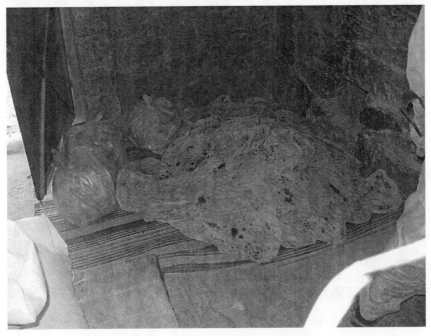

The bread ready to be served, lying in a pile on the floor.

At the former Ministry of Defense headquarters across the Tigris River in Baghdad, north of the IZ.

The author and my closest Iraqi co-worker at the Ministry of Defense Real Estate Branch.

One of the buildings at the former Ministry of Defense headquarters which was heavily bombed by the US.

The author at the former Ministry of Defense headquarters.

The US Army air base at Taji, about 20 miles north of Baghdad, the largest former Iraqi army and air force base in the country. The Coalition (US) took over many of these bases for its own use, but the Iraqis would occupy sections of them at the far end of the base. The US bases would be clean and well laid out, with Subway and Burger King, while the Iraqi camps down the road were dumps.

The former Iraqi army depot on the north side of Taji.

Scrap at Taji. The amount of scrap metal throughout the country was staggering. Near the end of my tour General Patraeus commissioned a study group just for this. An American contractor from Alexandria, Virginia, who had the scrap metal contract for Taji several years earlier, had been murdered.

More scrap at Taji.

Scrap Iraqi Soviet-designed T-72 tanks from the Gulf War and Operation Iraqi Freedom.

Scrap parts from destroyed Iraqi aircraft.

More scrap at Taji.

A renovated building at Taji. This was a typical construction project of J-7's that didn't involve building something new on raw land the Ministry of Defense didn't have clear title to. The building shown here would have been one of hundreds (thousand in the case of the Ministry of Interior) that J-7 had spent US dollars on and had never gotten the Iraqis to sign for to close out the books for the US Government.

The gate at the new Iraqi Air Force Headquarters at Taji. General Casey said the Iraqis were ready to take over the defense of their country any time they wanted to.

The Iraqi Air Force Headquarters building. No doubt they'll be able to stop an attack from Iran.

Preparing for a road convoy out of the IZ. These guys were from a reserve Infantry unit in the States who did nothing but road convoys. These were handled like a combat patrol with a full five-paragraph (situation, mission, execution, command and signal, service and support) field order briefing before each convoy departed. The unit did an excellent job. Contractors would ride in "up-armored" Chevrolet Suburbans, which had armor plating and bullet-proof windows. I took many of these convoys.

One of the convoy vehicles. The sign was not a joke. Warning shots would be fired at Iraqi drivers all the time if they got too close.

Passing underneath Assassins Gate leaving the IZ for "No Man's Land"—Baghdad.

Guarding the gate.

Iraqi army sentry at Assassins Gate.

Convoy through Baghdad.

We would have our sirens on and all traffic had to get out of our way. This was to prevent being slowed down and then attacked. If a truck or car got in front of the lead vehicle in the convoy and refused to move, it was fired upon and pushed out of the way, which was far better than the convoy being attacked.

Convoy through Baghdad.

Bridges and underpasses were the most dangerous place along any convoy route as bombs, RPG's and machine gun fire could be brought down from all directions onto the vehicles in the convoy below, leaving no place to escape.

Convoy through Baghdad.

Convoy through Baghdad.

Convoy through Baghdad.

Convoy through Baghdad.

Mom and her kids.

The old Iraqi army officers club pool at Zayuna.

Two veterans of the Iraq-Iran War waiting for their pension money at the Iraqi Veterans Affairs headquarters in Zayuna.

The US air base at Balad, about 60 miles north of Baghdad.

US Army Apaches in their "pens" at Balad. The concrete barricades in between the aircraft provide protection from shrapnel when mortar rounds hit.

Balad Air Base.

A Blackhawk about to land.

A US drone in its hanger at Balad.

Close-up.

US Army CH-47 "Chinook" cargo helicopter.

Crew chief of a US Army Blackhawk helicopter.

British helicopter and crew.

Helicopters arriving at Habbaniyah to take us back to Baghdad. The first two are Blackhawks, and the last two are Apaches providing escort for the others. This only occurred when a high ranking person was on one of the Blackhawks. That would not be the author. In this case it was the Norwegian admiral who was Deputy Commander of CMATT.

US Army Apache gunship in a hover before landing.

The US Army Apache attack helicopter, the most lethal helicopter in the world.

Scrap heap at Habbaniyah.

The bakery at the Iraqi army camp at Habbaniyah. This was the typical condition of any former Iraqi army building. They were essentially unusable.

The US Army "Sherpa." We flew one of these to Irbil, in Kurdistan, and also to Ur, both times at 100 feet above the ground and 250 knots.

Inside the "Sherpa."

Two of my closest friends at the Ministry of Defense about to travel with me.

The ziggurat at Ur during a dust storm. It is 5,000 years old.

After the dust storm.

Australian "Bushmaster" armored personnel carriers. These have V-shaped hulls to deflect IED's and EFP's. The US Army had plans to purchase about 1,500 of them for Iraq and Afghanistan. This was at Camp Tallil, near Ur.

Michael M. O'Brien

The gunner on the left, and the driver on the right, in the Bushmaster.

The gunner at his controls for the remote controlled roof-mounted machine gun.

The remotely controlled automatic machine gun on top of the Bushmaster.

Convoying from Tallil to Ur.

During the convoy to Ur. The two soldiers standing are providing lookout.

The Ur camp commander. Iraqis love to have their picture taken.

During our meeting.

The Ur camp commander preparing to eat lunch—and have his picture taken.

A latrine in one of the barracks at Ur. These buildings were a year and a half old when the pictures were taken. They were built by MNSTC-I J-7 for $118 million dollars.

Inside a ceiling.

A latrine.

Ur.

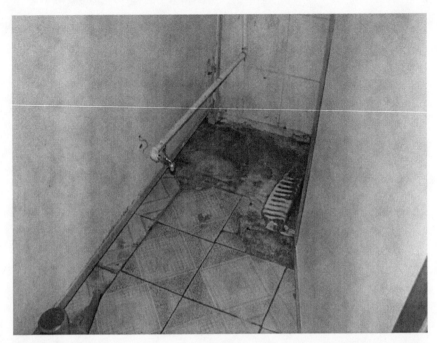

Ur.

Ur.

Ur.

Ur.

Shower at Ur.

Outside the "ablution building" at Ur. Ablution is the Iraqi custom of cleaning ones feet. Every camp, no matter how decrepit, had an ablution house, usually a separate facility just for this purpose. This building had been constructed after the other buildings in the camp: it was about six months old. Note the water pouring from the horizontal plastic pipe on the roof of the building, draining onto the walkway below.

Year and a half old J-7 construction. Notice the "drainage" for the rain water.

Inside the ablution building.

The doors to the stalls were so cheap they just hung there. Nothing worked. This building was constructed by J-7 after the others. It was six months old at the time these pictures were taken.

Ur.

Ur.

Ur.

Two Iraqi men of the countryside.

The author after coming inside the building where I worked at Phoenix Base. I had just removed my vest. I gained about 35 pounds in Iraq. There was simply too much food in the DFAC and eating was one of the few pleasures we had. The weight is gone now.

The author and my closest friend and co-worker from the Real Estate Division at the Ministry of Defense. We were on the road from Irbil to Diyanah in Kurdistan. This was one of only two trips the colonel from MNSTC-I J-5 included us on to locate sites for new units under the Prime Minister's Initiative. My friend was the acting chief of the Real Estate Branch, later made a Division. The permanent chief had left the job due to "health" reasons. He was gone the first nine months I was in Iraq, but continued to get paid because his brother was the Infrastructure Division Director.

13

A Lack of Leadership

WHY HAS AMERICA CONTINUALLY FAILED in its foreign policy efforts over the past several decades? There are those who would say the wars we have been involved in were mistakes, but certainly in the case of World War I and World War II we didn't start the conflict. Beginning with Vietnam, however, we began to get ourselves involved in conflicts we could have easily avoided, but we went into them stating it was for our "self defense" and to "save democracy."

Let's look at Vietnam. If we had avoided getting sucked into Vietnam, which is exactly what President Eisenhower was trying to do, what would have happened? If we place ourselves at that point in time, what would have happened if we had not gone into Vietnam in the first place? Of course, it is hard to place ourselves in a period in the past, which much of this very book has done, but people are paid a lot of money for their experience, knowledge and education in foreign affairs when the President asks them to come to Washington to join his team. If the "best and the brightest" were on such a team, all well educated in foreign affairs as they were supposed to have been, did any of them in the Kennedy and then the Johnson administrations ever think this question out? What would have been the threat to our "national security" if we had not gone into Vietnam in the early 1960's? The country is on the other side of the world, so any threat of Vietnam invading our soil was nil. What other threat could it have posed? The only other argument was the spread of communism. If Vietnam was going to go communist if the United States had not gone there, what would have been the threat to the security of the United States if that happened? At the time probably half the world was under communist rule anyway, so what difference would it have made if such a tiny country went communist as well? It bordered countries that were already communist, so going the same route would not have been as big an issue as, say, a country closer to our shores or one that was in a more strategic location and in a place that could have posed a realistic threat to our national security. Because JFK had achieved martyrdom by being assassinated, and had already begun to send troops to Vietnam (including my father, an advisor to the South Vietnamese army in 1961), LBJ followed suit to siphon off some of JFK's immense popularity. He lied to the American people about the Gulf of Tonkin affair as an excuse to get us involved in the conflict, just like FDR lied to us about the "surprise" attack on Pearl Harbor. Anyone who still thinks he and General George Marshal didn't know that attack was coming ahead of time must still believe in Santa Clause too.

The best example of a country that posed a serious threat to our national security and was being taken over by communism, was Cuba. If the spread of communism was our biggest concern, as well as defending our security, why did we do nothing about Cuba other than JFK's botched Bay of Pigs fiasco? Even today, can anyone deny that Cuba posed a threat to our security in 1961 if it fell into the wrong hands and was led by a pro-Soviet communist? Could anyone of the day deny that Cuba, being 90 miles from Florida, was located in close enough proximity to be a potential threat to the United States? When we had a country only 90 miles away and led by a communist dictator who hates America we did nothing. Yet we can go to Vietnam, which is half a world away, and waste 58,000 Americans lives for nothing. This is leadership? It shows how abysmal our "leadership" has been since the 1960's, and earlier. We let Cuba go down the drain, but we took up the fight in Vietnam! What were these "best and brightest" like McNamara thinking? Losing 58,000 American soldiers in Cuba would have at least made more sense than losing them in Vietnam. And let's not get into how things ended up in the long run. Cuba does go communist and is only 90 miles away, and we almost ended human civilization because it led to the Cuban Missile

Crisis as a result. Vietnam, half a world away, also goes communist and who cares? The fact is, it doesn't matter that it went communist in 1975 any more than it does now.

But it's these "best and brightest" who are supposed to know these things, who are supposed to study these historical events, and who are supposed to make sound recommendations to the Presidents they serve based on all they know. But who's kidding who? In reality they get their jobs because they know the new President and worked on his campaign. They get their jobs because they know someone who knows someone who knows someone in the White House and they get their job that way. Or, worse yet, they are from academia and *think* they know everything yet haven't got a clue what's going on in the real world. They have no practical experience in what they profess to know everything about, then they turn around and make policy. They talk a good line and get high level positions in the White House leading our country into these disasters. Where were these men coming from when they recommended we go into Iraq in 2003, when many of them were either serving in the administrations during Cuba and Vietnam, actually served in the military during these periods, or spent decades in academia studying and teaching about it?

Look at Vietnam and the damage it has caused our country since. Why did we get involved in Iraq, especially when the leaders of our country were all alive when Vietnam was being fought? How is it that men with high levels of education, men of vast experience in the government of our nation, and men from the professional military who fought in that conflict, could turn right around and repeat Vietnam almost as if it was scripted? There is no possible way that Vietnam and Operation Iraqi Freedom cannot be compared. The more I study the two, the more I read about them, the more strikingly similar they become. As I've said, McNamara and Rumsfeld even look like each other, which to me is some kind of weird parody. It may have been Winston Churchill, but possibly another scholar of history, who said that those who do not study history are doomed to repeat it. The operative word is "doomed." It stands to reason if one doesn't study history they will repeat it, but why "doomed" to repeat it? When history is repeated, and the lessons from the past are not headed and taken into consideration, the result is always negative. It just works out that way. It never turns out well. When an event in history such as war is not studied and analyzed, and is executed in the same manner as one that was fought before, especially with at least one of the "antagonists" being the same (e.g., the US), the results are always bad for that player. In the case of Vietnam, the United States fought a war that lasted from 1960 to 1975. Actually, we were indirectly involved in the early 1950's when the French got slaughtered at Dien Bien Phu. The Vietnam War was a disaster. It split our country in two. It created the liberal movement, and it was lived and experienced by all the "leaders" of our country today—draft dodger, military officer, political wonk or academic. We are now engaged in a conflict in Iraq, whose threat to our national security is as questionable as Vietnam, and it is having all of the same negative effects on our society that Vietnam did. Why does our nation do this? Why do our leaders keep making the same mistakes? Why do they continue to screw everything up? It is because we don't have real leaders any more, either politically or in our military. It is because we don't have leaders who possess common sense, and who are not afraid to speak their minds and take action when it is needed, regardless of what the media thinks.

Military officers, especially those aspiring for promotion to general, will not say anything contrary to what they believe their boss wants to hear for fear of hurting, or ending, their careers. We speak of courage under fire. Senior military officers may have courage on the battlefield, but they can turn into cowards in a heartbeat. I've seen this myself. Give a military man a mission and he will accomplish it, but ask him for his honest opinion on something that goes against the party line, and good luck. You will not get it. What you will get is what he thinks you (his boss) want to hear. It is only when the military officer feels comfortable enough to speak his mind you will get the truth, but that is usually when he has already submitted his retirement papers and he can't be touched. That's why US Army Major General John Batiste resigned mid-way through our current involvement in Iraq. He was so disgusted at what was going on he left, even after he was offered promotion to 3-star general. The promotion was most likely meant to muzzle him into silence so he wouldn't voice his opinion on the war. In our politically correct world, senior ranking generals are more afraid of a sexual harassment complaint being filed against them then they are a terrorist with a bomb. I don't say this lightly. I really believe it.

In his book *Fiasco*, Thomas Ricks describes the complete lack of leadership exhibited by both US Air Force General Richard Myers, the Chairman of the Joint Chiefs of Staff, and Marine General Peter Pace, the Vice Chairman. Both were in their respective jobs during the period leading up to Operation Iraqi Freedom, and both went out of their way to avoid confrontation with Donald Rumsfeld. This is another way of saying they never spoke up or objected to anything their boss ever said or did. How do two men of this rank and position avoid confrontation with their boss when the job of all three is the execution of our nation's warfare? Myers was a complete weenie, and Pace most likely got where he was because he cut a dashing figure in his fancy Marine uniform and never said a word contrary to what his boss wanted to hear. But when it came to actual leadership, they were completely lacking. Pace was personally involved in the lousy planning of OIF, to the point of insisting the number of invading troops remain absurdly low, as Rummy wanted, which led to the later disaster. And Myers would have done anything short of getting Rumsfeld's coffee and taking out his dry cleaning to keep him happy. When Tommy Franks called the Joint Chiefs of Staff "Title 10 mother fuckers," I wonder who he was referring to.

General Pace had two defining moments near the end of his career, when he was the Chairman of the Joint Chiefs of Staff. The first was when he was so overcome with emotion he started to cry in front of a Senate committee when asked the all-important question about what it was like growing up the son of Italian-American immigrants. As Pace dabbed at his tears, Senator Lindsey Graham of South Carolina made the moving comment, "It takes a strong Marine to cry." I get teary-eyed every time I think about this tender exchange. Actually, I can't think of a more pathetic display by the nation's most senior military officer. Big deal, his parents came from Italy. My grandmother came from Ireland. Are we all supposed to break out the handkerchiefs now? What has our country come to when this kind of nonsense is happening? Was General Pace able to look at himself in the mirror the next day? Sadly, he probably had no trouble with that at all. A real tough Marine, General

Pace. I'm sure the rest of the Marine Corps just loved that chapter in their history.

General Pace's other defining moment came when he was denied the recommendation of the new Secretary of Defense, Robert Gates, for another term as Chairman of the Joint Chiefs of Staff, which he had taken over after General Myers retired. Pace's job as Chairman had been questioned for some time, but the real reason he lost it was his comments about homosexuality several months earlier. No sooner did he say he felt that homosexuality was "immoral," he then said he supported the country's "don't ask-don't tell" policy of allowing gays in the military. General Pace committed the ultimate act of talking out of both sides of his mouth, typical of officers in high positions. If he supported the "don't ask-don't tell" policy, why on earth give his personal opinion on homosexuality, which is completely the opposite? But if he really thinks homosexuality is immoral, he had no problem keeping his mouth shut about gays in the military in order to get to the top of his profession.

This is another example of senior military officers thinking and feeling one way, and then turning a blind eye to, and going along with, policies they detest. Getting to the top is more important than their core beliefs and values. They are generals and admirals who are incapable of being true to themselves and to their country. As a result we get lackluster military leadership because these officers don't really know what they believe. Or, if they do believe in something but it happens to go against the politically correct line (which nowadays it probably does), they are completely afraid to act or speak for fear of jeopardizing their precious careers. In the end all we get are "yes men" who do and say whatever their civilian leaders want them to do and say, regardless of whether they believe in it or not. They won't stand up and say what's really on their mind and speak from experience because they're intimidated by their civilian boss who has no idea what's going on. And soldiers die as a result. And tens of thousands of innocent civilians die as a result. The only member of the Joint Chiefs who did say what he believed, and knew to be true based on his experience, was General Eric Shinseki of the Army. We know where he ended up.

Officers who do say what's on their minds don't make it to the top. They can't. To say what's on their mind could call into question what their civilian boss wants to do. If you have a boss like Donald Rumsfeld—who was an egomaniac and didn't have a clue what he was doing—to open your mouth meant your job. Either you say what's really going on and likely get fired, or you don't open your mouth and contribute to the needless death of thousands of soldiers and, in this case, Iraqi civilians. Or you resign. It's sad, but today there's really no other way to get to the top in the US military—and keep your job. The system's broken. The only way it can work is if the Secretary of Defense knows what he's doing (e.g., knows about warfare and the deliberate use of force), and a Joint Chiefs of Staff who work well with him. When's the last time we had that combination? What is such a waste is all the military education and training senior officers get during their careers, yet if they work for guys like Rumsfeld or McNamara they never get a chance to use it. What's the point of being a general and having attended the US Army War College, when your boss is a civilian who doesn't have a clue and tells you it's going to be his way or the highway? Hell, maybe he ran a big company, or better yet contributed to the President's campaign, so surely he knows how to invade a country. You can have stars on your shoulders and know global military strategy all day long, but if you work for clowns like Rumsfeld or McNamara all you need proficiency in is small unit tactics. They run everything else. The higher one gets in the military the less control and authority over things he has, things he has studied for 30 years. A platoon leader has more power than a four star general.

It has been mentioned that the Joint Chiefs of Staff during the Vietnam War were seriously considering mass resignation, so much was their disgust at the manner in which Johnson and McNamara were handling the war. In the end they decided not to. Why? I would venture to say it was nothing more than fear, plain old cowardice. After all, General Wheeler had never heard a shot fired in anger his entire military career, and he was the Chief. Imagine what would have happened if they had? The country would have known it wasn't the military who was botching the war, but their civilian leaders. In addition, I believe the country would have been very proud of those officers for resigning if they believed the war was a disaster. Hell, everyone else did. In the end, if they really felt that way about the war, to the point of contemplating resignation, how could they in good conscience stay in their jobs and continue to prosecute the war effort? But they did and the war went on, and look at the needless deaths that occurred after they wimped out?

What most people don't know is the Uniform Code of Military Justice (UCMJ), the legal code of the US armed forces, specifically allows a soldier or officer to refuse an unlawful or immoral order from his superior, whether civilian or military. After the Second World War the Germans tried to use the excuse that they were just following orders. But the Nuremburg trials clearly showed this doesn't work. No US soldier is obligated to follow an order he feels (and knows) to be illegal or immoral. This is tough stuff, but look at what happened in Vietnam. Look at what happened in Iraq. Did our senior generals have reason for not following orders in these conflicts? A case could be made they did. To say otherwise implies that no order is ever illegal or immoral, which is impossible.

And then there's McNamara himself, who wrote in his memoirs decades later he thought the Vietnam War was really a mistake—while he was running it—but he couldn't tell his boss, the President, that he felt that way. After all, he had a "duty" to continue working for his boss. The lives of 58,000 Americans was just the price he had to pay. Life sure is hard at the top, isn't it Bob? Apparently, after writing his book McNamara felt pretty darn good about himself, like he had undergone a soul cleansing. There was a political cartoon in the Washington Times after McNamara's book came out. It showed him standing in front of the Vietnam Memorial looking at the names of all the fallen with his book under his arm. The caption is his thought to himself, something to the effect, "I feel pretty good about myself now guys, how about you?" How could that man sleep at night all those years? For that matter, how can Paul Bremer now? McNamara was a corporate executive who thought he could win the war on statistical data. He couldn't, and his generals knew it, but they didn't have the nerve to do anything about it.

Vietnam. Iraq. Is there much difference between the two? There is one. Our political and military leaders had nothing before Vietnam to learn from in order to avoid the mistakes they made. But in Iraq they had Vietnam staring them in the face as a history lesson, and they allowed it to be repeated all over again. The two wars are exactly the same, but they didn't have to be.

Civilians in our national leadership, as opposed to military officers, are generally clueless when it comes to waging war, and from what this country has seen since Vietnam clueless in most other areas too, with the exception of Ronald Reagan. They don't spend their careers studying war. That's why they need to depend on the military for its advice in waging it. But the military has to have someone willing to listen, and of course they have to say what they believe is the right course of action. In the case of Iraq the military utterly failed to advise their civilian superiors, except for General Shinseki, the Chief of Staff of the Army during the initial planning of Operation Iraqi Freedom. But their civilian bosses weren't about to listen to anyone, so it hardly mattered. Not knowing anything about warfare is to be expected of our civilian leadership, save for rare occasions. Rumsfeld and McNamara both served in the military, Rumsfeld as a pilot and McNamara as a statistician (i.e., number cruncher). It's fair to say neither of them learned much more than their specific line of work and failed to grasp what military force, especially strategic military force, means and how to properly use it. The problem is that people like them make these terrible decisions, usually thought up over drinks in a DC bar, and are in positions of such power and influence with (and over) the President, that their dreams (or should I say daydreams) become reality. The ones called upon to implement these dreams, and the decision of the President to execute them, are the soldiers of our military.

The Unites Stated Government likes to waste money, and lots of it. We waste too many lives as well. Our political leaders make these crazy plans, send our soldiers half way around the world to risk their lives for a cause that doesn't make any sense to anyone except the clown who came up with the idea, and the President gives him the permission to do it. Iraq was Paul Wolfowitz's baby. He sold it to Dick Cheney. Cheney sold it to George W. Bush, who saw it as a way to vindicate his father's mess of 12 years before, and also as a way to spin his spurs and show the world he was from Texas and liked to kick some ass, just like Johnson tried to do in Vietnam. The same cockiness and ego of two different men from Texas got us involved in two wars that were disasters, and both places are about as far from the United States, and from being threats to us, as they could get. In the case of Vietnam, nothing at all was accomplished. In the case of Iraq, nothing has been accomplished. But we can't do anything about a communist dictator 90 miles away! If John F. Kennedy had not been assassinated he could very well have gotten himself into the same mess in Vietnam that George W. Bush is in today in Iraq, and would have ended up with the same lousy legacy. Both JFK and LBJ had Robert McNamara as their Secretary of Defense, and we know what a great job he did running the Vietnam disaster.

I am not a 4-star general, but I know that you never, ever, invade a country unless you use overwhelming force to do it, and are prepared to occupy it afterwards. If you bring too many forces, just send home what you don't need. But if you don't bring enough forces, you're up the creek. One other ingredient is absolutely required: the will and resolve to fight the conflict to a swift, decisive and complete victory.

Since World War II we've never pulled this off, even though our nation had an impeccable war record up to that time. It's as if we were great students who suddenly start screwing up and don't give a damn about school any more. In Vietnam we had the force to do the job, and essentially occupied the country, but we lacked the resolve to execute and finish the conflict to a clear and decisive victory. Even a stalemate would have been better. Instead we walked out. We left the field. We didn't have the will to finish the game we got ourselves into. We forfeited. McNamara was a clueless, egomaniac corporate executive who thought he knew more than his generals, all of whom were weak officers and went right along with whatever he wanted, except for General Green of the Marine Corps. He was the predecessor of General Shinseki 40 years later. The Joint Chiefs tried to win the war in Vietnam by asking for more troops after we got involved, but McNamara would never let them fight it, and Johnson sat on the sidelines doing nothing, wringing his hands with his head in the clouds. The result was the disaster we call "Vietnam."

Look at Grenada and Panama. True, they were small countries and small military operations, but look at the results they achieved. After President Reagan was briefed on the invasion of Granada he asked the commanding general if he had everything he needed to complete the mission as planned. The general said that he did. Reagan then told him to double the number of soldiers for the operation. He knew whatever the plan was, the unexpected had to be accounted for, so he sent in far more than what the general thought was needed. The result was a swift and overwhelming victory and the operation ended. That was it. Although we are discussing Iraq here, the principles are the same. They are *always* the same. There is no need to change them because the size of the country is greater. As a matter of fact, the principles hold even more based on the larger size of the country. The fewer soldiers we have to do the job, the worse the situation will become because the large geographic area involved will be impossible to fight across and manage effectively during the warfight, and after the initial operation is over. This is exactly what has happened in Iraq.

I started this book with a discussion of the Gulf War of 1991. If the principles I have discussed were followed then, we would not be in the situation we are in now in Iraq. But what makes the Gulf War of 1991 so depressing is that we had so much going into it. We had the overwhelming force and strength to do the job. We had half a million soldiers in the theater of operations, which included Saudi Arabia, Kuwait and Iraq. We had the political cover from the UN and world opinion. Because of this overwhelming force we were kicking the hell out of Saddam and his lousy tinker toy army, and had them on the run back to Baghdad, which we would have easily captured and occupied when we got there. Is this pie in the sky theory? No, it is not. Is there any way the Iraqi army would have stopped us as we kicked them up the road to Baghdad? Is there any way they would have been able to stop us, turn us around, and force us back to Kuwait? The fact is we had Saddam and his entire military and government on the ropes and we let him go. This was the single worst military-political decision the first President Bush could have possibly made.

However, the worst single performance of a US President was Lyndon Johnson's handling of the Vietnam War. I say this based on the body count of US soldiers. 58,000 during Vietnam is a lot higher than 4,300 during Operation Iraqi Freedom. But when looked upon in terms of the disastrous effects both wars have had on the social fabric of our country, Vietnam and the current conflict are extremely close.

Iraq didn't have to be so. It is, however, because of the terrible way it was planned and executed. The lessons from the previous conflicts were right in front of the planners of this one to see. They never bothered to look. Vietnam led to the beginnings of the liberal, anti-American, movement. This conflict has placed extreme liberalism (i.e., socialism) in the White House. All because of lousy leadership.

During the Gulf War of 1991 we had overwhelming force, and it appeared we also had the will and the resolve to use it toward the swift execution and culmination of the conflict. We were "winning!" What a concept—to win a war. We haven't done that in a while. Our total casualty rate was around 300 soldiers dead, mostly from car accidents with lousy Saudi Arabian drivers. The 82nd Airborne Division road into combat in buses! But you can bet they all got their CIB's (Combat Infantryman's Badge). But then Colin Powell and the President got together and ended the whole thing on a dime. I have a West Point classmate who was the pilot of the helicopter that carried Norman Schwarzkopf to the "treaty" signing at the conclusion of the Gulf War. He told me that Schwarzkopf was furious we were ending the war and letting the Iraqis get off. Well, he had his chance to tell the President how he felt and he blew it, so it was too late. He had no business being pissed off at these Iraqi generals now. When the aircraft landed and the Iraqi generals came out of the tent where the treaty was going to be signed, they all had shit-eating grins on their faces because they knew they had gotten away with the whole thing. They invaded Kuwait, were kicked out, but never had to suffer any consequences for what they had done. Saddam never suffered for the little stunt he pulled when he invaded Kuwait. The only ones who suffered were the Iraqi and Kuwaiti people. And if Saddam can gas his own countrymen, what does he care about how the economic sanctions are going to affect them? We had the overwhelming force, but we didn't have the resolve and the will to see the conflict through. That's because of one man—President George H.W. Bush. He obviously didn't have the desire to occupy the country if he didn't have the will to finish off Saddam. It is one of the saddest moments in our history that President Bush ended the Gulf War as he did. We now have a debacle on our hands because his son couldn't let a half-dead dog lie there. Now it's a whole new enemy: militant Islamic extremism that uses suicide mass murder as its weapon of choice. The less resolve we have to fight to a conclusive victory, the more enemies who are willing to take a shot at us. The DVD "Obsession" is a clear depiction of the true enemy of western civilization. Have we made a dent in that enemy by going into Iraq?

With the Gulf War ending as it did Bush's son, George W., decided to go back in and finish the job once and for all. This was supposedly prompted by the attacks of 9/11, but we will probably never know for sure if there was a plan to go in beforehand. Maybe there was, but it doesn't really matter now. The American people were told that because of the 9/11 attacks we were going into Afghanistan, and then we were told we had to expand the fight to Iraq, which doesn't even border Afghanistan. We seemed to be doing well in Afghanistan, having taken out the Taliban regime. But then we invaded Iraq and took forces away from an already good operation and sent them into Iraq, with a total force strength of only around 125,000 Coalition forces. If we had 500,000 soldiers in Vietnam and couldn't get the job done there, how were we going to get it done in Iraq with 125,000, which is about 33% larger, albeit desert versus dense jungle? If we had Saddam and his army on the run in 1991 with half a million soldiers kicking his butt, how did we think that only 125,000 would do the same job now? What had changed?

But we had "leaders" in place who thought everything had changed in just a dozen years, in the same location. Donald Rumsfeld thought we only needed 40,000 troops to destroy Iraq and its entire military structure and its government. Where did he come up with that number? I speculate he pulled it out of thin air. It's probably the number of soldiers and Marines who weren't scheduled to take vacation when Rumsfeld wanted to pull off the invasion. He just wanted to go into Iraq and kick Saddam's ass, and thought we could pull it off with an initial number of around 40,000! At least Tommy Franks got that number raised, but that's about all Franks did that made any sense. The number eventually got to around 100,000 US forces, but nowhere near what would constitute an "overwhelming force." How could it be close, with Iraq being a country 800-400 miles in size, with an army estimated to be as large as a million men, albeit not worth a damn? That's still a lot of firepower. All you have to do is tell them where to point their weapons and then tell them to pull the trigger. And George Tenant's "intelligence assessment" called for the invasion to be a slam dunk.

The cover story of Time magazine on March 23, 2003, begins with these words spoken by President George W. Bush, "Fuck Saddam. We're taking him out." Condoleezza Rice heard him say this in the hallway outside her West Wing office while she was meeting with three US Senators. This was the attitude Bush had going into the war. I don't disagree with his attitude toward Saddam Hussein. But taking that same attitude and applying it to estimates of the number of soldiers needed to execute a war is another thing entirely. Obviously, all objectivity in the planning of this conflict went out the window. And who pays the price for these awful decisions—the people in their cozy offices and high salaries and future jobs as lobbyists after they leave the administration? No. It's the soldier who's just trying to make a living.

After two and a half years running the show in Iraq, General George Casey was moved out of his job and promoted to Chief of Staff of the United States Army. During the time he was the Commander of the Multi-National Forces-Iraq (MNF-I) not only did he do nothing, he sat on his hands while the situation in Iraq went down the drain. If Bremer did his part to destroy the country by disbanding its military and national police, Casey added to the problem by doing nothing at all to stop the civil war that began to spread throughout the country afterwards. Had he done *something* it may not have gotten as bad as it did, but because he didn't want to do his job and fight the enemy things escalated to the point where thousands of Iraqis were being slaughtered weekly, sometimes daily. So what happened to Casey? Instead of being sacked as he should have been, he was promoted to the highest ranking officer in the US Army. The United States Senate didn't want to approve the nomination because of the lousy job he did in Iraq, but went along with it holding their noses because they were saving themselves for bigger fights down the road.

Why would President Bush nominate General Casey to this job when the results of his performance in Iraq were so abysmal? Obviously, if General Casey were sacked, as he should have been, that would have been an indication to the American people—and to the all important media—that things weren't going well at all in Iraq. And of course the

President didn't want the American people to be told the truth about the war. Instead, General Casey got promoted following two and a half years of telling the President time and again that things were going along just fine in Iraq. Based on the Woodward piece in the Washington Post, the guy Casey was selling the Brooklyn Bridge to (the President) went ahead and promoted him anyway. Not only did President Bush never hold anyone accountable for their screw ups, he actually promoted the guy who was blowing smoke in his face, and he knew Casey was doing it! It's incredible. Anyone with a shred of leadership ability would have ushered Casey to the back door, not caring whether it hit him in the ass on his way out or not.

But in the magical mystery tour that is Washington, if Casey got his promotion then he must be doing a great job, right? Not quite. No sooner did he get his promotion then General Abizaid, Casey's commander and the CENTCOM chief, got sacked. If Casey got promoted for doing a good job in Iraq, how could Abizaid get sacked for doing a lousy job as Casey's boss in over-all charge of operations in the Middle East? There's a big disconnect somewhere. It doesn't make any sense, but then again, it doesn't have to. It's just another example of "things are just fine" we've been getting from the White House from the outset of this war, and all during its operation.

The last point about George Casey getting promoted to Chief of Staff of the Army is the issue of "personal responsibility" that we heard from George W. Bush during his presidential campaign in the summer of 2000. We heard time and again how individuals should be held responsible for themselves and for their actions. Bush was the guy who was going to hold people responsible during his administration. He was the guy who was going to turn mediocrity and laziness around, and be surrounded by people who would get the job done, and done right. Well, just like he said we were invading Iraq to find weapons of mass destruction and we never found any, we also got the shaft from Bush on people being held responsible for the crappy job they did during his watch as Commander-in-Chief. What happened to the top level people in the administration after 9/11? The same thing that happened to the top people in the government and the military after we invaded Iraq—nothing.

If President Bush was a man of his word, and of basic principle: 1) Casey would have been forced to retire from the Army after doing nothing in Iraq while thousands were being slaughtered; 2) Bremer would have been sacked; 3) Rumsfeld would have gotten the same; 4) Wolfowitz the same; 5) Franks the same; 6) and George "Slam Dunk" Tenant would have been booted out of town with his tail between his legs after 9/11. Instead: 1) Bremer, Franks and Tenant got the Medal of Freedom presented to them by the President; 2) Wolfowitz was made head of the World Bank (where he hired his girl friend at top money—remember Parris Glendenning, the former Governor of Maryland?); 3) Tenant wrote a book telling everyone why nothing was his fault but everyone else's; 4) Franks wrote a book telling everyone about his poor country roots and what a great general he was and what lazy scumbags the Chiefs of Staff are; 5) Franks got away with allowing his wife to sit in on classified briefings that would get anyone else thrown in jail; and 6) Casey got the top job in the US Army after doing nothing in Iraq for two and a half years except fly back to Washington on his private jet to tell Congress and the President how great things were going. It's a sad joke, especially after the lessons learned from Vietnam.

General David Patraeus was selected as the new commander in Iraq. As mentioned, he had been the original commander of MNSTC-I, the organization that lost the 200,000 AK-47s and 9mm pistols. This is the same organization whose very existence is to un-do what Paul Bremer did when he disbanded the Iraqi military and national police. It's the same organization I was assigned to. General Patraeus said he would take the job (like he was really going to turn it down) only if the President would allow him to do what he felt was necessary in Iraq. Apparently, the President said OK. What was Bush going to say, "No, I want you to go over there and sit on your ass like George Casey has been doing for two and a half years." Somehow, I don't think that's how the conversation between the President and General Patraeus went. And of course it meant a fourth star for Patraeus, who was on top of the world. Not only was he getting away with losing 200,000 weapons that might possibly be used to kill his own soldiers, he was getting the all-coveted fourth star of a full general. What could be better?

One day, after I had been in Baghdad for about two months, a US Army full colonel I knew walked up to me in the chow line. He was one of the "good guys" I met in Iraq. Whenever we talked about the war he would do a 360 degree scan to make sure no one could overhear us. Because, you understand, we were about to talk about reality. (All military officers do this when they are about to ask a controversial question, such as "what the fuck is going on around this place," because they are afraid someone might overhear them asking something that everyone is talking about anyway, but is contrary to the party line.) He came up to me and asked, with his voice lowered so no one would hear him, what I thought of the war. I said, in a normal tone of voice, that I thought it was a "cluster fuck." He nodded his head in agreement. Then he asked me if I had been in the Infantry when I was in the Army. The question is important because it implied that by being in the Infantry, the US Army's combat branch, as opposed to one of its support branches, I would have a clue as to what was going on. I said I had been. Then he asked me an interesting question. He said, "What would you do?" I said, without the slightest hesitation, that I would take two US Army Infantry divisions and drop them right in the middle of Baghdad and clean the town up. I went on to say that Baghdad *is* Iraq, and if you secure Baghdad you secure Iraq. He just nodded his head in agreement again. I am telling this story exactly the way it happened. The reader will think me arrogant, but I'm not. I was asked these questions by the colonel just the way I have put them down here, and I answered them just as I have described. My answer made political and military common sense the moment I gave it, and it still does today. My only mistake when I said this was I underestimated the number of soldiers needed to clean the mess up. I said two divisions. I should have said at least five.

That was about 4 months before it was all over the papers that General Patraeus was going to take over Iraq from Casey, and that he was going to institute the "surge." What is the surge? It is exactly what I told my friend, the US Army full colonel, what I would do when he asked me in the chow line in the mess hall. I understand General Patraeus has a PhD and surrounded himself with "the best and the brightest" colonels in the US Army. I also know, for what is likely the first time in the history of the US Army, he was asked to participate in a promotion board to offer "suggestions" on the suitability of colonels being considered for promotion to brigadier general, rather than this important decision being made by a secret board of un-biased officers based on the records of those being considered, as it has been done for years. Politics always plays a role in promotion, but this was an outright hand dealt to General Patraeus to play any way he wanted. It gave him the authority to hand-pick his own people for promotion. This is unheard of. It means that one man is running the US Army. He isn't even the Chief of Staff, and he is making personal selections for promotion. This has never been done before, and it makes the entire promotion process an open admission of who you know in order to make the grade. It means promotion to brigadier general in the US Army today depends on whether you are one of David Patraeus' people or not.

I'm not a 4-star general. I never attended the US Army Command and General Staff College at Fort Leavenworth, Kansas, or the US Army War College in Carlisle, Pennsylvania, but I knew standing in a chow line what needed to be done in Iraq after being there four months. It's not rocket science. Put 25,000 US Army Infantry soldiers in one spot and tell them to start kicking butt, and what do you think is going to happen? They're going to start kicking some butt! That's what the "surge" is. It is 25,000 US Army Infantry soldiers—about two divisions, what a coincidence—who were put into the worst parts of Baghdad and told to start kicking some insurgent ass. Guess what happened, the insurgency dropped like a rock in those areas, the bombings dropped off the map in those areas, and now Iraqis who live in those areas feel safer walking down the street then they have in five years. But that's just a small piece of Iraq. Thank you General Casey for doing such a great job before getting moved up to Chief of Staff. We had an expression when I was in the Army—"Fuck up and move up!"

14

MY STORY

I RETURNED FROM IRAQ IN September 2007, after spending 14 months there as the Real Estate Advisor to the Iraqi Ministry of Defense. I worked at Phoenix Base in the International Zone in Baghdad. I was employed by a defense contractor in Alexandria, Virginia. While in Iraq on the MNSTC-I staff, I witnessed gross mismanagement of US-funded projects being executed by its Construction Branch, the J-7.

My former employer, which is owned by a huge US corporation and a publically traded company on the New York Stock Exchange, is responsible for taking on work in Iraq that it has secured through its Defense Department contacts in order to bill the US Government for services that are not wanted by the US military it was hired to support. It hires civilians and sends them to Iraq where the need for them to be there is highly suspect. Yet they are sent by my firm into a combat zone, where daily mortar and rocket attacks have claimed the lives of hundreds of civilians in the International Zone alone, not including the body count outside the IZ throughout the rest of Iraq. This is waste of US taxpayer dollars in figures I can't begin to imagine.

About one month after I arrived in Baghdad I discovered J-7 was building US-funded camps for the Iraqi military throughout the country without performing the due diligence to determine the ownership of land these camps were being constructed on. As the Real Estate Advisor to the Iraqi Ministry of Defense it was my duty to bring this to the attention of J-7, and to advise it this was needed to avoid land claims against the Iraqi government, the Iraqi Ministry of Defense, and quite possibly the United States Government. I had performed my own research on land ownership in Iraq and found there were multiple types of land ownership at the national level, as well as private ownership and long term leasehold interests. The J-7, under the leadership of a US Navy captain in the civil engineers had done nothing in this regard, and for three years it had been constructing camps for the Iraqi military, with US money, without any regard for ownership of the land the camps were being built on. I told J-7 that I would do whatever I could, working with the Ministry of Defense real estate staff I advised, to determine the ownership of land where J-7 had plans to build more Iraqi military camps. I soon discovered that this would be much more difficult than I could have imagined.

The only way to definitively determine land ownership in Iraq was by traveling to the Land Registration Offices located in each of the 19 provinces throughout the country. Because these offices were in Iraqi cities and towns across the country, and not on Coalition military camps, it wasn't possible to travel to them. As a civilian contractor I wasn't allowed to do anything like that. It wouldn't have been approved, nor was I willing to commit suicide by travelling to any of these places on my own. After realizing this was the only way to determine land title, and that travel to these offices was impossible for me or the Iraqis in the Real Estate Branch at MOD, I asked the Navy captain and the head of MODTT, David Murtagh, if they could meet with me to discuss this issue. I told them the Iraqis I advised could not travel to the provincial Land Registration Offices because they had no means to get to them, but the Coalition did. I asked the captain if he could assist me in this regard. I thought being a US Navy captain, and a primary MNSTC-I staff officer, he could arrange transportation for the Iraqis at MOD, who he was building these installations for. I told him he would be helping himself by helping the Iraqis determine land ownership, so his construction projects would have clear land title beneath them. I thought he would jump at the idea. Instead, he refused to assist me in any way. David Murtagh was no help at all because the captain wasn't receptive to the idea. Months went by with no resolution to this problem, yet J-7 continued to construct camps for the Ministry of Defense without determination of clear property rights and title. If the United States is supposed to be instilling democracy and the "rule of law" in Iraq, doesn't it make sense to have clear title to property before building on it—with US money? Of course it does, but the Navy captain couldn't have cared less.

I am convinced he would not have anything to do with my request because it was coming from a civilian contractor. If the exact same request had been made by a military officer he would have reacted in a completely different way. I saw this every day in Iraq. Anything said to a military person by a civilian got a completely different response than if the same thing was said by someone in the military. You would think this wasn't the case with reservists, who had just put on a uniform the month before they got to Iraq, because they were civilians in "real life." Not so. They were worse. We were from different worlds. There was absolutely no respect shown by the military on MNSTC-I staff toward its civilian advisors. And we were there to help the military at MNSTC-I do their jobs. I heard guys I worked with, who had been advisors to the US military at other locations, say they had never before experienced the disdain they received from the military at MNSTC-I.

A couple of years before, Paul Bremer had transferred all land owned by the Iraqi government under the Saddam Hussein regime over to the new Iraqi Ministry of Finance. He did this in order to place under one roof all assets of financial value owned by the Iraqi government. I had already discovered CPA Regulation #67, which stated all former Ministry of Defense land reverted from the new Ministry of Finance over to the new Ministry of Defense "as needed." I thought this would solve the land ownership problem of former MOD-owned camps, but when I asked the MNSTC-I Staff Judge Advocate (SJA, or "JAG") for a legal opinion of this CPA regulation, I was not able to get one. The job of the SJA was to advise MNSTC-I and its staff in all legal matters. If land title wasn't a legal matter, what was it? The colonel in charge of the SJA office put a lieutenant colonel on it, but he wasn't able to get anything done, although he did put some effort into it. I never got a definitive legal opinion from the JAG the entire time I was in Iraq assigned to MNSTC-I. It wasn't until the new MODTT legal advisor from my company arrived in Iraq that I finally got an answer. The civilian advisors were able to get things done the US military couldn't, or wouldn't, do themselves.

As always with MNSTC-I, months went by without a clear answer to this question. Because I couldn't get a straight answer from the MNSTC-I Staff Judge Advocate on MOD land title per CPA #67, I continued to work alone with the MOD real estate staff to determine land ownership of old MOD camps. The only method we could come up with to determine land ownership for new camps was travelling to the provincial Land Registration Offices, but the MOD staff I advised had no means of getting to them. And there was no way I could get there myself without the support of David Murtagh and his Chief of Staff, a US Army lieutenant colonel.

I was once asked by an Iraqi Brigadier General to assist him in developing a plan for the new Ministry of Defense headquarters building. The best location we could come up with was at Kademia, where the former Iraqi military intelligence command had been located. This was where all the tortures and executions under the Saddam regime took place. Kademia (also called Kazimiyah) is a point on the west bank of the Tigris River where the Imams Bridge (also called Aimma Bridge) is located. This is the bridge that connects Shi'ite and Sunni neighborhoods on opposite sides of the river from each other. In 2005 a pilgrimage was going across the bridge and a stampede began, killing over 1,000 people. I was supposed to go to Kademia to survey the location for the new headquarters building, but the MODTT Chief of Staff wouldn't let me go. He said it wasn't safe. The entire time the MODTT Chief of Staff was in Iraq, which was less than his required 12 month tour, he never left the IZ. But he wouldn't let me do my job by going there. Saddam Hussein was hanged at Kademia.

We weren't able to get a clear answer to the ownership of former MOD-owned camps until the new MODTT legal advisor came along, so the Ministry of Defense real estate staff appeared to come up with their own solution. They listed all old MOD camps in a memo that they sent it to the Minister of Defense, Abdul Qadir, requesting his approval for these locations to be placed in MOD's name. The Minister signed two of these memos. This method seemed to work, but the Iraqi Ministry of Finance (MOF) found out what MOD was doing and stopped it. MOF would not allow anything to be done without being in control of the situation, even if someone else came up with a system that worked. And with the jerk who was the IRMO advisor to the Ministry of Finance not willing to meet me, working with MOF was out of the question.

Later, MNSTC-I's J-5 and J-7 came up with their own joint memo, which was a "copy cat" of the Iraqi's two memos written earlier. This was the only time the US followed the lead of the Iraqis on anything. Their memo, which was signed by LTG Dempsey, was sent directly to the Minister of Defense, Abdul Qadir, for his approval. The memo listed dozens of *new* camps (not former MOD camps) J-7 planned to construct for the Iraqi army for the Prime Minister's Initiative, and it wanted to use the same technique the MOD Real Estate Branch had used by asking Abdul Qadir for his approval to have title for the land automatically put in MOD's name. If J-7 had collaborated with me and the MOD Real Estate Branch, instead of working completely on its own, we could have gotten Abdul Qadir's signature on the memo. I was never told of the memo, but I was identified in it as the primary point of contact for the Minister! What was interesting about this memo was it constituted an admission by J-7 that land ownership was indeed something that had to be determined for locations where it planned to build camps for the Iraqi military. How could J-7 act like land title didn't mean anything, including my request of the Navy captain in charge of it to provide travel for me and the Iraqis to the Land Registration Offices, when he had this memo written, signed by his commanding general, and delivered to the Iraqi Minister of Defense? He wouldn't have anything to do with my request for travel to the Land Registration Offices, which would help him do his job—legally—but turned around and wrote this memo and put me down as the point of contact on the issue without having the professional courtesy to tell me.

Because J-7, together with J-5, wrote the memo on their own and never went through the Ministry of Defense real estate staff, that I advised, we were never able to track it down to find out if it was signed and approved by Abdul Qadir. Even though I was listed as the point of contact in the memo, I was never asked for my assistance on how to best handle it within the Ministry and get it signed by the Minister of

Defense. It involved the area I was the primary advisor to the Ministry of Defense for, yet J-7 wrote it and didn't even tell me about it.

When the Navy captain in charge of J-7 was replaced by another one, I explained the J-7/J-5 memo to him and handed him a copy. A short time later he and I met with Brigadier General Wolff to discuss it, as it had General Dempsey's signature on it and General Wolff wanted to know what had happened to it. But the main reason for the meeting was because General Wolff was leaving Iraq and needed to close the loop on the issue. Why did it take his departure to do this? I provided General Wolff and the new Navy captain in charge of J-7 with copies of the memo, with all the supporting documents, even though I hadn't written it but the J-7 staff had. The meeting ended with no further action or decision from General Wolff. He was leaving for a fat job back in Washington, so what did he care. More weeks went by while we tried to find out where the memo was at MOD. One evening I was called into the new Navy captain's office. He was going over the memo line-by-line, and was crapping in his pants. He had been ordered by LTG Dempsey to report on the status of the memo immediately (e.g., the status of land J-7 was illegally constructing MOD bases on), and had discovered at least half the locations listed on it had changed because J-7 was building camps somewhere else. He was just finding out the list didn't match what he was building for MOD. If he had looked at the memo when I handed it to him in General Wolff's office he would have known what his staff was (and was not) building for the Iraqis before being called into LTG Dempsey's office. It was bad enough JHQTT, J-7, and the rest of MNSTC-I did everything on their own and never consulted with anyone else. But the Navy captain didn't even know what his own staff was doing. Being an MOD real estate issue, if J-7 had included me and the MOD Real Estate Branch in what it was doing for the ministry, we could have worked together to come up with an accurate list of locations where J-7 needed to build Iraqi camps, and collaborated on getting clear title. But more important, J-7 could have gotten help from the MOD Real Estate Branch on the best locations for new camps based the institutional knowledge of the MOD staff and their years of experience. Instead, J-7 created its own problem by doing things completely on its own, and not including me or the MOD Real Estate Branch on anything it did, or was planning to do, for the ministry. Yet here was the J-7 Navy captain asking me what camps were on his own memo and what camps weren't. If the captain had bothered to look at the memo when I gave it to him in the meeting with General Wolff, he would have covered his butt when LTG Dempsey finally started to make this an issue right before his departure, just like General Wolff had done before him. Of course, that was the only reason LTG Dempsey was making it an issue then—he was getting ready to leave and finally decided to tie up a few lose ends before he headed back to the States and a guaranteed fourth star on his collar. If asked at a Congressional hearing if he had done anything on this issue, he would be able to say that he had. Of course he hadn't, but he could cover himself by saying that, technically, he had.

If there had been any sort of coordination, cooperation, and collaboration between J-7 and MODTT this never would have happened. The Navy captain was constructing camps for MOD, and didn't even look at the memo I had given him weeks before listing where these camps were going—and his own staff had written the memo prior to his arrival in Iraq. Simple common sense would have told him he should read a memo his staff had written prior to his arrival in Iraq, because he was now responsible for what it said. But it was given to him by me, a contractor, so he didn't give a damn about it. I would bet that's why he never read it. The memo was now obsolete and full of errors, yet it was still floating around MOD for the Minister's signature. I was standing in front of his desk while the captain called in members of his staff to ask them about the locations listed in the memo. His deputy, the Navy commander, was also there and said that both he and his captain had just received the memo, which was bullshit. The captain had never looked at the memo before that day, and wouldn't acknowledge I had given him a copy of it at the meeting with BG Wolff. The fact that I had given it to him and he ignored it didn't make a bit of difference to him. But it should have. He was visibly freaking out over the list on the memo. It was written by his office and was signed by his boss, the MNSTC-I commander and a three star general, who was finally paying attention to the huge problem concerning land for MOD camps—all created by his organization. I figured LTG Dempsey had probably just woken up to the fact that MOD camps were being built on land the ministry didn't own, which I had been telling anyone who would listen for a year. He was probably also getting heat from the State Department and DoD in Washington over J-7's failure to get the documents signed by MOD to close the books on all the money that had been spent to build Iraqi army camps and individual facilities. The chickens were finally coming home to roost. For all I know J-7 is still constructing military installations for the Iraqi Ministry of Defense without any proof of land title in the name of the Ministry. Who knows how many individual projects have been signed for by MOD and MOI of the thousands J-7 has constructed for them over the past five years? It may have gotten these documents signed by now, but it's about five years late. But even if these documents have all been signed, what difference does it make if the projects don't have clear title to the land they were built on? What does J-7 or MNSTC-I care about that? By their actions, not at all. Everything J-7 did was a violation of Iraqi property law, and ran counter to the United States' intent of "transition" from Coalition control to Iraq's responsibility for its own destiny—under rules of law we are supposed to be following. It was also piss poor accountability of US Government funds on a grand scale.

About 10 months into my tour I was told by the Deputy Chief of J-7, the Mississippi school teacher, that General Dempsey had gotten word of all the claims for land that had been illegally taken from its rightful owners, essentially by J-7. According to the J-7 deputy, LTG Dempsey ordered a halt to all Ministry of Interior construction projects being done by J-7. When I heard this I was pleasantly surprised LTG Dempsey was finally taking action on this important issue. I assumed a similar order would be coming down from LTG Dempsey regarding Ministry of Defense construction projects too. But I never heard a thing about this. J-7 was doing the exact same thing regarding the illegal taking of land for both MOI and MOD projects, but a "cease work" order never came down regarding MOD projects. J-7 simply continued building camps for MOD like it was business as usual, and never even stopped to address the land taking issue for MOD camps in anticipation of a similar order coming down from LTG Dempsey. It was as though J-7 was going to keep taking land illegally for the construction of MOD camps until it got caught and ordered to stop by LTG Dempsey. And J-7 was commanded by a US Navy Captain. It was bizarre.

Because Paul Bremer had transferred all Iraqi government-owned land to the new Ministry of Finance, I attempted for months to meet with the snob at IRMO who was the US State Department liaison to the Iraqi Ministry of Finance. I have already mentioned my attempts to meet with him. The point is, there was no one within MNSTC-I who would assist in any way with the issue of land title or the rule of law associated with it. No one cared. But MNSTC-I kept rolling along with its camps for both the Ministry of Defense and the Ministry of Interior as if land ownership in Iraq didn't mean a thing. If this was so, why did the US Army Corps of Engineers go through all its efforts to secure land leases needed to build the Forward Operating Bases (FOB's) for the Coalition during the initial phases of the war? Why did J-7 and J-5 write the memo sent to Abdul Qadir? If private land ownership didn't exist, the Corps sure wasted a lot of time. The fact is it does exist in Iraq, but MNSTC-I just didn't give a damn—until I showed up and became a pebble in J-7's shoe.

When J-7 built a camp for the Iraqi military it constructed many buildings on the installation, each one being a stand-alone project for accounting purposes. Not only was there a land ownership issue associated with the new camps J-7 built, there was also an issue with the transfer of all these individual buildings over to the Iraqi Ministry of Defense. I hadn't been in Iraq a month when J-7 showed me a typical "transfer package" for a project it had built, and was asked for my opinion. I told J-7 the documents were too complicated and had too much extraneous material for the Iraqis to understand. I was told by J-7 the packages were not going to change. In other words, I was asked for my opinion but J-7 had no intention of changing the package. I had been hired for my real estate experience, which was over 20 years, to include a decade with the US General Services Administration. In addition to my experience, I was the Real Estate Advisor to the Iraq Ministry of Defense, who J-7 was building these projects for. It would stand to reason J-7 would want my opinion of the packages that it wanted my client to sign, so it could get these projects off its books. Hell, they asked for my opinion. But in the end my opinion meant nothing to them because it was contrary to the way they wanted to do things. My opinion counted in this as much as it counted for everything else. So much for being the real estate advisor to J-7's client, the MOD, and for being a "subject matter expert" in the real estate and facilities field. J-7 didn't care a bit. They just asked me for the hell of it. And the original idea of creating the position I was in had started with two officers from J-7 prior to its takeover by the Navy captain who was in charge of J-7 when I arrived. He wanted nothing to do with contractors on the MNSTC-I staff who were outside of his own J-7 staff, most of who were reserve Navy and Air Force officers who shouldn't have been in their jobs in the first place. A land war should be fought by a land force, to include all of its engineering and construction. US Army engineers know how to do these things, Navy and Air Force engineers don't. Air Force engineers build hangers, and Navy engineers build docks. You wouldn't ask an Army officer to fly a plane or steer a boat, so why would you ask a Navy or Air Force officer to construct an army camp in a desert in the middle of a land war. But that's our new and improved "joint force" way of doing things now. It's all PC nonsense. The pathetic (almost sickening) comment made by US Air Force General Allardice to the US Army full colonel, or the Marines not allowing US Army aircraft to fly into "its airspace" in Anbar Province, say all there is about how well the joint force concept really works. The military services got along better before. At least they all knew where they stood with each other instead of the touchy-feely "one team" garbage being shoved down their throats now. But don't ask a senior ranking officer what he thinks about it. You know what the answer will be. I'm sure MG Allardice would say it's a pleasure working with the US Army. And the Marines would say they just love working with everyone.

Around May 2007 the old J-7 staff was rotating out and being replaced by new staff, again all military reservists, again a new crop of people who didn't know facilities or real estate. But like their predecessors they all wore uniforms, so civilians didn't count. Another US Navy captain in the civil engineers was the new chief, and a Navy commander his deputy (mentioned above.) One day I found out there was going to be a meeting with the two staffs, about 10 minutes before it started, and I asked if I could attend. The purpose of the meeting was to discuss the Iraqi's signing for hundreds of these individual MOD projects, the same ones I offered to help J-7 get Iraqi signatures for 10 months earlier. The outgoing J-7 staff was in a panic to get these packages signed because LTG Dempsey, who was leaving in about two weeks, had ordered them to get this done. (LTG Dempsey should have been all over this a year earlier, but had done nothing.) A lieutenant colonel from the old J-7 staff said nothing had been done to get these packages signed and closed out. As he said this to the new staff he looked right at me. When he did this I told the whole group the MOD Real Estate Branch had been ready to help J-7 get this done for nearly a year. I wanted to make it very clear to the outgoing group, and their replacements, that the MOD Real Estate Branch (later Division) had been ready to help J-7 in this area all along, and the failure to get anything done was not the fault of MOD or its staff. In other words, don't even think of pinning the blame for this screw up on me or my client. Getting these documents signed wasn't my responsibility, it was J-7's. I had been trying to help J-7 get its documents signed for a nearly a year. Now I was getting the blame for this mess in front of the new crew because I was a contractor, and an easy target. That's what contractors are for. We should get "blame bonuses."

But the best part was after the meeting itself. I was told by the outgoing J-7 staff the packages were just being assembled by J-7's contractors. For the first time I was being told the contractors who built the facilities for J-7 had never provided the paperwork to assemble the packages for Iraqi signature. I was hearing for the first time that J-7 hadn't been able to assemble the packages for the Iraqis to sign, for projects going back nearly three years, because it couldn't get its own US contractors to provide the needed paperwork. This should have been required in their contracts with J-7. If it was, J-7 wasn't doing anything to ensure the paperwork was provided. If it wasn't included, the contracts J-7 executed with its contractors were seriously flawed. In all the years I have been in commercial real estate and construction, I have never heard of a project where the General Contractor does not provide all the documents and plans the client needs for its own purposes, and for the work the client contracted them to do. This is always written into the contract. Yet this was how all of J-7's projects were being executed. There was no routine provision of paperwork given to J-7 by its contractors, all of whom were American firms that had to know the requirements for submission of documents needed by their client. But then, J-7 may have never specified what it needed until years after the projects had begun. J-7 had to ask all its contractors to go back three years or more and provide the paperwork needed to close out projects it was managing on behalf of the US Government, in the billions of dollars. If I owned the US construction company that built the facilities at Ur, I wouldn't want to turn in the paperwork either! The problem was that J-7 was letting them get away with it.

This is an example of J-7's gross mismanagement of its projects and failure to properly account for the expenditure of US Government funds. Among all the staff working at J-7, there were at least two lieutenant colonels and a major whose job it was to manage the task of closing out these projects, yet the job couldn't get accomplished. When the initial group of J-7 staff was leaving, I witnessed five officers get the Bronze Star medal. Two of them were the officers who were responsible for closing out these projects. Another one was the officer responsible for building all the MOD bases on land the Ministry didn't own, and the hundreds of individual facilities on them.

The entire time I was in Iraq I asked J-7 to provide me with plans and documentation for the camps they had built for the Ministry of Defense, so that I could provide the MOD real estate staff with this information for its files and database. After all, the camps were built for their Ministry. I was never able to get any of this information except for two or three camps, and in those few cases the drawings were single sheets with a basic CAD (computer aided design) sketch, nothing more. I was actually told by a reserve US Army lieutenant colonel, one of the new bumper crop of J-7 staff, that there were no such files in existence. In other words, J-7 had contracted out to several American construction companies to have hundreds of facilities and dozens of camps built for the Iraqi Ministry of Defense, over a period of at least three years, yet the contractors who had performed the work never provided any of the drawings to their client, J-7. And to the best of my knowledge J-7 had never asked for it! I don't know if it was a J-7 requirement for the contractors to provide this, but it certainly should have been. I have never heard of a construction project being done where the General Contractor is not required to provide the client with multiple sets of drawings of the project, to include all architectural drawings for future use in case of alterations, renovations, etc. Based on this lapse alone, it was obvious J-7 had no concept of basic construction project management. I honestly believe because this was Iraq, J-7 just didn't give a damn about any of this, or simply wasn't aware of standard real estate and construction industry practices. Either way, it was inexcusable.

It was clear to me J-7 was inept in managing large scale construction projects and that, in reality, the entire staff were rank amateurs. No one on the J-7 staff had anything near the experience required to do what they were responsible for doing on behalf of the Iraqi Ministry of Defense. But that same staff wouldn't listen to any advice that was offered to help perform its services better for its client, the Ministry of Defense. I had over 20 years of experience doing this work and was hired, or so I thought, for my expertise in these areas. Yet when I arrived in Iraq I was marginalized by J-7, by my British boss David Murtagh, and in general ignored because I didn't wear a uniform.

By the time I left Iraq in September 2007, about 20 of these individual J-7 projects had been signed for by the Ministry of Defense, which showed some progress. These were 20 individual buildings, not 20 camps or military installations. These were 20 buildings out of roughly 300 that J-7 had built for MOD, and it had built at least 2,000 for MOI. But many more could have been signed for and accepted by MOD if J-7 had been on top of its contractors for the required documentation related to these projects. And, if J-7 and I could have worked together to get the Iraqis from MOD to these locations to inspect them, we could have gotten their signatures to close out the books. I was willing to, but J-7 wasn't. Unfortunately, the Navy captain in charge of J-7 would have nothing to do with the concept of cooperation, and he passed on this attitude to his successor. Along with the difficulty traveling to the Land Registration Offices to determine land ownership, travel was also needed for the Iraqis to get to these hundreds of projects J-7 had built for them, all with US funds, so the Iraqis could sign for their turnover and acceptance by the Iraqi Ministry of Defense. It seemed logical and rational to me that if J-7 was spending billions of US dollars to construct these facilities, and it required the Iraqis to sign for them, why not pay a little money to get them there to inspect the facilities. But no, this was out of the question for J-7, specifically the two Navy captains who ran it while I was there, who for some odd reason would have nothing to do with this solution to their problem. Instead, they blocked every attempt to get the Iraqis to these sites. And this was all in addition to the transfer of old Coalition FOB's to Iraqi control, which involved the real property staff of MNF-I and MNC-I. I couldn't get anywhere with them either.

I felt as though I was the only one who cared about getting any of these tasks done, yet they were J-7's responsibility, especially title to land and MOD signatures on transfer packages. The latter was a requirement of the Coalition and finance officials within the US Embassy. The Navy captains were incapable of doing their jobs using the most basic construction industry practices, not to mention any semblance of the rule of law. I don't know for certain, but I can only imagine the first of the two Navy captains was awarded the Silver Star upon departing Iraq. I say this because all of his senior officers were awarded the Bronze Star when they left. It is customary for the commander to get the next higher medal. All these awards were given out to these officers, yet in a year they couldn't even get a stack of paperwork signed to close the books on the expenditure of billions of US tax dollars

J-7 placed itself in a dilemma because it wanted the Iraqis from MOD to sign for hundreds of projects, yet refused to transport them to the same projects for the simple purpose of inspecting them before they signed for them. The Iraqis told me, and I passed this on to J-7, that they had no problem signing for the projects but would not do so unless they saw them first. I told J-7 the Iraqis had every right to inspect these facilities before they signed for and took possession of them. J-7 didn't see it that way. It wanted the Iraqis from MOD to sign for hundreds of projects (J-7 was just getting the paperwork from the contractors who built them) but would not let them see the projects first. This was ridiculous. At one meeting between a lieutenant colonel from J-7 and the Iraqi Director of Real Estate, a 2-star general, he asked if Google satellite photographs would be acceptable for the Iraqis' inspection of these facilities. I almost started laughing.

One of the main Iraqi camps in Baghdad that had to be turned over and signed for by the Iraqi Ministry of Defense was FOB Honor. FOB Honor was located on the grounds of one of Saddam Hussein's government complexes in the center of Baghdad and the International

Zone (IZ). This was the site of the ziggurat-shaped (pyramid-shaped) Council of Ministers building that was bombed and shown in flames the opening night of the war. The camp was the home of the 5th Brigade of the 6th Division of the Iraqi army, whose mission was the defense of that sector of Baghdad. J-7 had constructed 19 new buildings on FOB Honor for the purpose of providing barracks and office space for the brigade. Because the Ministry of Defense building, located across Haifa Street from FOB Honor, was so overcrowded the Ministry decided to take several of these new buildings away from the 5th Brigade and use them for its own needs. Regardless, all 19 buildings had to be signed for by MOD, just like the hundreds of other buildings J-7 had constructed for the Ministry of Defense throughout Iraq. Again, I told J-7 that I would assist in getting MOD to sign for the buildings. The funny thing was, every time I made an offer to help J-7 they would say OK, but when it came time to actually take me up on it J-7 was not around.

The Ministry of Defense wanted to begin moving people into the buildings on FOB Honor it had taken away from the 5th Brigade, but J-7 insisted they sign for them before taking occupancy. J-7 was finally figuring out the Iraqis had to conduct their inspection before signing for facilities it had built for them. Then the Iraqis could take possession of the keys to the front door and move their soldiers in. It was about time. In the past buildings and camps had been completed and the Iraqis had occupied them without J-7 getting their signature of acceptance first, which was one of the many problems J-7 was having yet taking no steps whatever to address. The Iraqis would say the buildings were in terrible shape, but J-7 would reply saying the Iraqis had moved in and trashed them. It was a Catch-22. The Iraqis even admitted their soldiers had trashed the buildings, but the Ministry of Defense would not sign for them unless Ministry representatives went and inspected them, even though Iraqi soldiers who were nearby had occupied the facilities. J-7 tried to get local Iraqi commanders at the camps to sign for them, but many would not, claiming that it wasn't their responsibility. It would always go back to the Ministry of Defense needing to sign for them, which it would not do unless its own representative had seen the camps and made the recommendation to accept them. But then J-7 wouldn't take any responsibility to get the Ministry's representatives there to look at them.

That was the only way J-7 was going to get the Ministry's signatures on the documents, as I tried to tell them, but it would not take the necessary steps to get this done. It was a relatively simple problem, but J-7 wouldn't move to correct it. All J-7 had to do was say, "OK, we will transport Iraqis from the Ministry of Defense to every camp and location we have built for them so they can inspect and sign for the facilities. It will take time, but we've been constructing facilities for three years and we don't have signatures for anything yet, so let's just do it!" Not these two US Navy captains. These men were both Captains in the US Navy, which is just below the rank of Admiral. They were primary staff officers to a 3-star general in combat. Yet they could not arrange for air support or ground convoy for their client, the Iraqi Ministry of Defense, to inspect what they had built for it, with US money. They could have if they cared to. But the suggestions were coming from a contractor, so they meant nothing to them. They just continued to procrastinate and talk about the problem, but wouldn't do anything about it. It was entirely MOD's right to send official representatives to inspect any facilities J-7 wanted it to sign for, regardless of whether the facilities had been occupied by the Iraqi army or not. All MOD wanted was one of its representatives to see the facilities first, and not take acceptance of it based on a Google Earth satellite photograph. MOD knew that once it signed for anything J-7 was off the hook and it (MOD) was then responsible for it. J-7 wanted MOD to sign for all of these facilities sight-unseen, which the Iraqis simply would not do. Under US law, when a person occupies a vacant building they often assume possession and responsibility for it. But this was Iraq, and that's the way MOD wanted to do things. As far as MOD was concerned, until they signed for these facilities, they belonged to the US Government. In Iraq, the signature of the person with authority is the only thing that matters. Ownership by mere occupancy of a building means nothing to them. The US (J-7) could just wait until the person with the authority to sign for the buildings was willing to. J-7 just refused to listen and insisted on doing things its own way, not MOD's. The two Navy captains should have paid attention when they attended their Total Quality Management courses back in the early 1990's—"Listen to what the customer is saying." But they were captains in the US Navy, and this was Iraq. Screw the customer. They should have gone into business with the guy who installed the generator behind the MOD building.

Many of these J-7 constructed projects had been occupied by Iraqi soldiers for three years, or had been trashed or looted by locals if they hadn't been occupied by the Iraqi army. Yet J-7 never made the effort to get the Iraqis to sign for them by doing what was needed to make this happen. It never addressed this issue, yet when I suggested getting the Iraqis to these locations J-7 discounted it out of hand. But it couldn't come up with any other way to get the Iraqis to sign for these projects. Like I've said earlier, if my suggestion to transport the Iraqis had come from someone wearing a uniform, I bet the Navy captains in charge of J-7 would have said, "Great idea! Let's do it." Instead J-7 made excuses.

To add to the problem, not only were these facilities constructed by J-7 without any proper turnover or signature to close out the books for the US Government, there were no maintenance plans put into place by J-7 after the facilities and camps were built. The Iraqis would move in with no formal turnover, their soldiers would trash the place, and the Iraqi camp engineer would not, or could not, do anything to maintain it. There is a huge cultural difference between the way Americans and Iraqis live, but if these camps were being built with US money there should have been a maintenance plan, and associated funding, included in the project budget. This had never been done by J-7. Instead, a camp would be built by J-7 (without any clear title to the land it was built on), never formally turned over and signed for by the Ministry of Defense, and the place would be practically destroyed by the Iraqi soldiers who moved in, all without a budget or a plan for the Iraqis to maintain it. The result was hundreds US-funded facilities that were not fit for human occupancy within only a few months, and with no proper close-out of the funding documents to reconcile the US dollars spent. It was a sloppy seat-of-the-pants operation by J-7, which was no better than the Iraqis at getting anything done by commercial real estate and construction industry standards. J-7 had no concept of land title, property rights, facility management, preventive maintenance, construction contracting, record and document control, or final inspection and close-out. Nothing. When I tried to help J-7 get these tasks done for the projects it had built for my client, MOD, it blew me off.

I was trying to coordinate the inspection of the 19 buildings at FOB Honor with J-7. After a couple of missed opportunities to get the inspections done, we finally decided on a day and time for the Iraqis from MOD to meet with the J-7 staff and the American contractor who had constructed the buildings. On the appointed day I assembled about six Iraqis, which was itself a monumental task, and was ready to bring them to FOB Honor. At the last minute we were informed the MOD Secretary General, the second ranking person in the Ministry of Defense, had issued a memorandum directing that a "committee" be formed for the inspections. The Iraqis could not do anything without first forming a committee to analyze and discuss the issue. It was one of the most frustrating things we had to contend with when dealing with them. Iraqis can't make a decision if their lives depend on it. They need to form a committee to go to the bathroom. As a result, the inspection was postponed until the following day. I e-mailed Mr. Saad, an Iraqi expatriate in the J-7 office, of the change and we both agreed the inspection would be the following morning at 10 am. At 10 am the next day I arrived with several Iraqis to conduct the inspection, but no one from J-7 was there. About 15 minutes later a vehicle showed up and a US Air Force major from J-7, and another Iraqi ex-pat from J-7, got out. The major said he didn't know anything about the inspection until 10 minutes earlier and was told by someone on the J-7 staff to get over to FOB Honor right away. I found out later the major was the Project Manager for all the 19 buildings! If he was the Project Manager how could he not have known about the inspection until 10 minutes before? I then asked him if he knew where the General Contractor was, and he said he had no idea. I had worked extremely hard to get this inspection to happen, in order to help J-7 and the Iraqis clear up the paperwork on the FOB Honor buildings, yet J-7 didn't even show up for the inspection of its own project. This was after J-7 had suddenly begun to make a big deal about the Iraqis signing for projects it had built for them, especially on FOB Honor. I asked where Mr. Saad was, and was told he had been ordered by his boss, the Navy captain in charge of J-7, onto something else. I could not believe Mr. Saad wasn't there, as he had told me he was in charge of the turnover of all the J-7 projects. If he was in charge, then where was he? He knew of this inspection, yet he went off and did something else. I realized J-7 didn't care at all about the inspection, so I told the J-7 major I was going back to MOD with the Iraqis and we left. When I returned to my office I sent an e-mail to the Navy captain in charge of J-7 explaining what had happened, and I copied the MNSTC-I Chief of Staff, a US Army full colonel, because I thought he should be made aware.

A few weeks later I was called into the office of the newly arrived Chief of Staff of MODTT, the organization I worked in. She was a US Army lieutenant colonel who had just arrived in Iraq to replace her predecessor, who was leaving after spending less than his full year there. His wife probably told him to get home because she needed help with the laundry.

The outgoing MODTT Chief of Staff had been in Iraq for about 10 months, and when he first arrived he and I had a conversation where he openly spoke about how he did not want to be in Iraq, did not agree with the war, and only wanted to be with his family in New Jersey. He had no problem telling people he did not want to be serving in Iraq, yet he was a career Army officer. Well, at least he was speaking his mind. While he was in Iraq he was selected for command of a line signal battalion back in the States when he returned. Instead, he turned it down and requested command of a training battalion. If he commanded a signal battalion, he was afraid he would get sent back to Iraq. He was not a good leader and had no business speaking about his personal feelings on the war, or his desire to be at home with his family rather than serving his country in combat. When I was in the Army the chance to command a line battalion was like gold. No one wanted to command a training battalion, with the responsibility of dealing with new recruits off the street. But this officer had no problem with this because he was not the leader in the "old school" sense. He was a modern day officer who just wanted to hold onto his wife's apron strings rather than command a line signal battalion. (He was a Signal Corps officer, which is the US Army's communications branch. He was not a combat soldier, or leader. He was a techie.) I was told he would get up in the middle of the night, waking his roommate, to talk to his wife at length over his computer voice hookup. What did he care if he woke up his roommate. He had to talk to his wife.

When she called me into her office, the new MODTT Chief of Staff handed me a Letter of Reprimand that had been written by her predecessor before he left Iraq two weeks earlier. The letter was being given to me because I had "violated" its probationary period. (I will discuss this in detail below.) The previous Chief of Staff had never given it to me. The letter was the result of several e-mails that had been sent to him from the J-7 staff. They related to the inspection at FOB Honor, that J-7 had blown off, as well as anything else I had done they didn't like. The Navy captain in charge of J-7, and his deputy, must have gotten their staff together after I e-mailed the MNSTC-I Chief of Staff about the FOB Honor inspection. These two senior officers likely ordered their people to write these e-mails to the MODTT Chief of Staff for the purpose of discrediting me and placing me in a negative light to my chain of command at MODTT. How else could a handful of e-mails, all from the J-7 staff, show up on the desk of the MODTT Chief of Staff at the same time? If true, this would constitute collusion on the part of United States military officers to discredit a US civilian contractor who was trying to do his job, a job he had been sent to Iraq to do by his employer, a DoD contractor, at the request of MNSTC-I and J-7.

This action, on the part of a US Navy captain and a commander, would constitute command influence over their subordinates for the purpose of discrediting me in retaliation for bringing to the attention of the MNSTC-I Chief of Staff the poor way in which J-7, specifically the captain, was managing its construction projects for the Ministry of Defense. When I sent my e-mail to the MNSTC-I Chief of Staff, the Navy captain in charge of J-7 most likely felt the need to protect himself by ordering his staff to write their e-mails to make me look bad, when all I was doing was my job, which was not what he wanted me to do. By doing my job I was highlighting flaws in the way J-7 was doing business which the captain in charge of J-7, and the captain before him, did not like. My job was to advise the Iraqi Ministry of Defense on its real estate issues, which were being adversely affected by the sloppy way J-7 was executing its mission to construct facilities for my client, MOD. J-7 blowing off the inspection at FOB Honor was the last straw for me, which is why I sent the e-mail to the MNSTC-I Chief of Staff. I had an obligation to bring to the MNSTC-I Chief of Staff's attention problems one of his staff sections was creating for my client. Anything less and I wasn't doing my job.

The US Air Force Center for Environmental Excellence, or AFCEE (which has been changed to the Air Force Center for Engineering and the Environment) is the Air Force equivalent of the US Army Corps of Engineers. J-7 uses AFCEE exclusively to provide contract management services for all of its construction projects in Iraq. When J-7 decides it is going to build a camp for the Iraqi military, it does not go to the Ministry of Defense Director General for Infrastructure, which is the engineering and real estate staff of the Ministry. Instead, J-7 plans to build a camp based on information it receives from MNSTC-I J-5 (Plans), which has decided where the camps are going to be placed, with minimal input from the Iraqi military. This entire process is contrary to the ideal of "transition" by the Coalition to Iraqi control of its own destiny and its ability to defend itself. In reality, J-5 would select new locations for Iraqi military camps, the Joint Headquarters Transition Team (JHQTT) would determine what Iraqi units would be stationed there, and J-7 would build it. I tried to get J-5 and J-7 to involve the Iraqis more, but was ignored.

J-7 would turn to the AFCEE Contracting Officer who sat in the same office as the J-7 staff, which eliminated any pretense of separation of responsibilities, and AFCEE would in turn go to its designated American construction companies to get the work done. It was AFCEE who was responsible for awarding the contracts to have all of the Ministry of Defense's camps built, but it was J-7 who ordered AFCEE to do it. By contrast, when Operation Iraqi Freedom first started in the spring of 2003, the US Army Corps of Engineers Gulf Region District (GRD) came to Iraq and actually secured the land from its Iraqi owners needed for the Forward Operating Bases, or FOBs, to locate Coalition troops for the warfight. The Corps of Engineers did the footwork and acquired title, or in most cases leased the land needed for these FOBs. By the time I arrived in Iraq GRD was gearing down, as all the FOBs that were needed for Coalition units for the initial warfight had long since been built. Now it was MNSTC-I's mission to reverse what Paul Bremer had done when he disbanded the Iraqi military and national police, and get the new Ministries of Defense and Interior on their feet and operational.

But instead of doing what the Corps of Engineers had done by securing title or leasehold interest in the land needed for the Coalition's FOBs, J-7 was simply ignoring this step entirely before it began building military camps and facilities for the Iraqi Ministries of Defense and Interior. When it turned to AFCEE to issue its construction contracts, the same thing happened. Not only was J-7 failing to secure land title for its construction projects, AFCEE was failing to make sure the contracts it awarded didn't have a "cloud" over them, meaning a legal flaw in the contract that would open it to dispute later on. If not having clear title to the land a project was being built on didn't open J-7, the United States Government, and the Iraqi Ministry of Defense to a future lawsuit, what did? But neither J-7 nor AFCEE cared a bit. I really don't think they even understood the implications of it all. When I tried to get J-7 to pay attention to the land ownership issue (before I even knew about the work the Corps of Engineers had done in this area prior to my arrival) I was brushed off by both the Navy captain and David Murtagh. Neither of them cared at all about the issue of Iraqi land ownership or property rights, but the US Army Corps of Engineers certainly did. It is interesting to note that one of the US contractors I met in Iraq actually told me AFCEE was liked by the contractors there because it wasn't a "big bloated bureaucracy like the Corps of Engineers," and was "lean and got things done" as a result. Real "lean," especially securing legal title for the land MOD camps were built on.

If J-7 was going to build all of MOD's installations with US money, and not allow MOD to build their own, then it had the responsibility to make sure AFCEE's contracts were legally sufficient and adhered to the Federal Acquisition Regulations—the FAR. In addition, J-7 was responsible for ensuring all that was needed to properly execute the construction of an Iraqi military camp was included in the Scope of Work of the AFCEE contracts. AFCEE was a contracting arm of the United States Government, and it had Contracting Officers who were warranted to sign contracts on the US Government's behalf that adhered to the FAR. After all, the contracts it was awarding were being paid for with US Treasury money. They were US Government contracts. It was J-7's responsibility to ensure land ownership was the first thing that was addressed when it planned for a new camp, before the first shovel was put in the ground. This was needed so the contracts to build the camps, and the money spent for them (US dollars), would not be encumbered later with un-clear title to the land upon which these facilities were built. In the States this would cause the entire project to end up in court. But what did J-7 know about any of this? It made no attempt whatsoever to do things correctly. Instead, J-7 operated as if it was building a house in the United States and not securing title to the land first, not caring at all what might happen later. Even though this was Iraq, it didn't mean this step was not needed. But J-7 didn't look at it that way. Both Navy captains just blew the whole thing off, rather than going out of their way to make sure these steps were followed to show the Iraqis they cared about property title and the new Iraqi rule of law.

They obviously felt, and this is evident by their actions, that because it was Iraq nothing needed to be done in this critical area. J-7's philosophy was, "show me where to built it and get out of my way." This was most apparent in the actions of the J-7 officer directly responsible for the construction of MOD projects, an Army reserve lieutenant colonel. He would not talk to me, even after I had asked to meet with him several times. All he did was sit at his computer and tell the AFCEE Contracting Officer what to do. (There was only one AFCEE Contracting Officer for all the projects J-7 was building for MOD. That was too much for one person to handle if J-7 expected to get the projects done right. At GSA, a typical Contracting Officer's workload might be 15 projects, 20 at most.) His carefree attitude towards the Iraqi rule of law and property ownership was evident. In addition, he made no effort to get the Iraqis to sign for the new projects he was building for them, as if three years of history of this same thing being done by his predecessors at J-7 meant nothing to him. He just continued doing what J-7 had been doing before he got there. Getting the Iraqis to sign for the projects J-7 had already built, and for the new projects he was building, fell on two lieutenant colonels and a major in J-7. Yet, after a year nothing had been done in this area. When they departed Iraq for the United States all but one of these officers were awarded the Bronze Star by the new captain in charge of J-7. The citations for these awards had been initiated by his predecessor. The Bronze Star is awarded for valor in combat. These officers didn't display anything close to valor in combat. They didn't display any valor (or integrity) in the management of their construction projects either.

When I first arrived at MOD I asked the Real Estate Branch staff what information they had on their camps and installations. They had none because Paul Bremer had taken it all away and given it to the Ministry of Finance. Because J-7 was constructing all the new camps for the Iraqis, I thought it logical that it would have all the plans and drawings related to them so I could give the MOD real estate staff their own copies to start building a data filing system. This was my first assignment when I arrived at MODTT, yet I couldn't get the most basic documents from J-7 to do this. I asked J-7 for any documents of the camps it had constructed for the Ministry of Defense. I was told there were none. I found this hard to believe, but it was true. I realized if the Ministry of Defense was ever going to stand on its own and manage its real estate and installations, it would have to develop its own system for surveying and drawing all the installations and camps J-7 had built for it, as well as all other real estate and installations that would someday come into its inventory. Of course, this is what J-7 should have been doing all along, but because it hadn't done its job properly I came up with this idea so the Iraqis could do it for themselves. Sort of like the "transition" we heard General Dempsey talk so much about, but never saw in action. I developed a Scope of Work (SOW) describing the tasks needed to do this, which would later be used as the basis for a contract to be awarded by MOD to get this work done by a contractor. I mentioned the SOW to two officers from J-7, and they asked me to give it to them so they could have an Independent Government Estimate (IGE) done to price the estimated cost of the work to be used in negotiations with prospective contractors. This is basic US Government contracting, the type of work AFCEE, J-7's contracting arm, would know inside and out. Or so I thought. I gave them the SOW that I had written thinking this would be a good way to work together with J-7 as a team on something. I was soon proven very wrong.

About two weeks later I was at KMTB, the Kirkush Military Training Base about 25 miles from the Iranian border. I needed to return to Baghdad early and was able to get a ride from KMTB back to Baghdad with the lead person in Iraq from one of the preferred US construction companies used by J-7 and AFCEE. We were in a private security convoy about half way back to Baghdad when he asked me if I knew anything about the RFP (Request for Proposal) that AFCEE had put out for bid on a project to survey all of MOD's military installations. This sounded exactly like my Scope of Work. I still hadn't received word back from the J-7 officers since I gave it to them to provide me with an Independent Government Estimate of its cost. I asked him if he had a copy of the RFP, and he said he had it on his computer and showed it to me. It was the exact same SOW I had written, word for word, and it was asking for cost proposals from contractors to do the work. I told him the RFP was not out nor had it been released yet. I told him I was going to look into it. When I returned to Baghdad I asked one of the J-7 officers I had given the SOW to what he had done with it, and told him it was now an RFP out on the street for bid. He said he knew nothing about it other than he had given it to the J-7 AFCEE Contracting Officer.

I went to the Contracting Officer that same day and asked him what was going on. He told me he was asking the contractors he used for all the work in Iraq for estimates of the cost of the project. I told him this was completely improper, a violation of procurement integrity, and a violation of the FAR to provide the same contactors he planned to bid the work out to with a copy of the SOW for them to come up with their own cost estimate of the job beforehand. That would mean they would be bidding against their own estimate of the cost of the job, which nullified the entire competitive process, as well as the US Government's ability to get the best price for the work on behalf of the Ministry of Defense. I don't think he even knew what an Independent Government Estimate was. If he did, he was completely ignoring this most vital step in awarding a US Government-sponsored contract. He got an attitude with me and started to make a joke of the whole thing. It was obvious he either knew nothing about the purpose of an IGE, or he didn't care. I told him I had been a warranted Contracting Officer at GSA, and what he was doing was grounds for an IG (Inspector General) complaint. When I said this he backed off and cancelled his RFP. Because of what he did I never went any further with the idea of having MOD contract for a firm to survey its installations, a task that was needed because J-7 and AFCEE hadn't done it themselves. Even when I tried to get the Iraqis to do something on their own, J-7 got involved and screwed the whole thing up. The AFCEE Contracting Officer was later fired.

I went back to the J-7 officers I had first given the SOW to and told them what had happened with the AFCEE Contracting Officer. The intent of the Scope of Work was for use by MOD in awarding its own contract, not J-7. But these two officers said J-7 had to do the work for MOD, that the ministry couldn't award the contract on its own. I knew MOD awarded contracts (not many), and because J-7 hadn't done anything to produce plans or drawings of the camps it had constructed for MOD, the ministry had to do this on its own. But J-7 wouldn't allow that. Here were two officers from J-7, a major and a lieutenant colonel, telling me MOD couldn't do its own contract. MOD had to because J-7 hadn't produced documents the ministry needed. J-7 didn't even know the steps needed to properly award a contract. I'm convinced the two J-7 officers had no intention of helping me when they asked for the SOW. They wanted it so J-7 could award the work to one of its preferred contractors.

About the time I had been in Iraq a year a co-worker from my company who was leaving came up to me with a printed copy of an e-mail that had been sent to him. He handed it to me and said I could keep it. The e-mail was written by a British Brigadier (General) named Rob Weighill. In his message, that he sent to the MNSTC-I Chief of Staff and copied several other senior MNSTC-I officers as well, Brigadier Weighill said: "Now that I have surfaced from my trip to the UK I have picked up the traffic on the [he wrote the name of my firm here, which I have deleted] moratorium. [MNSTC-I had implemented a hiring freeze on my firm due to serious questions about our value.] Emphatically I agree with you that we must not pay contractors (and their companies [i.e., my firm]) huge sums of money for the benefit of their 'advise' only. Where possible we should ensure that each and every contractor has the capacity to determine specific outputs over a period of time and create the ability to monitor and assess the fruits of their labour. The TRA helps here (although it remains crude – I think the CMM will help) but it will remain a challenge to determine an objective assessment model and define a means of remediation."

After all this wordy bullshit Brigadier Weighill proceeded to contradict himself by making the case to retain the legal advisor on his staff who had given me the e-mail, and who was employed by my company that the Brigadier had just blasted, and who was leaving in disgust over the whole situation at MNSTC-I.

What was Brigadier Weighill getting at? Simply this: he was coming right out and saying that my firm (and its people in Iraq), was making way too much money and he couldn't see what the Coalition was getting for it in return. If this wasn't a public announcement that my company was on thin ice, I don't know what was. It upset me because I wanted to do something in Iraq, wasn't being listened to at all, and this guy was saying to very senior officers at MNSTC-I that people like me, employed by companies like mine, were all lard asses and didn't do anything but collect money.

But Brigadier Weighill's e-mail went way beyond this. It was an indication that a very senior Coalition officer had no concept of the role of my company and its staff at MNSTC-I, and probably the rest of the advisors who were there as well. He was not alone in his shear ignorance of why we were there and what we had to offer. There is a saying: "People hate what they don't understand." Well, at MNSTC-I we were getting a real life taste of just what that means. This moron had no idea we were hired for our "advice" in the first place. All of us had years of experience to offer, and the vast majority were "subject matter experts" in our respective fields. The US Government was paying top dollar for us, and why the hell not. He probably thought we were there to dish out food in the DFAC (dining facility, i.e., mess hall) and drive trucks—"the fruits of our labour." Not quite old chap. In all candor, I knew more about real estate, land title, construction and facilities than any other person at MNSTC-I, especially the Coalition military who were assigned to Iraq to do just these tasks. If Brigadier Weighill wanted to bitch about people getting paid a lot of money for doing nothing, he should have started with people there in uniform doing jobs they had no clue how to do. Case in point: the officers and staff of J-7. He should have asked why the deputy in charge of J-7, a high school teacher from Mississippi, was the second ranking person in the entire country responsible for the construction of every single building, camp, police station and frontier border station for the Iraqi Ministry of Defense and Ministry of Interior. Why didn't Brigadier Weighill question how the deputy J-7 got his job and what experience he had in that line of work before pointing the finger at my firm and its staff? But we didn't wear uniforms and guys like the J-7 deputy did, so he was totally off limits. And let's not even talk about the fact that we volunteered, that we committed to stay for a full year, and that US Air Force personnel had tours as short as 3 months in Iraq. Was MNSTC-I getting its money's worth out of them? But in Brigadier Weighill's opinion, because I didn't wear a uniform, I was dead weight and collecting fees for sitting on my ass. Brigadier Weighill's e-mail said all I needed to know about how my firm, its staff, and guys like me, were viewed by the military officers at MNSTC-I we were hired to support.

But maybe his e-mail said something else. Because we weren't treated with any respect by the military at MNSTC-I and were in most cases marginalized, our value was in fact minimal. It was a foregone conclusion that if we weren't allowed to add value, then we had no value to add. My case is as good an example as I can come up with. If I was hired for my experience and knowledge, yet was unable to voice my opinion or have any say in how things were conducted, then in a perverted way Brigadier Weighill's point was true. If you don't treat subject matter experts as they deserve to be treated, beginning with courtesy and respect as volunteers and then moving up to what they have to offer professionally, then you are left with a pool of folks making a lot of money and not contributing to the effort. And you end up getting bullshit e-mails sent out like Brigadier Weighill's. But no one bothers to ask the simple questions: why aren't these people contributing more if we asked for them, and paid their way here?

I wasn't just upset at the implications made by Brigadier Weighill, a British subject whose country didn't even pay for my company's services. At an MODTT staff meeting weeks before, John Cochrane, the British civil servant who had replaced David Murtagh as head of MODTT, made a rather surprising comment to his entire staff that General Dubik, the new MNSTC-I commander, did not like my firm. (I bet the guys at the Pentagon weren't saying that to the two retired 4-stars who ran my company back in Alexandria, Virginia.) Nothing prompted Mr. Cochrane to say this. It appeared he just had the need to get it out. What was interesting was that at least 80% of Mr. Cochrane's staff were employees from my firm. What he was telling us was that the commanding general, who we all worked for, really didn't care for us or our company. I told this to a military friend of mine who worked at the US Embassy, and he said General Patraeus did not like my firm either. My friend told me General Patraeus' comment was heard by very reliable source and then passed on to him.

I had already experienced being treated like a second class citizen by MNSTC-I military staff. In addition, I had been going through all the things I have described above for the previous 11 months. As a result, I didn't appreciate a British brigadier making off-the-cuff derogatory comments about employees from my firm, which included me, all of whom had volunteered to come to Iraq. I went to Iraq to try and make a difference and have a positive impact. I was having a difficult enough time doing this without these bogus comments from a British general whose country didn't even pay for my services. I decided to do something about it.

I electronically scanned the general's e-mail (which was not classified) and e-mailed it to my colleagues. I wanted to let them know our company was not particularly liked by MNSTC-I senior staff. I also did this to make my firm's management aware there was a big problem with its MNSTC-I contract, as if they didn't already know. What would the shareholders of our parent corporation do when they found out our client was openly showing dissatisfaction with our firm, yet our local management in Iraq failed to do anything about it? If my firm lost its MNSTC-I contract, and its managers failed to act beforehand, heads would roll. Not that this would be a bad thing. The brigadier's e-mail, and the other negative comments being made about my firm, were all my company's management needed to see. I was doing my fellow employees, and the company, a favor by sending the brigadier's e-mail to them. But did my manager in Baghdad give a damn about Brigadier Weighill's e-mail? Not for a minute. All he cared about was that I had sent it out and the MNSTC-I Chief of Staff had gotten wind of it and was pissed off. He couldn't have cared less about what the e-mail said, or about his own people, how we were viewed by the MNSTC-I senior staff, or that we were all miserable at the way we were being treated.

The following day I was called into the office of the MODTT Chief of Staff and handed the letter of reprimand written by her predecessor two weeks before, but which I had never seen or even knew existed until she handed it to me. This was the same letter that had been written concerning the events at FOB Honor. She was giving me a letter of reprimand written by someone else, and was applying its probationary period to my sending out the British brigadier's e-mail, which I did *before* I was given the letter. So how could I know I was under probation? I told her she could not do this, but she handed it to me anyway. The following day my manager called me into his office and told me the MODTT Chief of Staff, John Cochrane and the MNSTC-I Chief of Staff, "want you out of here." He told me I could resign or be terminated. After some discussion I decided to resign.

I was going to be terminated (but offered to resign instead), for sending out the British brigadier's message, which pissed everyone off. Yet, the basis of my termination was my violation of the probation in the Letter of Reprimand written by the previous MODTT Chief of Staff—that I didn't know existed at the time I sent out the brigadier's e-mail. I did something people didn't like and was being punished with a letter of reprimand that was written before the fact, when it was not given to me at the time it was written or by the person who wrote it, or for the reason it was written in the first place. It was as if the previous MODTT Chief of Staff wrote the letter of reprimand, tucked it away in his desk drawer, and then told his successor it was there for her to save for a rainy day.

If this wasn't bad enough, the newly arrived MODTT Chief of Staff lied. My manager asked me why I had sent the brigadier's message out when I had been placed on probation by the previous MODTT Chief of Staff's letter of reprimand, which was dated two weeks before. I told him I didn't know the letter of reprimand existed until after I sent out the brigadier's e-mail message. He said he had met with the new MODTT Chief of Staff the previous day, and she had given him a copy of the letter of reprimand and said I had violated its probation. I asked my manager if he realized I had no idea the letter of reprimand existed until just the day before, when the new MODTT Chief of Staff handed it to me, but he refused to answer me. I asked him again if she told him I didn't know about the letter of reprimand until the day before, which meant I wasn't aware it existed when I sent out the British brigadier's e-mail, and therefore the letter of reprimand could not be applied to that action. He still would not answer me, but I would not let the issue end. Finally, he admitted the MODTT Chief of Staff had **not** told him she had just given me the letter the previous day, clearly misleading him into thinking I had been given the letter on the date it was written two weeks earlier.

By not telling my manager I had just received the letter of reprimand the day before, which was after I had sent the British brigadier's message out that had everyone so upset, the new MODTT Chief of Staff committed a gross act of unprofessionalism and dishonesty. By not telling him this key fact she purposely led him to believe I had already received the letter of reprimand before I sent out the British brigadier's message. This would then give him the false impression I had violated of the letter of reprimand's probationary period. After pressure from me, my manager finally realized what was going on with the MODTT Chief of Staff's disingenuous act (he probably knew already but didn't want to say so, but I wouldn't let him off the hook), and reversed himself on the statement he had made about me being terminated. He said he would look into the timing of when I was given the Letter of Reprimand. He told me not to resign but to wait for him to get back to me.

Around this same time I was asked by my co-worker for information on the warehouse project mentioned above. I gave her the information and asked what she wanted it for because she wasn't involved in the project. She grinned and said the Navy captain who had taken over M-4-TT from the Marine colonel had asked her for it. I told her this was all very interesting because the captain had pulled himself and his staff off the project weeks before, and now he wanted information on it, but he wasn't coming to me for it. I figured he must have been directed to stay involved in the project by someone of higher rank. Then my associate asked me to come over to her computer and she showed me an e-mail recently sent out by the captain to several people. The e-mail was all about me, accused me of not doing my job, and said I had completely messed up the warehouse project. The message was entirely false. He even went so far as to say I had no files or information from the trips I had made with the MOD real estate staff to the locations we had visited, and that I had no information on the sites for the warehouse locations. This was a lie, as I had everything he was accusing me in his e-mail of not having. It was a lie because he had never asked me for this information, and would therefore have no idea whether I did or didn't have it. He was simply making up accusations and telling people about them behind my back. My colleague asked me for the same information the captain said in his e-mail I didn't have, because he asked her to. In other words, he was stating in his e-mail that I didn't have this information, a flat lie, yet at the same time asking her to get it from me because he probably figured I would have it. He was right, I did. I gave it all to her within an hour.

About two days later I was at my desk when this same Navy captain came into the area where I worked and walked over to the desk of the US Navy captain who had been placed in charge of me and my two associates at MODTT, the captain who didn't know squat about real estate or facilities. These two men constantly hung out together, with the one coming over to our building to stand by the other's desk and watch him type on his computer. When the captain in charge of M-4-TT got to the other's desk this particular day I was very busy at my computer. I was working on something that was taking all of my attention, and I was talking in a low voice to myself. This was helping me keep my concentration. Suddenly I heard the M-4-TT captain say to the other, in a loud and very sarcastic voice, "Listen, he's talking to himself." He had a big shit-eating grin on his face, thinking himself to be rather funny. I stopped what I was doing and asked him if he ever talked to himself, and he said no. At that the captain sitting at his desk joked and said he talks to himself all the time. I then said to the captain from M-4-TT that if he wanted to insult me and tell lies about me, he should do so to my face instead of doing it behind my back in his e-mails. At this he snapped and started yelling at me. I asked him why he had taken it upon himself to discredit me, which only made him more mad and he started yelling at me even louder. The other captain just sat there and did nothing, when he could have defused the whole matter instantly. He was probably enjoying it. The MODTT Chief of Staff, whose office was around the corner, heard this and came out to the area where the captain was standing and yelling at me. She told me to come into her office, which I said I would do only if he joined us. I told her, in front of the captain, that he had provoked the entire incident. She was not about to deal with him, her superior officer, so she walked away. A minute later I followed her into her office. I tried to explain to her what I had gone through with the captain and his behavior toward me in recent weeks. I asked her if she was going to make an issue of what had just happened with the captain, and she said she would not.

The following day my manager called me into his office and said I was going to be terminated. This was after he had instructed me to wait until he got to the bottom of the issue with the MODTT Chief of Staff and the Letter of Reprimand. I had not heard a thing from him since, which by that time was about three days prior. His statement that he would get back to me when he figured out what had happened with the Letter of Reprimand, specifically the timing of when the MODTT Chief of Staff gave it to me, and that I should not resign until he got to the bottom of it, was all out the window now. He told me the MODTT Chief of Staff had ordered that I was not allowed to return to my office at Phoenix Base. I was not allowed to go to work. I was not allowed to come to work from that day until the day I left Baghdad, nine days later. I had to get up in the middle of the night and walk into the office at 2:00 a.m., when no one was there, to logon to my computer to get my e-mails. I had been in Iraq for almost 14 months by that time and was being treated this way by military people who had just arrived in country weeks before. I was given a Letter of Reprimand by someone other than the person who wrote it, because the one who wrote it didn't have the professional decency (i.e., the balls), to hand it to me himself, and he wrote it two weeks before he left Iraq. He left that for his female replacement to do. When his replacement gave it to me she applied it retroactively to something I did that people didn't like because it exposed huge problems within MNSTC-I between its senior officers and the civilians on its staff who were there to support them. And she lied to my manager concerning the timing of its delivery to me. I was being harassed by a US Navy Captain who hardly knew me, but who had taken it upon himself to go out of his way to lie about me in his e-mails to others, and to discredit me for work I had done on a project that began with his staff before he got there, that he knew nothing about until a few weeks before, and that I had been involved in for six months.

The treatment I received as a result of trying to do my job and help the Iraqi people and the Ministry of Defense was absurd. What is more, the waste of US taxpayer money due to the inept mismanagement by J-7 of US funded contracts, executed for the benefit of the Iraqi Ministry of Defense, constituted gross negligence and mismanagement, at a minimum. Senior US military officers on MNSTC-I staff have lied, acted unprofessionally, and failed in their duty as commissioned officers to behave with integrity. And a US Government Contracting Officer did much of the same.

When my manager originally offered me the opportunity to resign, his assistant e-mailed me the standard company resignation letter to complete and turn in. I never filled it out because my manager told me to wait until he verified when the MODTT Chief of Staff had given me the Letter of Reprimand written by her predecessor. I never heard anything more from him about his offer allowing me to resign. It was never mentioned again by him. In the meantime the Navy captain from M-4-TT insulted me, which I refused to put up with, and then I was told I was out. Whatever happened to the fact that I had accepted my manager's resignation offer? I had accepted his offer, had been told by him to wait, was then harassed and intimidated by a US Navy captain, and was now being fired for standing up for myself and not putting up with his crap. I decided to fill out the resignation letter and e-mailed it to my manager. I asked him to confirm its receipt, which he did.

The day I arrived in Baghdad, July 19, 2006, my manager said to me and the others who arrived the same day that we may be doing what we had been hired to do, but we may not. He told us things change a lot in Baghdad, and we may end up doing something entirely different than what we had been hired to do by our firm. In other words, our employer was sending us half way around the world and into a combat zone simply to be in Iraq and collect fees for our presence there, yet whatever we ended up doing was not relevant. This was an open, yet indirect, admission by our manager in Baghdad that our main function was not to do the job we had been hired to do as "Subject Matter Experts," but to collect fees for our company by simply being present—and staying alive. His comment was the first thing that came to my mind when I read Brigadier Weighill's e-mail. With attitudes like my manager's I could almost see where military officers like Weighill could feel that way toward us. The problem stemmed from the fact that the US military hired us, but then didn't use us. So it would be easy for MNSTC-I officers to think we didn't do anything. And with managers like the one we had in Baghdad, who should have been making sure we were put to work in the areas we were hired for and treated with the respect we were legitimately due, the problem just got worse.

Throughout MNSTC-I the prevailing attitude of the military personnel was one of envy of civilian contractors because of the high income we earned, and disdain toward us because we were not wearing uniforms—the worst possible combination. The military in MNSTC-I treated the civilian contractors like second class citizens, with nothing to add or to offer, and this was facilitated and condoned by the general officers in command. They felt the same way. A perfect example of this was the e-mail written by British Brigadier Weighill, mentioned above. His message said my firm's employees don't really do anything except talk a lot and make a lot of money. His e-mail was sent to several other senior officers at MNSTC-I. After I sent his e-mail out to my colleagues, who he was referring to in his e-mail, I was threatened with termination. All this when I was trying to make my colleagues and my firm aware that there was a major problem with our contract on the part of our client. Nothing was done about Brigadier Weighill's e-mail, only that I had sent it out. Being a publically traded company, if our contract was terminated, which it looked like it might be with the attitude shown by Brigadier Weighill that he shared with a dozen senior military staff at MNSTC-I, what would the shareholders of my firm think when they found out nothing had been done by our management to prevent it from happening? Instead, my firm and its management, especially my manager in Baghdad, allowed its staff in Iraq to be treated like crap by the MNSTC-I military, doing nothing on our behalf that would upset anyone in the MNSTC-I command structure. In effect, anyone could do anything they wanted to us, and say anything about us they wanted to say, and our own management had no problem with it. When my crack manager saw the e-mail from Brigadier Weighill that I sent out, rather than going into panic mode that our contract was in jeopardy and doing something about it, all he cared about was going after me because the MNSTC-I Chief of Staff wanted my hide. If my firm's employees didn't like their treatment by the MNSTC-I military staff, screw them. They could just go home and that was OK with our management. The situation in Iraq would go on.

All US Government contracts in Iraq are under the overall control of the Joint Contracting Command-Iraq, or the JCCI, which was commanded by a US Air Force major general while I was there. I never met the JCCI Contracting Officer who was responsible for the contract I was on. He and I never spoke about what was happening to me. I was being told by my manager that sending out the British brigadier's e-mail was grounds for termination. He backed off when he realized the MODTT Chief of Staff had lied to him about when I had been given the Letter of Reprimand written by her predecessor, with a date on it that was more than two weeks prior to the date it was given to me. Then the dipshit US Navy captain harassed and intimidated me. After I stood up for myself, I was told by my manager the MNSTC-I Chief of Staff, and the MODTT Chief of Staff, "want you out of here." Those were his words. My employer was ordered by the MNSTC-I Chief of Staff, a US Army full colonel, to terminate me, but the only person who can do that is the Contracting Officer. The Contracting Officer can't be commanded by a senior officer to do anything. This is against US Government contract law. But this is exactly what happened to me. Only the Contracting Officer can decide that someone on a contract he or she manages can be terminated, and he/she must have valid reasons for doing so. The Contracting Officer is supposed to reach his own conclusion as to what should be done with anyone on his contract. Instead, the MNSTC-I chain of command had complete say over which contractors were allowed to stay and who they wanted gone, and they simply ordered the Contracting Officer to make it happen. The managers of the companies that employ these contractors, like my manager, did as they were told. Instead of asking what had happened and trying to sort things out, in other words coming to my aid, he just rolled over like a lap dog and did whatever the military at MNSTC-I told him to do with me. The way in which my company managed its contract with MNSTC-I, and that by all appearances our services in Iraq weren't needed, give the distinct impression that people like me are nothing more than sources of revenue. We aren't wanted for anything other than revenue for our companies, under contracts awarded to them under the crony system at the Pentagon. This is a gross waste of US taxpayer money.

The mismanagement of construction projects executed by MNSTC-I J-7 for the Iraqi Ministry of Defense (and the Ministry of Interior) is overwhelming. Not only do the Iraqis have hardly any involvement in the construction of their own camps, the camps are built by J-7 without any regard to the ownership of the land they are built on. The US Army Corps of Engineers took this matter seriously during combat operations, but the US Navy officers running J-7 didn't think it was important, even after the intense fighting of the initial assaults was over and they didn't have the high level of combat dangers the Corps did. The contracting mechanism J-7 uses to build these camps, AFCEE, is run by Contracting Officers who don't know the Federal Acquisition Regulations. The AFCEE Contracting Officers, the JCCI Contracting Officers, and the contract managers from companies hired to support MNSTC-I, are pawns who do whatever the MNSTC-I senior military officers tell them to do. This is bad enough, but many of those same officers aren't competent and proficient at their own tasks, and in the worst cases act in ways that are unprofessional and bring discredit to their uniform. And the lack of accountability of the dollars spent on the projects managed by J-7 is astounding.

The amount of money spent by J-7 is probably known, but what it has been spent on is a complete mystery to the organization charged with spending it. When I asked a lieutenant colonel from J-7 for plans of the buildings and camps J-7 had constructed for MOD, he replied there were none. That told me J-7 had no idea what it had spent billions of US taxpayer dollars on, just for the Iraqi Ministry of Defense alone. It can only be assumed the same was true for the Ministry of Interior projects J-7 had built, which numbered up to 2,000 or more. This complete lack of financial accountability has been going on since at least 2004, when MNSTC-I was created under the initial command of General David Patraeus, the same officer whose unit (MNSTC-I) lost the 200,000 weapons. General Patraeus was the commander, and as such he was responsible for **everything** that occurred during, under, and within his command. If the loss of 200,000 weapons can be brushed aside and not impede his promotion to 4-star general, what else has been brushed aside in Iraq that we don't know about? The things I experienced firsthand and have written about in this book happened under the command of LTG

Martin Dempsey. And like General Patraeus, he's getting his fourth star too. One might say there's a pattern here.

Every month LTG Dempsey held a Transition Readiness Assessment (TRA) run by MNSTC-I, which he personally chaired. The TRA was "Death by PowerPoint." The PowerPoint slides would go on and on, in graphic splendor, and everyone's eyes would glaze over. The print was so small you couldn't read it, and it covered the entire page of every slide, the worst use of this otherwise effective presentation tool. I have heard that officers at the US Army's senior staff colleges get training in PowerPoint. I'm not surprised. They probably e-mail letters home to their families in PowerPoint. The purpose of the TRA was to track every aspect related to the transition from Coalition to Iraqi control at the Ministries of Defense and Interior, yet the Iraqis were not invited to the TRA by LTG Dempsey. I attended many of these TRAs during the 14 months I spent in Iraq, and never saw an Iraqi officer or senior MOD civilian there once. I was in Iraq for eight months of LTG Dempsey's tour of command. Colleagues of mine who had been in Iraq the entire time LTG Dempsey was in command of MNSTC-I told me they hadn't seen any Iraqis at the TRA either. How could the Iraqis play a role in their own "transition" if they weren't at the TRA to see what the Coalition was doing for them, was planning for them, and what was about to be transitioned to them that they would soon be responsible for themselves? How could the TRA be held if the "client" wasn't invited to have input? In reality, however, nothing was being transitioned over to the Iraqi Ministry of Defense and Ministry of Interior, so maybe that's why LTG Dempsey didn't feel the need to invite them. That's the way everything was done at MNSTC-I. The TRA was the "capstone" of everything MNSTC-I was there to do—to stand up these two Iraqi security ministries. Every senior staff officer and advisor was present, to include the heads of all the "J" staffs and the Transition Teams. They were all assembled at one location at the same time to discuss the "transition" of the Iraqi Ministry of Defense (General Dempsey chaired a separate TRA for the Ministry of Interior). What better opportunity to directly tell the Iraqis what was going on and where the problems were, and then work together to figure out solutions. General Dempsey chaired it. He could have invited Abdul Qadir, the Iraqi Minister of Defense, as well as the senior military and civilian staffs of MOD to go over the things that were slowing the transition down. With the joint influence of the Minister of Defense and the commander of MNSTC-I, chairing the meeting together, the message would have gotten across to everyone present. Instead, all we did was shit our collective trousers the week before the TRA to make sure the green bar at the bottom of the power point slide was moving to the right, to show General Dempsey what "progress" was being made in our respective areas. The Ministry of Defense could only execute one contract for goods and services in a six month period, but damn if we weren't going to find some way to move the bar to the right to show progress for the Directorate of Acquisition, Logistics and Infrastructure at MOD. And this was just one component of the ministry. The TRA could have been used to get things done, but in the end it was just another "dog and pony show."

To the best of my knowledge, General Dempsey didn't invite the Iraqis the entire time he was the MNSTC-I commander until the month he left, most likely because he didn't want it to get out they had "never" attended a single TRA. It was obvious enough to my colleagues and me that we talked about it. Well, at least General Dempsey can say the Iraqis did attend the TRA—once. The gross lack of cooperation, and collaboration, between the Coalition and the Iraqis we were all there to support, and also within MNSTC-I itself, started at the top with LTG Dempsey and trickled down to my level and below. Because MNSTC-I is a small place, this could be seen by everyone there. Chairing the TRA's without the Iraqis was one of the most inept failures committed by LTG Dempsey. He is being promoted to his fourth star.

In the spring of 2007 the US House of Representatives Committee on Armed Services issued its report entitled "Continuing Challenge of Building the Iraqi Security Forces," which described in detail the complete chaos at MNSTC-I, specifically its total lack of accountability. The report concluded with the very strongly worded "recommendation" that MNSTC-I report its doings to Congress on a regular basis. This was a huge red flag that MNSTC-I was completely out of control, and that it was not doing its job, yet Lieutenant General Dempsey was still getting promoted to full 4-star general, the same rank as General George Casey and General David Patraeus.

The construction contractors hired by J-7 to perform work should be under scrutiny, but the US military in J-7 who hires and manages them should be too. It is the military at MNSTC-I who hire the contractors in the first place, and it is the military within that command who are responsible for the work the contractors do and for what goes wrong. Civilians like me, who actually know what we're doing and do this kind of work for a living, are hired to go to Iraq thinking we're going to be put to work, but end up being ignored. But we get paid well, so we're supposed to keep our mouths shut and be grateful.

About a month before I left Iraq, I decided to make a formal complaint concerning many of the things I have written about in this book to the MNF-I Inspector General at Camp Victory, the lakeside resort home of General Casey, General Patraeus, and now General Odierno. The IG was a US Army full colonel who I had never met. As we introduced ourselves he saw my West Point class ring and asked me when I had graduated. I said 1977, to which he replied he had once been a classmate of mine. I didn't remember him. It turned out he had indeed been a classmate, for about three years. He told me he was one of the 150 of our class who were kicked out of West Point in the electrical engineering cheating scandal in the spring of 1976. The Secretary of the Army, Clifford Alexander, allowed anyone who had been kicked out to return (under certain conditions) to West Point and re-enter the academy into the Class of 1978, which the colonel had done. Allowing cadets to return to West Point after having been kicked out for an honor violation had never been done before. Now here he was a full colonel and the Inspector General for the entire Multi-National Forces-Iraq, commanded by a 4-star general. And what does the IG do? It investigates, among other things, lying and cheating.

I was sitting in the IG's office and his deputy, a Marine lieutenant colonel, was sitting nearby at his own desk. I began to tell my story to the full colonel when the Marine walked over and sat near me. He kept interrupted me when I tried to say something, arguing with me on every point I tried to make. It was ridiculous. The IG is a place where people go to file complaints, which are then investigated. It's not a place where you're interrogated while you file your complaint. He was committing an IG violation every time he opened his mouth. I wasn't even speaking to the Marine but to the Army full colonel I had made the appointment with. I had to look directly at him while I spoke, with the Marine off to the side harassing me at the same time. I kept trying to tell my story, but the Marine wouldn't stop. Finally, I had it with the Marine and told him if he said one more thing to me I would get up and walk out. He got so pissed off he went back across the room and pouted at his desk. I had the nerve to stand up to this ass, and he couldn't handle it. I wonder if he treated people in uniform that way. The colonel just rolled his eyes and let me continue. Needles to say I never heard another thing from the MNF-I Inspector General's office.

I went to the office of the Special Inspector General for Iraq Reconstruction, SIGIR, in the Republican Palace in the IZ. SIGIR exists to investigate corruption, waste, fraud, abuse, and mismanagement related to the US involvement in Iraq. I met with one of the senior staff there, who gave me some assistance on how to file a complaint about the things I have described in this story. He said he would send some of my information to his superiors in the SIGIR office back in Washington (Crystal City in Arlington, Virginia, to be precise). I decided to follow up with a formal complaint to SIGIR when I returned home, which I did. I never received any word back from SIGIR other than an e-mail informing me my complaint had been forwarded to the Department of Defense "Hotline."

15

My Tour

I had originally decided to leave Iraq at the end of my one-year obligation. My firm sent over resumes of candidates to take my place, and I was asked to review them. One of the candidates had absolutely no experience at all in real estate. He had worked as a dispatcher for a trucking company and as a clerk in a hotel, but because his resume said he was a graduate of the US Army Command and General Staff College at Fort Leavenworth, he was recommended for the job. His resume didn't even say he had been in the Army. But the senior advisor in my group, also employed by my firm, recommended this guy for my job. I took this not only as an insult to my experience, but proof once again that we were just there to collect fees. In other words, anybody could get a job in Iraq regardless of their qualifications. You might not end up doing what you were hired to do once you got there, so what difference did it make what your qualifications were. This was sobering news, and certainly a blow to my ego. I actually thought, for a very short time, that I had gotten the job because I was the best candidate for it. My associate and I disagreed with the senior advisor in our group and they decided not to make the offer to the guy. I decided to stay beyond one year, which turned out to be a **BIG** mistake. (But maybe it wasn't after all.) I did this partly for the money, but in very large part because my firm couldn't find someone to take my place who was at all qualified to do my job, and who could be of some help to the Iraqis I advised. Call it professional pride, but it's the truth. I didn't want to leave with some moron, who didn't know squat about my field, taking my place and destroying what I had tried to build to help the Ministry of Defense and the staff of the Real Estate Division.

This meant that many contractors, but certainly not all, had no experience in, or qualifications for, the jobs they were hired to do. When I was first introduced to a couple of officers in J-7 one of them, a US Air Force Academy graduate and a civil engineer, and also one of the few active duty officers on the J-7 staff, told me I was the first contactor he had met in Iraq who actually did the same type of work in real life. I did do that type of work in real life. Many of the contractors and advisors to the MOD that I worked with had years of experience doing many things, some directly related to what they were doing there, and some not so directly related. But the one thing we all had was our more senior age, and with that our overall experience in matters that could help the situation in Iraq. That was the most important asset we brought with us. And I honestly believe most of us really wanted to get something done. We wanted to earn our pay. In my case I was also bringing experience directly related to the subject matter I was advising, which made me all the more upset when I was ignored and brushed aside. If I hadn't been experienced, then being blown off wouldn't have bothered me as much. I would have just walked away hoping not to be found out. Maybe that's why my manager wanted us to keep our mouths shut. He didn't want anyone to say anything and be discovered for the sham "subject matter expert" they really were. He had to keep those contract dollars coming in.

After I arrived in Iraq I was told the story of the fellow who had been offered my job before me. Apparently, a guy had applied for the job as the Real Estate Advisor to the Iraqi Ministry of Defense, the job that eventually went to me. He was made a formal offer by my firm, and was soon contacted by my associate from Iraq. (She contacted me before I arrived as well.) In no time this clown started calling her and others before he departed the States, telling them about his plans to fly his private plane to Iraq so he could use it to survey the land needed for Iraqi bases. (My associate informed me that my job would be to travel the country conducting land surveys, etc., for the Iraqi Ministry of Defense.

I didn't find out until I got there it would take an act of Congress to travel five miles, and if there was a single cloud in the sky the Marines would ground their aircraft due to weather. Of course the whole issue with J-7 made anything I was hired to do impossible. It was all bait and switch to get me to go over there.) He also told everyone he was going to bring his personal weapons over with him too. My company received my resume and immediately rescinded their offer to him. Bad for him, good for me. Or maybe I have that backwards. The point is, anyone could get a job over there regardless of their qualifications. If the senior advisor from our firm thought a guy who had been a dispatcher for a trucking company and worked the front desk at a hotel could do what my job entailed (i.e., what it should have entailed), then anyone would have qualified to be hired by my firm, for any position, and sent to Iraq. The guy who was offered the job before me was so stupid he would have gotten himself killed. That wouldn't have been so bad, but he would have gotten someone else killed along with him. All because my firm had no legitimate candidate screening process beyond making sure the person was breathing. It didn't matter to my firm if a candidate had nothing qualifying them for the position, much less anything to offer its clients—the Ministry of Defense and the Iraqi people.

The "warm body" syndrome was alive and well when I was in Iraq, and it still is. Some of the guys I worked with who had left at the end of their year commitment went back to Iraq after only a few months. Why would anyone do that? Either they are desperate for the money, which most folks who go to Iraq are, or they are running away from something or someone. One guy I worked with, who went back after six months, was on his fourth marriage. To guys like him marriage is just an extended date. If you have nothing going on in the States, and you can go over to Iraq and make $200,000 or more a year, doing nothing if you don't feel like it, why not go. Especially if you're running away from a wife breaking your balls because of your drinking, or the fact that you're broke. My roommate, the full colonel who left the Army on a month's notice, came to Iraq for the money, nothing more. His first wife had built up so much debt he could never get out from under it, even six years later. She had 38 credit cards when they split up, every one maxed out. But when he used his credit card to buy a gift for his new girlfriend, while he was still married, his soon-to-be ex-wife nailed him to the wall for adultery. All this time later he was still paying off the money she got out of him for his little slip. In the five years he had been married to his second wife, they had been together under the same roof for about 7 months. The rest of the time he had been deployed to the Middle East—in uniform during the first part of OIF, and now as a contractor, all the while making great money. I knew another guy who was there simply to support his wife's spending habits. She wanted him to go to Iraq because of the money, nothing more. They had small kids. He was in Kuwait before coming to Iraq and had nearly been killed when he was hit by a truck. He had undergone half a dozen operations on his shoulder, and went back to Iraq because the money was simply too good to pass up, and his wife made him. When he was on the phone with his wife all they talked about was money. She was spending them into the poorhouse, and he was making $200,000 a year.

One particular case of the "warm body" syndrome could have easily turned out to be the "cold body" syndrome. Early in my tour I was called into my manager's office and his deputy asked me if I was willing to escort someone from Baghdad back to Kuwait. I said sure, and was told the reason. My firm hired a guy who had just arrived in Baghdad the day before. He needed to return to the States immediately. The man was 67 years old, and in such poor health he couldn't even wear his helmet, must less his 35 pound vest. Someone had removed the SAPI plates (SAPI—Small Arms Protective Insert) from his vest because he couldn't wear it with them still inside. (The vests had ballistic ceramic plates in them which gave them their weight. The plates could stop a 5.62mm AK-47 round, and could be removed by sliding them out of their pouches in the vest. Most of the women in Iraq didn't have the plates in their vests because of the weight, and they didn't look nice with the plates inside. Comfort and fashion are far more important than protection from an AK-47 round. Most of the civilian women simply refused to wear helmets because it messed up their hair. They carried them instead, which provided absolutely no head protection in the event of a bullet or shrapnel. One female nurse was killed by shrapnel from an exploding mortar round that landed a block down Haifa Street from the US hospital. I don't know if she had her SAPI plates in her vest or not. The women started wearing all their protective gear after that.) Apparently, when he arrived at Ali Al Saleem Air Base in Kuwait everyone noticed him. He was in terrible shape. He had a heart condition, and by the time he got to Baghdad he couldn't make it up a flight of stairs. He should never have been allowed to leave the States, but the Army doctors who screened him at Fort Bliss weren't allowed to give him a physical. No one was given a physical before they left for Iraq. I honestly think it was because DoD knew half of them wouldn't pass it. (Many of the contractors who went to Iraq wouldn't have made it past a drug screening. The guy who had been married four times was a walking pharmacy. He had something for anything that ailed you. He had been a Medical Services officer in the Navy and was a prescription drug addict. He violated General Order #1 frequently.) The doctors at Fort Bliss had to go by the report from the guy's doctor in his home town in upstate New York, which wasn't worth the paper it was written on. My company never even met him in the first place, so how would they know his condition. Everyone is so concerned with people's privacy, they can't make the determination that someone is physically incapable of the rigors of Baghdad. In short, there was no screening process whatsoever before you went to Iraq, professionally or otherwise. I had to stay with the man until he walked down the jet-way at Kuwait International Airport to make sure he didn't die while under my care. I had to carry his empty vest and Kevlar helmet for him. He didn't have the strength to carry them himself.

Many of the contractors who worked in Iraq were on their third, fourth and even fifth year there. I ran into a construction contractor who had been there for over four years. He had a family in the States, and had a six year old daughter. She has never known her father. But to some the money is just too good. It's the only thing they have. It's an addiction. Many people have made the decision to place money over everything else. There is a culture of pure love for money, and nothing more, in Iraq. I realized after I had been there for a while it was simply the money that mattered to most contractors there. But the military were not exempt. They were making the best money of their lives, all tax free up to the level of pay of a Sergeant Major. I knew an Army major who was making over $100,000—tax free.

Sure, the money was great. I loved it. I would get paid $7,000 every two weeks, before taxes. I've never made that kind of money in my life. But I really wanted to do something while I was there. It was my desire to do the job I was hired to do. Why go there if not to get something done? The place is a mess, so why not try to fix it. I really wasn't thinking of just myself when I went there, and especially after I had been there just a short time and had worked with the Iraqis at MOD, who just wanted to live their lives. I didn't want to go there for the money alone.

When I started working at MOD I saw what the Iraqi people were going through as a result of the war. The hallway walls in the MOD building had photographs of MOD staff who had been killed within the past week or so. Once there was a picture of a very pretty young woman around 23 years old. I asked my translator about her. She said the girl had left the MOD building one afternoon, walked down the street to the gate that was the main entrance and exit to the IZ called "Assassins Gate." The girl walked past the checkpoint at the gate and was standing on the Baghdad side. A car drove by and they shot and killed her. There was no reason for it. She wasn't involved with insurgents or other bad people. They probably just felt like killing someone who was leaving the IZ because they worked for the Coalition or the new Iraqi government. I wonder what the person who shot her was thinking when he spotted her? I doubt it was anything a normal man thinks like, "Hey, she's pretty cute, I wonder if she's available for a date." No, probably something like, "Kill the pig whore who works for the infidels." Really nice guys. Once my translator told me about her trip into work that day. She and her father would drive in together. They were turning a corner and there was a pile of dead bodies on the sidewalk. I asked her how many there were, and she said "about 25 or 30." Just a pile of bodies. About a mile from the MOD building, just beyond the IZ wall, a house was discovered that had 60 decapitated bodies in it. And the whole time he was in command General Casey insisted everything was just fine and the Iraqis could take over any time they wanted to. General George Casey was incompetent. There's no other way say it. All of this was happening right under his nose—for two and a half years.

My desire to get something done and be useful was in direct conflict with those at MNSTC-I, and the manager from my firm, who didn't want me to do anything if it meant exposing what the US military, specifically J-7, was doing wrong. If J-7 and I had worked together, which of course meant doing things legally and the way they are done in the commercial real estate and construction industry, things would have worked out better. Not that everything would have been perfect, but the things J-7 was doing that were screwed up, like those I've mentioned in this book, could have been addressed. Maybe the US Navy captain who took over J-7 wouldn't have been crapping in his pants when General Dempsey wanted to know the status of the list they had sent to MOD for Abdul Qadir's signature, which by the way was never found. I knew how to correct many of the things J-7 was doing wrong. But J-7 was just a bunch of guys who thought their shit didn't stink because they were wearing uniforms, like a kid feels when he's wearing a crossing guard belt in elementary school. They just wanted to continue doing things the way they had been done for three years, to include not securing clear title to land and not getting the documents signed to close out the books on J-7's projects. They certainly weren't going to do anything that was suggested by a guy in civilian clothes. That was out of the question. Who cares if what he says makes any sense.

Was I wrong in trying to help J-7 in these areas? Was I "out of my lane" when I was trying to help fix what it had screwed up that directly affected my client, the Ministry of Defense and its real property program? No, I was not. J-7 just didn't want to hear anything I had to offer, and idiots like my manager were completely on the side of the military at MNSTC-I and not the side of their own employees who they had hired to go to Iraq. Of course, my manager had nothing to do with my being hired. But he did have the responsibility to take me on when I arrived and treat me, and my colleagues, with respect as volunteers and Subject Matter Experts in our respective fields. But no, he didn't give a damn about that. He just cared about us continuing to generate revenue for the company and not pissing anybody off wearing a uniform, US or foreign. He was incapable of dealing with anyone's issues or problems. Who in Iraq is not going to have issues or problems? Instead, he would babble about Vietnam or Afghanistan, anything other than what you came to talk to him about, and kick you out of his office if you had any disagreement with him. And he was our Contract Manager. He was a joke, and our company knew it but let him sit there making probably $300,000 a year. He had no skills at all to do his job, especially dealing with people, but like everyone else over there he probably got it because he knew someone and he needed a job.

If you're employed overseas by a US company and are subject to Federal income tax, the first $82,400 of income earned is completely tax free, but you have to be physically outside the United States for 330 days out of 365. If you follow that rule you only pay taxes on whatever you earn above $82,400 in a 365 day period. I made $210,000 a year and got a $10,000 bonus, for a total of $220,000. The first $82,400 was tax free as long as I stayed outside the US for 330 days out of 365. Let's say taxes on $82,400 is $20,000. Because I didn't have to pay that, I was making the equivalent of $220,000 + $20,000 = $240,000 per year before taxes. Quite a sum when you consider no one wanted to hear anything I had to say concerning legal title to the land MOD's camps were being built on by J-7. Not bad when you consider no one wanted to hear anything I had to say about the way MNSTC-I was constructing military installations for the Iraqi army, or that US taxpayer money was being poorly spent with minimal accountability (or none at all) by the US military with the responsibility to manage it. Not bad when no one would let me assist in the transfer of FOB's from the Coalition to the Ministry of Defense. Not bad for another high-paid contractor who no one cared was around, was treated like dirt by the company he worked for, the military officers he reported to, and the State Department staff who ignored him.

When I arrived in Iraq I wanted to do something. That was my problem. I wanted to get something done and serve a useful purpose. I say this with the utmost sincerity. I can't stand having nothing to do. Sure, I went to Iraq for the adventure, but also to add more to my life. I wanted to make good money, who doesn't, but I wanted to earn it. That was my first mistake. And I wanted to be treated with respect. That was my second. I was barking up the wrong tree from the day I got off the plane at Baghdad International Airport. The lowest private was a field marshal compared to the most experienced civilian contractor in Iraq. Because he was wearing a uniform, the private who had been ordered to Iraq against his will was more valuable than the contractor who had volunteered to go there. At the PX (Post Exchange) in the IZ there were two lines at the checkout counter, one for soldiers and one for everyone else. There would be a couple of soldiers in their line, and 50 people in the other one. Whenever a register opened up, they would call for the next soldier to come up, while we stood there and watched. Our line moved only when the soldiers' line was empty, or when one of the people at the register felt sorry for us. We'd wait for 30 minutes while a soldier wouldn't wait at all, he'd just go right on through.

All the stuff we hear about the military "volunteering" to go to Iraq is mostly nonsense. They might volunteer to join the military, but most of them have no desire whatsoever to go to Iraq. This is especially true of the reserves and the National Guard. How many times have we seen bleeding heart stories of the mom who has to leave her kids to go to Iraq or Afghanistan, tears flowing? The military is so cruel. She volunteered, but this wasn't supposed to happen. She was just supposed to get her monthly the pay check.

Contractors made good money but didn't wear uniforms, and that's all that mattered. But the psychology of it makes sense. Because most of the military don't want to be there, especially reservists, and because we contractors get paid more than they do, they can use their uniform to screw with us. It's their way of coping. We were their scapegoats. It's nothing more than petty jealously and an outlet for their anger.

But no one ever talks about the danger contractors are in along with the military, the fact that we were getting killed too, and the fact that we didn't have to be there but had volunteered. No one back home ever heard about the number of civilian contractors who got killed over there all the time. In the first six months of 2007, nearly 60 contractors were killed in the IZ alone. That doesn't count the rest of Iraq. The Republican Palace serves as the US Embassy and the MWR (morale, welfare and recreation) facility. Behind the palace are trailers where hundreds of military and contractors live, along with a huge swimming pool from Saddam days, and the dry cleaners. There is also a trailer for the KBR (Kellogg Brown & Root) staff who handle the housing, assigning trailers to people when they arrive. I probably walked in front of this trailer 10 times a week. One day a woman who worked in the trailer went outside for five minutes to take a break, and never made it back inside. A mortar round landed right next to her killing her and an

Army sergeant, and wounding a third person. She had been in Iraq for three years and was leaving in two days. She was going home to see her brand new grand-daughter.

No one hears of this back in the States because the US military doesn't want anyone to know how many civilians are getting killed, which would really have an impact back home. Of course the civilians are there because we don't have enough military. Because our military is too small, we have to augment it with civilians. But when they get killed the American people are kept in the dark about it. So what's it going to be—either increase our military so we don't need civilians, or treat the civilians with the honor and dignity of a military person? Well, almost. Instead our country does neither. And it is the military that doesn't want to report the high number of civilian deaths that hired the civilians in the first place because it can't handle the job on its own.

The only time I heard of anything being written about the number of contractor deaths in Iraq was a New York Times story written on May 19, 2007, by John Broder and James Risen. The article referred to these deaths as the "hidden casualties of the war." At the time the article was written 917 contractors had been killed and over 12,000 had been wounded since the beginning of the war in the spring of 2003. In the first three months of 2007, right in the middle of my tour, 146 had been killed. This was the highest number for any 3-month period of the war, and the closest ever to the number of military deaths (244) during any other 3-month period of the conflict. When I read the article it was no surprise to me. I was there when mortar rounds and rockets were coming into the IZ every day. One day in particular, 22 rounds landed in succession in an area about a half mile wide. The closest rounds were landing about 200 yards away from where I sat at my desk.

While I was in Iraq a US Army brigadier general made the astonishing statement to the world on cable news that the US would not return "counter-battery" fire to wipe out locations where enemy mortar rounds and rockets were being fired from. We have the ability to fire off a round within seconds of an enemy round being fired at us, and destroy the place the insurgents have fired their round from. We can do this fast enough to kill them before they can pack up and take off to fire at us another day. But the general said we didn't want to inflict "collateral damage," i.e., kill innocent civilians. Of course we don't, but this is war. When we invaded did we think there wouldn't be any civilian casualties? How many Iraqi civilians have died because we invaded, yet this general was telling everyone we wouldn't defend ourselves if it meant one civilian might become a casualty. In effect, the general was telling the insurgents they could fire at us all day long and we wouldn't fire back. That's all they needed to hear. We were declared open season by one of our own general officers. But if we did fire back and wipe them out, maybe they would get the message and stop. That would make too much sense though. I wonder how much money has been spent to develop that counter-battery technology. Too bad we couldn't even use it.

But all anyone ever hears about are the military deaths. Death is death. I'm an American as much as any soldier over there. But if I had been killed I would have been put in a box and shipped home and that would have been it. If a soldier was killed, as sad as it was, it was treated like the Chief of Staff of the Army himself had become a casualty. There's a major disconnect going on in Iraq over the way civilians are treated, both alive and in death. One wears a uniform and his death is treated like a state funeral, while one doesn't and his death is the equivalent of a pauper's burial. Very often the civilian contractors do just as much, and sometimes more, than the military. This was especially true in the case of the civilian advisors to the Ministry of Interior, who worked side by side with the Iraqi national police in the villages and towns throughout the country, and of course Baghdad itself. The casualty list of civilians who do this work is extensive, yet no one ever hears about it back home. Just the beheadings. We always hear "Support the Troops." That's great. But what about supporting the contractors? They are ignored at home as much as they are in Iraq.

But there are inequities cross the board. While I was there a US Navy Commander who was in the branch that awarded contracts was killed by an IED. He was assigned to MNSCT-I and worked in the building called "The Barn" across from mine. The memorial service held for him was beautiful, it really was. It was in our DFAC. It was attended by General Patraeus, and half a dozen other flag (general and admiral) officers. The place was packed. As I walked away from the DFAC back to my office I thought to myself, "Why don't they have services like that for everyone who gets killed over here?" But the ceremony was so elaborate, I knew this wasn't possible. So why did they pick this one officer? I had to ask myself what was so special about the Navy commander. The reader will think this a very callous thing to say, but if you were at that memorial service, and had seen the things I saw over there, you might think the same way. Why have such an incredible service for just one person, and not everyone who serves under the exact same conditions as the Navy commander? Then it hit me. The commander was not a combat soldier, but in the Navy and in contracting. Being both in the Navy and in contracting in Iraq, you're not a combat type by a long stretch. I figured that was the reason for the ceremony, to make the death of a non-combat officer like every other soldier or Marine killed over there. His death was an anomaly due to his military branch and his job. The vast majority of the US military deaths in Iraq are Army and Marine. He was neither. Do they get memorial services like the Commander's? Did General Patraeus attend all of their memorial services too? I tend to think this memorial service was to show all the military at MNSTC-I they were held in as much regard as the soldiers and Marines who were outside the "safety" of the IZ. (I wasn't going to waste a brain cell on a civilian getting a service like that.) But the IZ wasn't safe at all because we (military and civilian alike) were easy targets for mortar and rocket fire from 360 degrees and within a couple of miles radius. We were sitting ducks. There should be equal treatment across the board, in life and in death, combat military and non-combat military, and civilian. Hell, we're all in "combat" in Iraq, so what makes one's death any more special than another's?

The US military also doesn't want anyone home to know about the high number of accidental shootings. One of the biggest causes is the clearing of pistols outside all the mess halls (DFAC's) in Iraq. Because all the US military carry a side arm, a 9mm semi-automatic pistol, they have to "clear" them before entering mess halls to avoid the accidental discharge of a round while inside. As soon as I arrived in Iraq I noticed the improper way all the US military were clearing their pistols. It made no sense to me at all. When I served in the Army in the late 1970's and early 1980's, we were taught one way to clear our .45 caliber semi-automatic pistol, which is the same type of weapon as the newer M-9 carried today, only far more lethal. (One shot from a .45 will drop anyone, often killing them. That's why it was developed by the US Army for the Philippine Campaign from 1899-1902. The US Army was fighting Moro guerillas who often used drugs to eliminate the sensation of pain, thus allowing them to continue attacking after being shot multiple times by the standard weapons of the day. The .45 semi-automatic pistol was introduced for its one unique characteristic—stopping power. One shot from a 9mm might slow down the average size person, but it will often take more than one to drop them. Getting off more shots takes more time, which a person being attacked may not have. You may only have time for one shot, or it's too late. A visual comparison of the two rounds tells the story. The .45 round is about twice the size of the 9mm. Its mass is huge in comparison. Add velocity to that and the results speak for themselves.) You would take the .45 out of the holster, point it toward the clearing barrel, push the button on the side of the weapon to let the magazine drop out of the pistol grip (even if there wasn't a magazine in the weapon), pull the slide back to eject a round if one was still in the chamber, look to make sure no round was still inside, release the slide forward, point the weapon into a clearing barrel full of sand, and pull the trigger. If by some fluke there was still a round in the chamber of the weapon after all these steps, it would be fired safely into the clearing barrel and no one would be hurt. This was always done deliberately, and we took our time because we were dealing with loaded weapons. It made sense to me then, and it still makes sense to me today.

 But not in Iraq. Everyone would take their M-9 out of its holster, and with their index finger on or near the trigger pull the slide back as they pointed the weapon in the general direction of the clearing barrel, pulling the trigger at the same time. This was done as a single motion, with no attempt at all to take time and deliberately ensure each step was done correctly. Not once did I ever see anyone check to see if they had a magazine in their weapon. They didn't because they *assumed* one wasn't there. But they also didn't check because that's the way they had been trained to clear their weapon. One day a lieutenant colonel on MNSTC-I staff was entering the mess hall. As he walked up to the clearing barrel he pulled the slide back. He had neglected to make sure there wasn't a magazine still in the weapon. He had been walking around Phoenix Base all morning with a loaded magazine in his weapon. When he "cleared" his weapon he failed to make sure the magazine had been disengaged. Instead of ejecting a round that might have been in the chamber, he did just the opposite and chambered a round from the top of the loaded magazine still in his weapon. Because he did this so fast and in one sweeping motion, when he slipped the M-9 back into his holster he pulled the trigger and fired a 9mm round into his leg. The round went from where it entered his thigh above the knee, all the way down to his ankle, an extremely bad wound. This happened just across from the front door of my office, about 75 feet away. We ran outside and saw him lying on the sidewalk covered in blood from the wound. We heard afterward that he might lose his leg. We also heard he was probably going to be discharged with a negative efficiency report due to his negligence and the danger he had posed to everyone around him while carrying a loaded weapon all day. Harsh punishment, but he deserved it. He could have killed someone, or himself.

The officer was a reservist who had no clue how to properly clear his weapon. But he was doing it the exact same way everyone else was. I found the whole thing a gross safety violation, yet it seemed to be condoned by everyone. I had to assume this was the new method of clearing one's weapon that was being taught back in the States, but that didn't make it right. I heard afterward this was happening all over Iraq, with hundreds of these cases having been reported. Why wasn't the US chain of command doing anything about this? The sad irony is if the lieutenant colonel had been carrying a .45 he most certainly would have lost his leg. It would have turned into meat. Is the sloppy method of clearing weapons in Iraq because the 9mm is less dangerous than the .45 if a round accidentally goes off? Is that why we took so much care to clear our .45's when I was in the Army? Maybe it's better our soldiers carry the M-9 now. Because it's not as lethal as the .45 they won't kill themselves.

What bothered me the most about being in Iraq was that we civilian contractors were completely ignored, when many of us had incredible experience and so much to offer the US military. Yet, the military didn't give a damn about us, except a small handful who appreciated us being there and what we had to offer, not the least of which was to help them do their jobs more effectively. What made things worse was that the company I worked for couldn't have care less about us either, its own employees. All of this on top of the fact we had travelled half way around the world, were in a combat zone, had to wear a 35 pound ballistic vest and a 10 pound Kevlar helmet everywhere we went in 110 degree heat and higher, and had to undergo the exact same living conditions the military did, or worse. I lived in a 9 x 12 (108 square feet) foot room, which was half a trailer that had another 9 x 12 room on the other side. We shared the same bathroom, which always ran out of hot water. I shared my room with another guy, so we each had 54 square feet to live in. But most lieutenant colonels, and all full colonels, had their own room with a private bath depending on the design of the trailer. In Iraq this was huge! Most of the contractors were retired military, many of them retired lieutenant and full colonels themselves. But now they were contractors, so they could stick it. Of course my manager had to kick one of his own people out of a room he had to himself into a room with someone else so he (my manager) could have his own room. A real peach. The guy he kicked out was a retired Command Sergeant Major. He was a great guy, and was so fed up with our manager after that he went home.

After being in Iraq about two months I realized I needed a security clearance. I had a Top Secret/Sensitive Compartmented Information (TS/SCI) clearance when I was in the While House working for Tom Ridge, but it had been taken away the day I left. The job I had taken in Iraq didn't require a clearance. I soon realized that I needed one because MNSTC-I and the rest of the Coalition military was classifying everything, almost to the point of classifying the menu at the DFAC. I went to my manager's deputy and asked what I could do to get a clearance. He was a great guy. He had been Special Forces his entire Army career, and was very down to earth. (While I was home for vacation in December of 2006, he had a massive heart attack and was sent back to the States. He survived only because he was about 100 feet from a defibrillator at the Embassy. I was told he had turned blue, and was as close to buying the farm as anyone had ever seen. He was replaced by another good guy.) He told me to go online and fill out the clearance form on the Government's web-based application called "eQip." I filled it out, the Standard Form 86, and submitted it on-line to the Office of Personnel Management (OPM), the agency of the Federal Government that handles all security applications.

Some time later our cracker jack manager poked his head into my office and said something about my "interim clearance" being denied, and then he left. He said it so fast I didn't understand him at first, so I followed him down the hall to his office and asked him what he had said. He told me the Security Officer at our company had denied my interim clearance because of my answer to one of the questions on the application. I asked him what an interim clearance was, because I had never heard of it before. He said it was a temporary clearance the company had the authority to issue while a person waited for their full background check to be completed and their permanent clearance to be granted. He told me I could e-mail the women at our firm who handled clearances, and gave me her name and e-mail address.

I contacted the lady at my firm who was responsible for security clearances for all employees. I e-mailed her and asked what the problem was. She said I had answered the question about having seen a "mental health professional" in such a way that it had raised questions. She said the way I had answered the question led "the adjudicator" to think I was a "violent" person. I couldn't believe what I was hearing. I asked her who "the adjudicator" was, and she wouldn't answer me. It had to be her, but she was playing word games with me and blaming it on "the adjudicator." I asked her why "the adjudicator" had come to this conclusion, and she referred me to question #21 on the SF-86, the security clearance application.

Question #21 on the form addresses whether you have ever seen a mental health professional. I have seen a therapist for several years. The question has two parts. The first asks about ever having seen a mental health professional, and requires a yes or no answer. The second part says: "If you answered "Yes," provide an entry for each treatment to report, unless the consultation(s) involved only marital, family, or grief counseling, not related to violence by you." I could not figure out the meaning of the question. I thought, I have seen a therapist, so I'll answer yes to the first part of the question. But I hadn't seen my therapist because of marital, family or grief counseling, or any violence by me, so I thought that meant I put down the counselor's name and the dates of treatment. It didn't make much sense to me, but that's the way the question is written, and that's the way I understood it to mean. I was reading it literally, which was my mistake. Well, she (or should I say "the adjudicator") had other ideas. She told me because I had put the name of the therapist and the dates of treatment, it meant the treatment *was* because of violence by me! Nothing could have been further from the truth. I tried to explain the reason why I had answered the question as I had, but this woman would not listen to a word I said. The decision had been made by "the adjudicator," and that was that. There was nothing I could do. She said I could send a registered letter to an agency in Columbus, Ohio explaining my answer, and that I would hear back from them in ten days. I did, and I never heard a thing. (I have answered the same question the exact same way before, and never had a problem. I had a TS/SCI clearance in the White House. But what did "the adjudicator" care? The question is so poorly worded, it reads like it was written by a fourth grader.)

The day I was hired by my firm, I reported to its corporate headquarters in Alexandria, Virginia. Four other guys showed up along with me that day, all headed for Iraq. We were going to get in-briefed and go through the new employee paperwork drill. But before we got started a guy walked in and introduced himself. He was the Senior Vice President for Personnel. He came into the conference room and walked around shaking everyone's hand, and handing out his business card. In his introduction he made a point of telling us he had been a brigade commander in the 82nd Airborne Division, so that we would be duly impressed with him. Then he told us if we needed anything, anything at all, we should contact him. "Anything I can do for you guys, you just let me know," blah, blah, blah....... So, when I was getting screwed by the woman in charge of security clearances ("the adjudicator"), I took Mr. Senior VP up on his offer and e-mailed him. I told him the problem I was having with the security clearance application, specifically the part about the woman not giving me the time of day when all I wanted to do was explain to her why I answered the question the way I did. I never heard back from Mr. Senior VP, the former brigade commander in the 82nd Airborne Division, who told us to contact him "any time" we needed his help.

To add to this circus the lady ("the adjudicator") told me she was putting my application into the system for normal processing, and I'd get my clearance when that was completed. So, if she could say that, why couldn't she ("the adjudicator") give me the interim clearance right then? I had to wait for the clearance process to run its full course, which takes about a year, all because of my answer to one stupid question "the adjudicator" didn't like.

Around February 2007, I figured I would check on my security clearance application to see how things were moving along. After all, the lady said I would get the clearance, didn't she? I contacted her via e-mail, but instead got a reply from the guy at our firm who handled all of us in Iraq. He told me the lady had been fired, and wanted to know what I was asking about. I told him I wanted to check on the status of my security clearance application, and he said he would get back to me. The next day he e-mailed me and simply asked me to re-submit my application! Just like that. Like I could just whip it out. What about the application I had submitted five months before? I asked him why I had to re-submit my application. He said my finger print cards, which I had submitted along with my application back in September, had been thrown out by the woman ("the adjudicator"). The entire application process had stopped, and I didn't even know about it. I was never in the "system" in the first place. It takes about 12-18 months to get a security clearance from the Federal Government. I had just lost five months for nothing. But now I also had a black mark on my record for having had an interim clearance denied. It could have all been avoided if Mr. Senior VP had answered my e-mail and helped me. She ("the adjudicator") worked for him. But I didn't count except as a warm body to collect fees for my firm in Iraq. He just hires bodies. He didn't care beyond that. I told the guy who handled the employees in Iraq the story about the VP walking into the conference room my first day and what he said to us, and that I had e-mailed him asking for his help, never receiving a reply. He said the VP was "a very important guy" and had "other things to worry about." My personal needs didn't mean anything to the company, the US military, or anyone else. I was on my own and half a world away in a war zone. Not a good feeling.

16

Aftermath

I have been home for almost two years. The "surge" has been successful, and the violence in Iraq has dropped drastically. All good news. But that is not what this story is about. This story is about America's failure in Iraq. How can we have failed if the surge is a success, as the conservative radio talk show pundits all say? Although I am a conservative, on this point I strongly disagree.

Barack Hussein Obama changed his website during summer 2008 from the surge being a failure to the surge being a success, but his campaign made it clear he wasn't "flip-flopping." He was just clarifying his website to make it more accurate with the times. How nice. No one cared whether Obama was flip-flopping or not. He was going to get elected anyway.

I was in a pizza parlor on MacArthur Boulevard in Washington, DC the night of September 5th, 2008. *Larry King Live* was on TV and he was interviewing Michael Moore. Because I was in the pizza parlor I had to sit and watch the interview without throwing up. Larry King was asking Moore about the upcoming presidential election, when the topic turned to the Iraq war and the surge. Moore said something I will never forget. He said the Iraq war was like a kid in the kitchen who is screwing around and spills a glass of milk. He cleans it up and wants to get all the credit for it. But the milk wouldn't have spilled if he hadn't been screwing around and made the mess in the first place. To Moore, that was the same as the surge. We screwed up the war, conducted the surge, and now wanted to take all the credit for being so great. Moore said one more thing. He said the surge wouldn't bring back the dead American soldiers or the "100,000" dead Iraqis that were the result of the war. His estimate was low.

(It is important to note this same Michael Moore doesn't think there is any threat at all to the United States from Islamic terrorism. (See the DVD, "Obsession.") In his opinion it's all bull and exists in the imagination of conservatives. So liberal is Moore that he most likely thinks the events of 9/11 are all the fault of the United States, and specifically George W. Bush who was in office only 8 months. Moore probably thinks Bush and the CIA did it. Does Moore have any opinion on the way Bill Clinton and Madeline Albright handled the situation when Osama bin Laden was offered to the US on a silver platter by Sudan, or the fact that bin Laden was pulling his little pranks the entire time Clinton was in office? While Clinton was president 59 Americans died from acts of Islamic terrorism, and our nation's leaders did absolutely nothing other than talk a lot. (Lopez, NRO) What does Moore have to say about that? But then again, I already know what he would say. Moore would say that's all nonsense and Clinton did everything he could to stop bin Laden. Who's the one with the vivid imagination?)

On May 31, 2008, the Washington Post reported on a study that had been conducted by eight Iraqi physicians estimating the total death toll as a result of the war to be 655,000. But nothing is reported about this here in America except on a rare occasion. Although the "main stream" media is biased against the war, it is amazing this information is seldom discussed. As much bad press as George W. Bush receives, he has been treated lightly on this significant statistic. We will never know the total death count from this war. But we do know it is very high. What is really important, however, is regardless how many have died—American, Iraqi, Coalition and contractor—**none of them would be gone if we had not invaded Iraq in 2003.** But if we had entered into this conflict with an honest reason for doing so, and a clearly defined objective to accomplish and the resources to do it, at least those who died would have for a legitimate reason. We can only assume the number of total deaths would be significantly lower as well. Even a timeline for withdrawal wouldn't have been so important as long as we knew why we were there and what our objectives were. We had none of these things.

And what of our real enemy, the fanatic Islamic terrorist who wants to kill every non-believer in the world? What are we doing about him? What has our involvement in Iraq done to address this killer, to wipe him out before he destroys our world as we know it? The battle is not in Iraq, it is world-wide. It is right here in America. Some say we took the fight to Iraq so it wouldn't be here in America. That is plausible, but a pipe dream when looked at in relation to the magnitude of the actual problem. The problem with Islamic terrorism is that it is everywhere, and there are millions of young men willing to die for what they believe in, even if what they believe in is nonsense. But it isn't nonsense to them, and that's all that counts. After 9/11 President Bush should have reinstituted the draft. We will need hundreds of thousands of men and women to take on our new enemy, creating a pipeline of fresh recruits coming in to take the load off the ones who have been fighting before them. We can't do it with technology alone, or with air power alone, or with ships alone. It will take everything our country has, to include all of these resources. But it will take combat troops in the hundreds of thousands, who will fight on the ground in very harsh conditions, to combat this new enemy. We don't have this capability now, and if we don't do something about it soon we won't have it when we need it.

Our deputy contract manager in Iraq spent 35 years in the US Army Special Forces (Green Berets). He once told me the only way to win in Iraq was to have small teams of elite forces, like the SF, in the villages and towns throughout the country. By doing this we would be living among the people, in their homes and side-by-side with them in their fight for freedom. But no, we are still fighting with conventional tactics, like the way we came up from Kuwait in the opening phase of Operation Iraqi Freedom. That's good for some types of warfare, against conventional forces, but it is worthless against the new enemy we, and the rest of western civilization, are going to face in the years to come. The United States military has done nothing in Iraq to demonstrate it is aware of this new enemy, much less that it is able to fight it. Instead of base camps all over the county of Iraq, with Subway, Pizza Hut and Burger King, we should have hundreds of thousands of special operators and elite soldiers in civilian clothes, just like their opponent, living and working with the Iraqi people to help them start a new life in freedom. If we can do it there, we can do it other places too. But we're not even close. We care more for the creature comforts of our soldiers and generals than preparing for the real battle we will face, and are already in.

I have tried to describe life of the typical Iraqi today, and how it was before the war. The only conclusion I can come to is they would have been better off if we had never invaded. What could I say when the Iraqis I worked with asked me why we were conducting the war on terrorism in their country instead of someplace else? I felt like a jerk. I was even a little afraid they would take it out on me. But they were too nice. And they were too used to war to be angry at an American who wasn't the cause of the war himself. No one disputes that Saddam Hussein was a prick. But I know Iraqis who never had a problem with the man or his thugs—as long as they kept their noses clean. Sure, no one would argue this is a lousy way to live, but is dying better? To the Founders of our country, such as Nathan Hale, dying was. As he said, "Give me liberty or give me death." But our Founders were fighting for themselves, for their own freedom. The Iraqi people are dying for our version of freedom for them, in their country. Let them decide on their own if they want to be free and how to achieve that, just like our Founders did. No Iraqi ever took out Saddam Hussein, although many may have wanted to. But just like Nathan Hale, if they really wanted Hussein gone, someone would have made the ultimate sacrifice and done something about it. The fact is, the average Iraqi was content to live under Saddam, no matter how bad he was. If they didn't want to make the ultimate sacrifice and kill him in order to live in freedom, wasn't that their choice? But no, we had to make that choice for them.

The United States has a policy that forbids assassination of foreign government officials. We don't want to get into the business of assassination, primarily because we wouldn't want someone to try it here. If Saddam Hussein had to go, as President Bush declared, were 500,000 to 1,000,000 people worth the price of his life? That's what has been paid. The only reason to invade another country is to occupy it or stop its assault on another. If Iraq wasn't invading a neighbor, and we had no intention of taking it over ourselves, what was the point? It was all to get rid of Saddam. All those people died to get rid of him. He wasn't worth it.

If the people of Iraq wanted our help, we would have been there. No one ever asked us to come. That's the difference, and that is why the United States is disliked so much. We stick our nose under way too many tents. If people don't ask for our help, we should stay out of their business. Why do we have to decide it for them? If we espouse freedom, doesn't that imply leaving other nations alone and staying out of their business, leaving them "free" to make their own decisions how they want to live their lives? And if the reason for entering the war in Iraq was WMD, what about all the other countries in the world who we know for certain have these, yet we do nothing? This war was a pipe dream, plain and simple. The only conclusion for entering this war was that Bush had an issue about Saddam's threat against his father, and he wanted to show the world how tough he was. Can any other conclusion be reached, especially in light of no WMD ever being found, which was Bush's case for going in? Unless that was just an excuse, which it most likely was.

I have often wondered what George W. Bush's presidency would be like had he never invaded Iraq. What would it look like today if he had grabbed the bull by the horns the day after 9/11 and went into Afghanistan and wiped out the Taliban and Al-Qaeda, not stopping until Osama Bin Laden's head was stuck on top of a pole where it belongs? What would things be like today if Bush had reinstituted the draft, growing our military to a decent size to fight the "War on Terrorism" in a serious manner, and not half-assed like he has done in Iraq? He lost the best opportunity a president in modern history has had to seize the moment and do what needed to be done to prepare for a new enemy and a new battle. But George W. Bush was weak like his father, and was too easily swayed by neoconservatives like Douglas Feith, James Wolfowitz, Donald Rumsfeld and Dick Cheney, with dupes like Colin Powell playing along so he could remain on the world stage. And of course George Tenant was throwing his two cents in. If Saddam posed such a serious threat, why couldn't we have parked a fleet in the Persian Gulf off the coast of Iraq at Al Faw while we waited for him to pull something? He wouldn't have done a thing. He wouldn't have had the nerve. Despots like Saddam Hussein are easy to deal with. Force. Just rap them on the head a few times and they back right down. They know force when they see it. They use it on their people every day, so when someone uses it on them they have great respect for its value. But the United States is too worried about "water boarding" and panties wrapped around the heads of killers at Abu Ghraib prison. We will spin our collective wheels as a lazy nation until the shit really hits the fan, and then we won't know what to do or how to deal with it. The enemy is just waiting and watching, in disbelief at our stupidity.

I am continually amazed at the lack of will on the part of our leaders, namely our past presidents, to use the force we have that our taxes have paid for, to good effect. Why have a military at all if we don't even use it to rattle our sword to deter rogues like Saddam Hussein? Instead, we defer to the United Nations to send inspectors. But when that fails we overreact and invade the place, but do it with a fraction of the forces needed to properly execute the mission. We could have shown some force, and the will to use it, and keep an eye on him. Of course, it follows that when we used it we would have gone in with *overwhelming force*, then leave or occupy the place depending on how the situation developed. But all this would have taken cool heads, good planning, the will to use all the forces we have, the determination to get the job done right and in a timely manner, and the flexibility to adapt to conditions in the combat theater. It can safely be said of Operation Iraqi Freedom that none of this was done.

We declare a global war on "terror" (as Bush says, not "terrorism"), yet we don't enact a draft to fight it. If our national leadership, the President and the Congress, force our nation into a war, how can they not force people of age into service to fight it? Instead, we are forced into a war but ask for volunteers to fight it, always with disastrous results either way. Rather than a draft to beef up our regular forces, we call up the reserves and national guard who are only in it for the extra cash and have no desire to get called into active service and deployed. Yet we send them right into the thick of things because our full-time military is spread too thin. It is spread too thin because it isn't big enough. And it isn't big enough because our country won't reinstitute the draft and can't afford to pay the salaries of a larger full-time active force along with the rest of the money it spends on things far less important and vital to our nation. So our Government has to depend on the reserves and the National Guard, like a Federal agency depends on contractors. A contractor is simply a part-time employee. The company he or she works for makes money as long as they are employed at the agency, which has the option to not renew the contract when it ends. The reserves are the same thing. We send them in to fight our wars, and send them back to the grocery store where they came from when they are no longer needed. It's a stretch, but is there much difference between a mercenary and a reservist? We pay them when we need them, and send them away when we don't. The United States gets around this little obstacle by including the reserves and the National Guard in along with the regular military. But they really aren't the same. The National Guard belongs to the individual states, yet the uniforms of the Army National Guard say "US Army" on them. This is technically incorrect. The Army National Guard only becomes part of the US Army when the President federalizes it and includes it into the ranks of the active duty military forces. Do Army National Guard uniforms say "US Army" on them so we can save on the cost of a name tag? The president rarely calls up the National Guard, so what's the point of having "US Army" on the uniform? Have the name of the state on the uniform and switch to "US Army" if the President activates the state's militia. That's what Velcro is for. It's all smoke and mirrors written into the United States Code to avoid accusations of our country having a mercenary force.

(During the Hurricane Katrina disaster, Louisiana Governor Kathleen Blanco pleaded with President Bush to send in the Louisiana National Guard. Bush told her the Louisiana National Guard belonged to her. She was the Commander-In-Chief of her state's National Guard, and she didn't even know it. She was later defeated and kicked out of office. Now there's a leader for you! We'll leave for another time any discussion of New Orleans Mayor Ray Nagin.)

Iraq is crawling with reservists and national guardsmen who don't do this sort of work for a living. So what purpose do they serve? Their highest and best use (as we say in commercial real estate) should be to back-fill the full-time components of our national defense structure. For example, if the 24th Infantry Division is sent to Iraq (or Afghanistan), and has to leave Fort Riley, Kansas, a reserve unit should come in to run the installation while the 24th is deployed. Reserve and guard units should be used to do all the "back office" staffing of the full-time components of our military, not go right into combat on the front lines like they have been doing since Dessert Storm. The only time this should ever happen is as a last resort, when we need every fighting unit we have, like we did in World War II. Isn't that what "reserve" means? In that conflict we had millions of men in uniform, so sending a reserve or guard unit into front line combat made sense. They are not full-time soldiers and therefore don't have the level of training, unit discipline, equipment, and commitment to fight our wars that full-timers do. If someone is a full-time soldier, he will have the commitment to stay as long as he is needed (and if he knows he's getting a reenlistment bonus to buy a new car). But no, our leadership doesn't even make the full-time soldiers stay in Iraq longer than one year at a time because they are spread too thin, even with the high number of reservists and guardsmen that are sent over to augment their numbers. Our military is so small by comparison to when I was on active duty it boggles my mind. When I was in the US Army there were 16 active duty divisions. Today there are around 10, but I won't venture a guess because the number may go down by the time this book is published. By the way, I should have used a different unit instead of the 24th Infantry Division in my example above. The 24th has been deactivated. It no longer exists.

To add insult to injury the tours of duty in Iraq are a joke. There's no other way to describe it. Soon after arriving I saw how one component of the military had a completely different schedule than the others, yet they were all working side by side in the same office or at the same camp and for the same commander. The Air Force was the biggest offender. This is typical, as the Air Force has a reputation among the services as being a county club. (There is a joke about the new Air Force base. The first thing that is built is the Officers Club, then the golf course, then the Enlisted Men's Club, then the PX, and then the commissary. The Air Force runs out of money and has to go back to Congress to ask for more to build the runway.) There were two young officers, a captain and a major, who showed up at Phoenix Base to work at CAFTT, advising the new Iraqi Air Force. Their job was to come up with locations and facilities for the new air force and its fleet of aircraft. Of course, the Iraqi

Air Force consists of about a half dozen C-130 transports and about the same number of Bell Jet Ranger helicopters. But Iraq had just purchased a number of former Polish Air Force Mi-17 "Hip" helicopters, which were pretty sharp when painted with the Iraqi colors. One day I saw the major walking along with some typical party-like things sticking out of his plastic shopping bag. When people left Iraq their co-workers would throw a going away party for them, getting things that were sold at the PX or the local "Haji Shop" as gifts. I asked the major who was leaving, and he said Captain So-And-So, the other officer. I was concerned, because the captain had just arrived, so I asked the major if everything was OK with him. He's fine, the major said, his tour is over and he's on his way home. The captain had been in Iraq three months! I was stunned. The major just smiled at me like it was a big joke. The captain was an Air Force Academy graduate. That's what our country got for all that training and money. Three months. I hope he didn't break a nail packing his bags.

What made this so ridiculous was that we all had to work together. What is the point, and the effect on morale, when one person leaves after three months and the guy at the desk next to him has to stay for a year? There is no consistency at all in Iraq, because there is no consistency to the length of military's tours. As I mentioned previously, the contractors were the only ones who gave any stability to the place, along with their institutional knowledge, but in return for our expertise and our service we were treated like crap by the military (US and British), many of whom left after a few months. Yet the military in MNSTC-I thought they were the only ones getting anything done. Who's kidding who? We didn't wear uniforms so we didn't count, and we made a lot of money so they were envious of us. But we were the ones who knew anything because of the time we had over there and the relationships we had built with our Iraqi counterparts (and friends).

The amount of money spent to send someone to Iraq is staggering. When you consider the training before they go, the cost of replacing them at their old job, the transportation costs involved, and of course the hardship, it is tremendous. But to go through all of that and only send someone there for three months is pathetic. And, of course, the biggest impact on our effort in Iraq with these absurdly short tours is their affect on the overall military strength of our forces there. If people are rotated out every three or six months, then you need two to four times the number of people to get a full year of service out of them in Iraq, a full "man-year." For example, if one person goes to Iraq for a year, that's the same as four going for three months each, one after the other. That's assuming one always arrives as the one before them leaves. With such huge turnover the chances of a gap between tours of duty is much greater, resulting in periods when no one is serving in a particular position at all. One year tours drastically reduce the potential for gaps because the turnover rate is that much lower, not to mention the effectiveness of our forces due to cohesiveness between staff and their institutional knowledge. It takes a month just to figure out where the laundry is, and the Air Force captain was leaving after three! But of course, what I'm saying makes sense. That's the problem.

We have a huge problem with force numbers in Iraq, and it's all our own doing because the Secretary of Defense and the President allow services like the Air Force to get away with three and six month tours. Are they afraid the Air Force will throw a tantrum? If we are using the "combined force" structure in Iraq, whereby all four services are working side by side, we should also demand all those in the combined force serve the same length of time there. But that would take leadership to make these tough decisions, which we don't have. What would have been tough about the Secretary of Defense ordering the Secretary of the Air Force to make all tours one year? Let the Air Force bitch for a few days, and then move on.

Before anyone went to Iraq, military or civilian, they were sent to a CRC, or CONUS Replacement Center (CONUS stands for Continental United States). There were several of these, but the one I went to was at Fort Bliss, Texas. We spent a week there for training and the issue of our equipment, including our ballistic vest, Kevlar helmet, and protective (gas) mask. I was not issued a weapon. The cost of this training, and the time and effort to send us there, was huge. All the more reason to make the lengths of tours in Iraq, especially for the military, at least one year to make it cost effective and to maximize the benefit of the training. We attended one lecture after the next during this week. But the one subject we were given more lectures on than any other prior to being sent to Iraq and into a combat zone was—you guessed it—*sexual harassment!* We were given three lectures about it, more than on IED's, nerve agents, heat exhaustion, or anything else. It's easy to see where our nation's priorities really are.

I mentioned that I was not issued a weapon. When I got to Iraq the subject of weapons for contractors was huge. We were in a combat zone, yet MNSTC-I (i.e., LTG Dempsey) wouldn't allow us to carry side arms. We were told we would be protected by the military we served side-by-side with. Following that logic, I was safe as long as I was near a soldier with a rifle or pistol. How nice. And what about when I wasn't near a soldier, like I was all the time? Did LTG Dempsey have a solution for that scenario, or did that simply mean I wasn't safe when caught in that situation—but I still wasn't going to be issued a side arm. The real reasons we weren't issued weapons was the US military didn't want to bother with the extra work, and they didn't trust us to carry them. So if we found ourselves in need of self defense, we were screwed. Right before I left for Iraq there were several beheadings of contractors who had been captured by insurgents. Many contractors wanted a side arm to avoid being captured alive. Who could blame them. But LTG Dempsey had about 20 security guards protecting him, so what did he care if one of us got captured? He didn't want us there anyway. And from the levels of experience of the contractors in Iraq, almost all of whom were former military, I would bet most of them were far more familiar with weapons than most of the military were. We would have been protecting the soldiers, not the other way around.

The "Bush Doctrine" of preemptive strike has proven a dismal failure. I do not for a moment think the left in American would like George Bush had he *not* invaded Iraq in the spring of 2003. But it is safe to say they would not hate him as much as they do. Likewise, I do not for a moment think liberals will ever like a Republican president, no matter how good a job he does, and the same could be said in reverse. But it's another thing entirely when liberals are right on something, even for the wrong reason. If George W. Bush had not invaded Iraq, all other things remaining the same, he could have been a very popular president. He prevented another terrorist attack on our soil, which is monumental. Had he done what he could easily have done the day after 9/11, when he was given a mandate few presidents ever get, he could have led the country on a legitimate path toward the defeat of Al Qaeda and the Taliban and the destruction of Osama Bin Laden, without ever invading Iraq unless he was given provocation to do so, which he wasn't. He could have made an inroad into the destruction of radical Islamic fanaticism by increasing the size of our **active duty** military, especially the US Army and Marines, and preparing the country for a new enemy and a new type of warfare. If he had done this he would have been going after the real enemy, and building up the force strength we will need in the near future. Hell, even Rosy O'Donnell backed Bush for a short time after 9/11, appearing on *The O'Rielly Factor* disgusted at her elite Hollywood friends for not supporting the President. Instead, Bush let Rumsfeld use World War II tactics against an unknown enemy in Iraq, which is just the tip of the iceberg compared to what we will face in the future, and never increased the size of our active duty military a bit. Even during the war Rumsfeld was "reinventing" the US Army, as if we were in the slumbers of peace time, when the Army was up to its ass in a war half way around the world. Bush completely blew his opportunity to build what our country will need very soon. And thousands of American, Coalition and Iraqis have died as a result.

Would George W. Bush be vilified as his is now if he had stayed on course in Afghanistan, which was going very well, and left Iraq alone? No, he wouldn't have been. But instead he was sucked into a game plan devised by a handful of self serving, high ranking snobs in his administration, who led him into this conflict and who all left his administration to get their huge incomes as lobbyists and consultants to the rich and powerful. Do they care about the dead soldiers, contractors, or Iraqis? Probably no more than Paul Bremer does. It's all about them, not their fellow man.

Iraq can not be looked at today without looking back to the Gulf War of 1991, because it was the pathetic manner in which that war ended that led to this one. But the main cause of this conflict is George W. Bush himself. Even though his father screwed up the previous conflict, with the help of Colin Powell and Norman Schwarzkopf, that didn't mean the son had to repeat the same mistake. There is really no excuse for it. As the saying goes, "the acorn doesn't fall far from the tree." My last assignment in the Army was in Texas. There are acorn trees all over the place down there.

How is Iraq today, and how is the United States doing there now? A good example of American might and influence, and how we have performed in Iraq, is the construction of the new US Embassy in Baghdad. It's a complete disaster. The "Embassy" is really a campus of many buildings, obviously designed this way to prevent extensive damage and loss of life that will result when the mortar rounds start coming in after it is occupied. If the Embassy was one huge building and a mortar or rocket hit it, an entire wing of the building would be wiped out. But if the Embassy is made up of many individual buildings, and a round hits one of them, so what. But of course, everything is "going great" in Iraq, so why worry about some stupid old mortar round—like the one that killed the lady from the KBR housing office.

The Embassy has been a nightmare construction project for none other than my former boss, General Charles Williams. He put in complete charge of the project, the largest US Embassy in the world, a woman from OBO who is about five feet tall and wears glasses. Before the reader calls me a male chauvinist pig, stop and think about it. Why would we put a woman in charge of a construction project in a Muslim country? That's insane for the simple reason she will not be respected by the contractors and sub-contractors on the job, all of whom are middle-eastern men, all of whom are Muslim. Women don't lead huge construction projects in the Middle East. The woman is a very nice person who I worked with at OBO. She's an architect, and very good at what she does. But she was fed to the lions when put in that job, whether she had asked for it or not. It's another example of political correctness in America. It doesn't matter who's right for the job, it only matters that it's someone from a particular "class." The result has been a disaster. The project is not only over budget and years behind schedule, but is completely infiltrated with corruption on the part of the Kuwaiti general contractor and sub-contractors because, well, that's the way they do business over there. But it's being built with US dollars, so that's a problem.

And if the Embassy is being built with US dollars, why are we having it done by a foreign contractor? All US embassies and consulates used to be constructed by American contractors and with American labor. Every person on the project had to get a security clearance before they went over to start working on the project. Our embassies and consulates were built right—the first time. But in the 1970's Jimmy Carter started to screw the whole thing up. (What else is new?) He ordered that the US Embassy in Moscow be built by Russian workers. We all know what happened there. The place was so full of electronic "bugs" it could have flown away. It had to be re-built, almost from the ground up. On the wall outside General Williams' Office at OBO there was a large chunk of marble that had been taken out of the US Embassy in Moscow. It was marked where you could see the tiny microphone the Russians had planted in it when they constructed the building. Funny, the chunk of marble was on a wall at the very same Federal agency responsible for building US embassies. Too bad Carter didn't use FBO (now OBO) for what it was there for. He preferred Russians over his own US government agency to build the Embassy in Moscow. If one needs an example of the abysmal leadership our country has been stuck with the last few decades, they need look no further than Jimmy Carter to see why we're in such a lousy state of affairs. But we can't dismiss the fact that Jimmy Carter got the Nobel Peace Prize. Was it for brokering the deal with North Korea (without presidential authority to make the trip there) that allowed it to continue its nuclear weapons program? Or was it giving away the Panama Canal, the primary strategic transit for our naval vessels between the Atlantic and Pacific Oceans, and the main link for commercial shipping in the northern hemisphere? There are so many examples of Jimmy Carter's brilliant statesmanship, I simply can't keep track of them all.

But why did Bush have to make the same mistake? The Embassy in Baghdad was severely delayed when it was discovered the Kuwaiti general contractor has used unauthorized pipe for the fire suppression (sprinkler) system, even though he had been told not to. OBO brought in a firm to inspect the sprinkler system and found it to be unsatisfactory, failing it on inspection. The Kuwaiti contractor hired its own firm to conduct its own inspection, finding it to be satisfactory. What a surprise! In the end the sprinkler system failed to meet US State Department construction standards, most likely because the woman from OBO had the wool pulled over her eyes by Arab contractors who didn't want her in charge of the project—and in charge of them. General Williams signed off on the sprinkler system as being compliant with State Department construction standards on his last day at OBO. But it didn't pass OBO inspection, and he ran OBO. I'm still trying to figure that one out.

Billions of Iraqi dinars are held in US banks for the Iraqi government to spend through a US Government program called Foreign Military Sales, or FMS. The purpose of FMS is to enable Iraq to order American and foreign military equipment, and pay for it with funds the country has already placed in American banks, collecting interest while held in deposit. The Iraqi government can go through the FMS procurement system, managed by the US government, and order what it needs. It all sounds good in theory, but in reality it is a disaster.

When I was at MOD we were trying to order furniture for the buildings at FOB Honor the Ministry was taking away from the 5th Brigade. Because the Ministry of Defense's procurement system was so broken and inept, they wanted to use FMS to buy desks. FMS is supposed to be used to buy tanks. But what difference does it make? Mid-way through my tour I heard that 600 HUMVEE's had been purchased by the Iraqi army through the FMS system and shipped from the United States to Iraq, but no one knew where they were. A fully "up-armored" HUMVEE costs about $500,000. If FMS was such a great system, why did half a year go by with only one contract being awarded for the entire Ministry of Defense? In the first half of 2007 the MOD awarded one contract! One contract in a six month period for the entire Iraqi military that was started from scratch after Paul Bremer disbanded it. Just a year prior to that same six month period General George Casey was saying Iraq was just around the corner from being able to completely take over and run its own show. How was Iraq going to do that if it couldn't even order clothes for its soldier or pay for a generator cable that costs $48,000? How was it going to do that when it lost 600 HUMVEES it had ordered from the States, and when 200,000 weapons General Patraeus bought for them disappeared? One contract in six months to feed, cloth, equip, train and arm the entire Iraqi army. And this was after we had been there for four years. The situation in Iraq is a mess. The violence has gone down only because of the surge, a purely US military operation.

The day we leave Iraq it will go right down the toilet for two reasons: 1) we're gone, and; 2) Iraq has had the ability to defend itself taken away by us, thanks primarily to Paul Bremer, and partly due to LTG Martin Dempsey, the commander of MNSTC-I. We know the damage Paul Bremer caused. But LTG Dempsey did nothing to make effective use of his time as commander of MNSTC-I to get the Iraqi security forces on their feet to the level needed to defend their country. We will be there for years doing the heavy lifting for the Iraqis mostly because of LTG Dempsey, who talked about "transition" all the time but who never made it a reality. At this point the only solution is to leave as many as 100,000 US military there indefinitely.

Paul Bremer dissolved Iraq's military and national police, and we didn't do anything for years under General Casey while the country went to hell in a hand basket. On top of that we are forcing the Iraqis to do things our way down to the level of spending their own money the way we want them to, which they will never be able to do because it goes against their culture and they don't understand it. The only positive things to come of all this is the money being made by US contractors, the promotions being handed out to military officers, and the adventure for State Department employees.

Everything in Iraq is dysfunctional, from top to bottom, both Iraqi and Coalition (US). The only thing that keeps the wheels from falling off completely are US contractors, who are there because our military isn't big enough to do all the things it needs to on its own. Yet at MNSTC-I we were treated worse than insurgents. Contractors are there primarily to make money, which keeps them from leaving the day their tour is over like the US military does. If the US military are jealous of the money contractors make, do they ever stop to think who would bother going to Iraq if they were making the same money there as in the States? Who are they kidding? American contractors are the only continuity in Iraq today, and have been for the past six years. The US military leaves as fast as it can get on the plane, greeted like conquering heroes upon their return, but bitching and moaning the entire time they are there and complaining about the money contractors make. But if it wasn't for the contractors there would be nothing in Iraq to keep the place together. The contractors are the only institutional knowledge in Iraq, and have been from Day 1. The contractors are the ones who cook the food for the US military because there are no military cooks any more. But back in the States no one ever hears about the contractors in Iraq except when the media blasts Dick Cheney and Halliburton. Without firms like Halliburton, Iraq would be in worse shape than it is. The woman who was killed by the mortar round behind the US Embassy in the IZ was employed by KBR, a former subsidiary of Halliburton. Halliburton's employees, and those of every firm in Iraq, are in danger every day. The contractors are the ones who drive the truck convoys hundreds of miles to feed the soldiers and fuel their vehicles, because the US military doesn't have enough trucks and drivers to do it. The contractors run the precious PX (Post Exchange), but when one of them gets killed no one except their family even knows about it. And it is contractors like me and my colleagues who jerks like British Brigadier Weighill say aren't doing anything. In the hallway outside his office were pictures of dozens of contractors who had been killed in Iraq. Brigadier Weighill sat behind his desk on Phoenix Base in the IZ, and lived in the lap of luxury at the British Embassy that was on par with a resort hotel. And he had the nerve to complain about US civilian contractors, all of whom are volunteers, some working for British civilians and officers whose country doesn't even have to pay for their services. The saddest part of all is that we were treated this same way by our own employer and our own military.

One final note on contractors. There are primarily two types of contractors in Iraq: security contractors and everyone else. It is estimated that security contractors have billed the United States Government for as much as $5 billion dollars since the war began. The last week of June 2006, the week before I started my job, I saw the documentary film "Shadow Company" by Nick Bicanic and Jason Bourque. The film had recently come out about security contractors in Iraq. It was very sobering. I saw the same contractors (not the same individuals) when I arrived there. The theme of the film was simply this: are these contractors really mercenaries? After spending 14 months in Iraq I have absolutely no doubt they are.

The best example I can give to support this claim are the security contractors who protect Unites States military flag officers—generals and admirals. Every day I saw civilian security contractors guarding US general officers. Why were they not being guarded by soldiers? Why wasn't the admiral or general telling them to split and asking for soldiers or Marines to provide security? They were driven around in black up-armored Chevy Suburbans, with an entourage of plain clothes "security contractors" wherever they went, sunglasses and all. Actually, I think it made these officers feel more important, kind of like rock stars. There was no legitimate explanation for it. (Whenever a general in Iraq is photographed he always has his helmet off so his face can be seen by the cameras. He's out of uniform, but a good photograph is more important. So much for setting a safety example to his troops by wearing his helmet.) If the governor of a state goes someplace he or she is protected by plain clothes state police. The President and Vice President are protected by the US Secret Service. They aren't protected by civilian contractors. But US general officers in Iraq are. This is absurd. If security contractors are doing this, which is clearly the job of a soldier, then they are doing what soldiers do, which means they are mercenaries.

The way our Government gets around this is with semantics, with words. Security contractors in Iraq are called PSD's, for Personal Security Detail. In the case of general officers, contractors are providing "personal security" protection for them. So, our Government simply says they are "security contractors," making it sound like they're security guards protecting an office building so the American people won't know what they really do for a living. This is extremely misleading. PSD's, like Blackwater and many others, are fully equipped combat forces, capable of engaging with any enemy force in Iraq. The truck driver hauling fuel is there because the US Army doesn't have its own trucks and drivers to do this, like it used to. The PSD's are there because the US Army doesn't have enough soldiers to guard high ranking military officers. This is true because I saw US soldiers doing the exact same thing PSD's were doing. In rare cases US soldiers were providing security for general officers, like protecting LTG Hunzeker, which is their job. We should not have any PSD's in Iraq. None. But we do for two reasons: 1) our military isn't big enough, and; 2) we need to feed the military-industrial complex President Eisenhower warned us of all those years ago. Well, here we are. If we didn't have PSD's, maybe we would have to increase the size of our military. But the private security companies wouldn't be making all that money. One would think they are largely responsible for limiting the size of our armed forces. We are hiring PSD's to cut corners and "privatize" how we fight our wars, just like a Federal agency hires private contractors to augment its lack of full-time employees. When you privatize warfare, you've got a mercenary force for hire. What is there not to understand?

So then, why aren't we reinstituting the draft? Because it's politically incorrect to even say the word, that's why. But to not reinstitute the draft in the face of the dangers posed from fanatical Islamic terrorism is insane. Logic then follows that political correctness is insane, because it leads to insane responses in the face of overwhelming rational evidence to do the opposite. Political correctness is more important in our country today than rational thought and behavior. The evidence of this is everywhere anyone cares to look.

The most widely known example of the issue surrounding security contractors in Iraq is that involving Blackwater, the largest and most profitable firm providing these services in the world. Blackwater was founded by a former US Navy SEAL, who touts his firm's expertise by claiming that all his employees are ex-SEALs, Rangers or Delta Force. Based on my own observations while in Iraq for 14 months, as well as personally knowing a few security contractors, I am convinced this is nonsense. Anyone who wanted to go to Iraq and be a badass could get a job with one of these firms. If you really wanted to experience the "thrill" of killing someone, without any consequences, what better job than as a security contractor in Iraq? They were as well armed, or better armed, than any soldier because they could "pack" whatever weapon they felt like, whereas soldiers can only carry what they are issued. And they had carte blanche to shoot at anyone or anything they wanted to, for whatever reason, and get away with it. There were no "Rules of Engagement" for our security contractors in Iraq. For them, it was the Wild West. Too bad Iraqi civilians who got in their way didn't know that.

Just about every PSD in Iraq looked exactly the same, as if they had come out of a "PSD factory." They all had long sideburns, goatees, tan baseball caps with the beak in a tight curl, sunglasses (which we all needed), tan slacks with cargo pouches, black golf shirts—and tattoos, lots and lots of tattoos. In fact, they had more body art than I had ever seen. One moron actually had Roman "armor" all over his body. They all thought they were total studs. In reality, we thought most of them were clowns. They did nothing but hang out at the gym, and it was obvious most were steroid freaks. I knew one who said the drug problem inside the PSD compound was out of control. There was no way they would have been able to get away with their behavior if they were soldiers, at least not to the extent they were. And if they look like jerks, they will act that way too.

The incident on September 16, 2007, where Blackwater employees killed 17 Iraqi civilians at Nisour Square in Baghdad, was nothing more than a legally sanctioned (by the US Government) massacre. If the incident itself wasn't bad enough, idiots from the State Department's Diplomatic Security Division, which oversees all security contractors in Iraq, gave the massacre's perpetrators immunity if they would give their statements, eliminating any possibility they would be prosecuted for what they had done. I guess that means if I killed someone here in the States, I could just cut a deal and tell the cops I did it in return for immunity from prosecution for my statement. Sounds pretty good to me. But this massacre happened in Iraq, so anything goes. If a US soldier had done such a thing he would have been court marshaled and thrown in jail for the rest of his life. But not Blackwater. They get off scot free. One even got drunk at the "Tiki Bar" behind the US Embassy on Christmas Eve 2006 and killed an Iraqi in the IZ. He was sent home and went on his way. To the best of my knowledge no charges were ever filed against him because it happened overseas in a combat zone, and because he is a "security contractor." Blackwater agreed to pay the dead Iraqi's family a chunk of money, and that was it. (I heard the dead Iraqi's family hired an American lawyer to sue the Blackwater employee, and Blackwater itself. It seems Blackwater didn't even pay the dead man's family what it had promised. Not only was the dead Iraqi's life not worth anything, the promise to pay off his family wasn't either. Hey, it's Iraq.) So, if someone really does want to experience what it's like to kill someone, without any cause or consequences, they can get a job as a security contractor in Iraq and experience it for themselves. All at the US taxpayer's expense.

At the time this book was written Blackwater had lost its contract in Iraq. It had also changed its name to "Xe Services LLC," obviously to sever any connection to its tainted reputation. Blackwater has been in litigation for months over its various problems. It's "co-defendant" should be the US State Department.

Conclusion

For the Unites States, Iraq is many things. It is an example of mismanagement of United States Government contracts, private companies who send people to Iraq without regard for what they do and then turn their backs on their employees, murder by private security contractors, waste, fraud and abuse of US taxpayer dollars, gross dereliction of duty by senior military officers and senior State Department employees, useless involvement in a strictly American operation of British and other foreigners, negligent management of US military and civilian staff by these same foreigners who have no regard for their well being and expertise, gross inequalities in the tours of duty of the different US military branches, and waste of time and effort to maintain a "Coalition" of countries that looks like the bar scene in Star Wars. It's a mess, almost to the point of being laughable. But it's not funny. How many Iraqis have died because we invaded in the spring of 2003? How many Iraqis have died because we didn't finish the job we should have in 1991? How many Iraqis and American soldiers have died because we're more concerned with political correctness and the "sensitivities" of other people than killing insurgents who murder innocent people by the thousands? How many have died because of gross incompetence on the part of the Bush administration? How many have died because of senior US military officers who cared more for their own careers then the Iraqi people they were sent there to protect and defend? How many US soldiers have died due to inept planning and pathetic execution by these same senior military officers? How badly has the reputation of the United States suffered as a result?

Barack Hussein Obama has now been elected President of the United States. We don't even know if he was born in the United States, as required by the Constitution. But that is being overlooked, even though he had no qualifications for the job. (He said during his campaign that he wanted to be the "Commander-of-Chief," not the "Commander-in-Chief." He didn't even know what the correct title of the job was, but he wanted it anyway. And now he's got it.) If we don't adhere to our own laws, why bother in Iraq? Under Bush the US Treasury has doled out $700 billion dollars to bail out AIG and the banking and credit industry. Barack Hussein Obama's stimulus bill has just been passed by Congress with no evidence it is anything other than New Deal (i.e., socialist) growth of the Federal Government that will take over of the economy. This will eventually lead to a one-party political system controlled by liberal Democrats, who will be able to buy votes with their newly minted treasure chest that working Americans are paying for. Socialism and the welfare state are around the corner, and the fate of the US defense and homeland security structure hang in the balance. Are we going to be attacked from outside while we decay within?

The first President Bush gave us Bill Clinton. The second President Bush gave us Barack Hussein Obama. What is to become of our country?

Barack Hussein Obama pledged during his victorious presidential campaign that he would pull all US forces out of Iraq within a year to 18 months. He now says he's going to leave around 50,000 there. Why the change? I submit the reason is a combination of two things: 1) he said he would pull all of our forces out as a campaign promise with no evidence to support it, and; 2) when he go into the Oval Office and found out what's really going on in Iraq he realized there was no way we could pull out now. But if we have been led to believe everything is going great in Iraq, as General Casey was saying at least three years ago, what's the problem?

Because of what we have done in Iraq, the world hates the United States as much as liberals hate George W. Bush. He is one of the reasons for the hatred we are receiving, both at home and abroad. But he certainly isn't the only reason. Although I had such high hopes for him when he was elected, thinking that maybe he would be another Ronald

Reagan, I was soon proven very wrong. But President Bush succeeded in the single most important job of the President—he defended our country. However, just about everything else he did was a disaster: from immigration reform; to the nomination of Harriet Myers; to Katrina; to the recent bailout orchestrated by his Treasury Secretary Henry Paulson, which is nothing more than the first step toward the nationalization of our economy.

But the disaster in Iraq would not have happened if George W. Bush had just stayed in Afghanistan instead of creating a reason for invading Iraq in the spring of 2003. If he had just focused on Al Qaeda, Afghanistan, and the real threats to our nation's security from global Islamic fanaticism, as he said we were indeed facing: the world wouldn't hate our country as much; liberals would still hate Bush simply because he's a Republican; and Americans in general wouldn't feel as bad about themselves, our country, or our nation's fate. Can we say this is the case now? Sadly, we can't.

At the beginning of this story I quoted the wise saying: "Those who do not study history are doomed to repeat it." I mentioned it along the way as well. It is very evident the United States repeated the same mistakes made by previous administrations when it invaded Iraq in 2003. Anyone who disagrees with this is entitled to their opinion, but is also in serious denial. I also said at the beginning of this story what my intention was in writing it. It is worth repeating. I hope our country never repeats what we have done in Iraq, which began at the end of the Gulf War and continues through to the present day. There's no need for these mistakes. Too many *innocent* people have died teaching us our lesson.

In November 2008, a former co-worker from Iraq e-mailed to say he was back in the States. He wanted to tell me our employer in Iraq had lost its contract. My translator e-mailed me a few weeks later and told me the new company that had taken over sent a woman to be the real estate advisor who was an accountant and didn't know a thing about real estate. The woman left after a couple of months. Her replacement is a guy who doesn't know anything about real estate either. Some things never change.

LaVergne, TN USA
17 November 2009
164027LV00002BC/23/P